Looking for Mrs Livingstone

Looking for
Mrs Livingstone

Julie Davidson

SAINT ANDREW PRESS
Edinburgh

First published in 2012 by Saint Andrew Press
SAINT ANDREW PRESS
121 George Street
Edinburgh EH2 4YN

ISBN 978 0 7152 0964 6 hardback
978 0 7152 0966 0 paperback

British Library Cataloguing in Publication Data
A catalogue record for this book is available from the British Library.

It is the publisher's policy to only use papers that are natural and recyclable
and that have been manufactured from timber grown in renewable, properly
managed forests. All of the manufacturing processes of the papers are expected
to conform to the environmental regulations of the country of origin.

Typeset in Sabon by Regent Typesetting, London
Printed and bound in the United Kingdom by
CPI Group (UK) Ltd, Croydon, Surrey

This book is for

Marion Moffat
Mike Muyafula
Janet Wagner Parsons
Keith Rampton
Catherine Reid
Harry Reid

Contents

Personal Acknowledgements

In Africa: I made three long road trips to the places where Mary Livingstone lived and died – journeys which took me to some obscure corners of the countries which are now South Africa, Botswana, Malawi and Mozambique. I have no experience of off-road driving, I'm mechanically incompetent, and, unlike other, more intrepid women travellers in sub-Saharan Africa, I would have found these expeditions too intimidating to attempt alone. For this reason, I must thank first and foremost the two people who drove, guided and gave me their cheerful and solicitous company over nearly 3,000 miles of tar roads, dirt roads and bush tracks: Mike Muyafula of Central African Wilderness Safaris (CAWS), Lilongwe, Malawi, and Keith Rampton of Explorer Safaris, Johannesburg, South Africa. Without them, I could not have gone looking for Mrs Livingstone.

I must also thank warmly the people who offered me hospitality and in other ways helped to subsidise my travels. The Strathmartine Trust, which supports education and research in Scottish history with a range of grants to assist projects and their publication, awarded me the grant which covered some of my international flights. Chris Badger, managing director of CAWS, Mike's employer, released his valuable and popular guide for five days at no cost, put together our itinerary and gave me the use of a Land Rover for the price of its fuel, while Caroline Rampton, Keith's wife, twice interrupted her own busy career to welcome me into their home in Johannesburg. My Kalahari explorations at Meno a Kwena on the Boteti River and Camp Kalahari at Makgadikgadi Pans were made possible by the generosity of their owners and the expertise of the guides who looked after me, Jeff Gush and Super Sande.

There were many others along the road who helped me in different ways, notably Gaia Allison, whose command of Portuguese and experience of Sofala province in Mozambique laid all the groundwork for our meeting with the priest at Chupanga Church, where Padre Medard introduced us to Antonio Loli John, the village elder whose childhood memories of the house where Mary died held a startling revelation. Gaia also came up with the idea of putting Mary's grave on a 'heritage trail', and was our guide and interpreter at Inhaminga and Afrika wa Jesu. Although I never met them, Rod and Ellie Hein of Afrika wa Jesu provided first-hand information on Chupanga Mission and its condition in the aftermath of the civil war, while Ant and Pat White of M'Phingwe Lodge and their son Graeme, along with Michelle Gilardi, filled in several gaps.

An essential link between the UK and Botswana was Alice Gully, director of Aardvark Safaris, who organised part of my Botswana itinerary and funded its international and internal flights. From her delightful farmhouse office in the Scottish Borders, Alice has been responsible for sending me on my most thrilling safaris, and it is thanks to her that I have met the experts who have given me some understanding of the African wilderness, its wildlife and the interface between conservation and community interests. I can't mention them all, but key mentors in repeat visits to Zambia have been Grant and Lynsey Cumings of Chiawa Camp on the Lower Zambezi; Robin Pope, Jo Pope, Rocky Simachila and Deb Tittle of Robin Pope Safaris in the Luangwa Valley; and Abraham Banda of Norman Carr Safaris, also in the Luangwa Valley. Other memorable guides with whom I've walked in the bush include Sean Lues, Graeme Lemon and Dean MacGregor in Zimbabwe, Elikana Nyaru (a Maasai chief) in Tanzania, and Matt Gurney and the late Peter Faulls in Kenya. I never got to know their surnames, but when I trekked in the Karisia Hills of northern Kenya with Peter and his wife Rosalie we were given rare insights into Ndorobo and Samburu culture by their local guides, Lekermogo and Lentaiya. Although I have turned only a few pages, all these people have opened for me what has been called 'the never-ending book of the bush'.

Few Africans have no time to spare for you. On the highways and byways of my road trips, those who shared an eager interest in the story of Mary Livingstone included the Reverend Harry Ngwale, choirmaster at Blantyre Mission; Brian Mullins of Grahamstown in the Eastern Cape; Hetta Hager, curator of the Mary Moffat Museum in Griquatown; Hester Groenewald of Wildebeest Guest Farm in the Northern Cape; and the Reverend Kudzani Ndebele, director of Kuruman Moffat Mission. There were nameless others who nudged me along with directions, information and ardent good wishes. To all those who have given me an experience of sub-Saharan Africa which has been hopeful, heartwarming, humbling and inspiring, I dedicate this book.

In the United Kingdom: archive and bibliographic acknowledgements are cited at the end of the book, but there is an entire cast of other supporters whom I must thank, one of whom deserves a double credit. Janet Wagner Parsons, author of *The Livingstones at Kolobeng*, spent fifteen years, two of them in Botswana, researching the history of the Livingstone mission at Kolobeng, and had a significant role in the conservation of the site, which is now a national monument. More than anyone, she has written with authority and insight about Mary's relationship with her husband and the dynamics of their early family life. For permission to 'mine' her research and to quote from her book, for which she alone holds the copyright, I am hugely grateful. In a series of e-mails and phone calls, Janet has not only vetted and endorsed my use of her material but also given *Looking for Mrs Livingstone* her blessing; or, as she put it, 'I am so pleased the big topic of Mary and the Crowd That Was All Around Her is going to get another good airing' (a reference to the New Testament account of Mary, mother of Christ, identifying her son on his painful progress through noisy crowds to the Stations of the Cross).

An early enthusiast, and my first point of contact when I began to explore Mary's story, was Karen Carruthers, curator of the David Livingstone Centre in Blantyre, Scotland. Karen has been consistently helpful (in Zambia, in 2005, we both attended the 150th-anniversary events which commemorated Livingstone's arrival at the Victoria Falls), and I owe thanks to the DLC and the National Trust for Scotland for the use of photographs of Mary, her husband and children. The three maps were created by Christine Johnston, a freelance Edinburgh cartographer who has worked for many publishers, including the celebrated map-makers Bartholomew. She produced the maps with Quantum GIS and Natural Earth data, along with details of routes and place names provided by me.

Encouragement came from many sources, among them the African explorers' historian *par excellence*, Tim Jeal, author of *Livingstone*, of *Stanley: The Impossible Life of Africa's Greatest Explorer* and of *Explorers of the Nile: The Triumph and Tragedy of a Great Victorian Adventure*, his latest book. The late Andrew Ross, author of *David Livingstone: Mission and Empire* and a principal of the University of Edinburgh's Faculty of Divinity, entertained me to coffee at New College and offered his assessment of the Livingstone marriage, while another leading cleric, Andrew McLellan, former Moderator of the General Assembly of the Church of Scotland and the current convener of its World Mission Council, could not have been more ebullient in his enthusiasm.

An Edinburgh friend, Kenyan-born Claire Foottit, travel writer, photographer and author of the *Bradt Guide to Kenya*, gave me valuable personal details about her great-great-uncle, William Cotton Oswell, who trekked with the Livingstone family across the Kalahari. Another leading travel writer who deserves to be remembered with affection and gratitude is my old friend Jill Crawshaw, who introduced me to Africa on my first safari, and with whom I shared many more. And, on Mumbo Island in Lake Malawi, I made two new friends who became old friends as soon as we met: Jessica Fagerhaugh and Deborah Tomkins, taking a break between working in Johannesburg and going home to Washington DC. Jess and Deb, feminists to their fingertips, have been monitoring my progress with Mary ever since and, when necessary, urging me on.

The book's addendum, 'Loose Ends' (in the Epilogue), owes everything to the keen collaboration and vigorous research of Mary's great-great-niece Marion Moffat, the Moffat family historian, and her husband Lewis Carlin. I am more generally indebted for their co-operation to other members of the Moffat family, including Dr Howard Moffat of Gaborone, Botswana and Neil Wilson of Kendal, Cumbria, and to my dear friend Ann Wilson, who renewed a long-lost friendship from her youthful years in Canada to put me in touch with Flora Moffat.

It has been a long journey in more ways than one to the publication of *Looking for Mrs Livingstone*. With me every step of the way, in spirit if not in flesh, has been Ann Crawford, publishing editor of Saint Andrew Press, whose guidance and patience (some might call it forbearance) have been invaluable. Ann was the only person who read the manuscript in its early stages and, indeed, read the completed work before it went to its scrupulous copy-editor, Ivor Normand – and, if Ann hadn't claimed to be 'thrilled' by Mary's story and by my treatment of it, I might have failed to meet her deadline. Doing so was a close-run thing, handled with unflappable efficiency by Rebecca Goldsmith, rights and editorial administrator of Hymns Ancient and Modern, the new stewards of Saint Andrew Press.

Finally, I want to identify the two people who have lived longest with my search for Mary Livingstone, and who have been required to indulge its claims on my time and presence. My daughter, Catherine Reid, shares my love of African travel, has been the best of companions on some of my safaris and has spent two seasons working in the industry in Zambia and South Africa. My husband, Harry Reid, has never been to the African continent and has little interest in going there, but tolerates my periodic absences and tales from the bush with good humour. As a historian and writer, he has been more interested in this project than in any of my wildlife yarns, and back in 2000 he gave me the copy of Tim Jeal's *Livingstone* which first triggered my interest in Mary – and my sense of injustice on her behalf. He has been immeasurably supportive during my occasional crises of confidence, and, as the author of five books, he has given that support with the experience of one who knows what he's talking about. I thank both Harry and Catherine with all my heart.

Timeline

1821   Born in Griquatown, 'Bechuanaland', 800 miles north of Cape Town; she is the first child of missionary couple Robert Moffat of Ormiston, East Lothian, and Mary Smith of Dukinfield, Lancashire

1825   The Moffats and their children move to the mission station of Kuruman, the most remote in southern Africa

1830   Sent to boarding school at Salem, near Grahamstown, in the Eastern Cape

1835   Further education in Cape Town, including teacher training

1839   Arrives in the United Kingdom with her parents and five siblings. Her father is lauded for Kuruman's achievements and preaches and lectures throughout the country. Among those he inspires to volunteer for Africa is David Livingstone

1843   Sails for the Cape with her family. Livingstone has been based at Kuruman since 1841, and rides out to meet them

1845   Marries Livingstone in Kuruman Church, 'the cathedral of the Kalahari', and treks deeper into the interior to the mission station of Mabotsa

1846   Her son Robert is born. Livingstone moves his wife and child to Chonuane to preach among the Bakwena, while Mary continues to teach women and children

1847   Her daughter Agnes is born on a visit to Kuruman. The family move to Kolobeng, 300 miles to the north, where the Bakwena paramount chief Sechele has settled with his people

1848   Her son Thomas is born at Kolobeng. Livingstone sends his family to Kuruman while he makes his first expedition to Lake Ngami; before he returns, Mary takes the children back to Kolobeng

1850   Pregnant again, she and the children trek across the Kalahari with Livingstone and reach Lake Ngami. On their return her second daughter, Elizabeth, is born and Mary suffers a stroke. The baby survives for only a few weeks and the family retreats to Kuruman

1851   Returns to Kolobeng to make second trek with Livingstone and their children across the Kalahari, this time to the Chobe River, where her status as 'Moffat's daughter' opens doors for her husband. Her fifth child, Oswell, is born by the Boteti River on the return journey

1851   Leaves Kolobeng for the last time to travel to the Cape. Livingstone has made the decision to send his family to the United Kingdom while he continues his exploration of central Africa. In October Mary and her four young children arrive at his parents' home in Hamilton, Lanarkshire

1852–4   Quarrels with her parents-in-law, leaves Scotland with the children for Hackney, near London, then moves every few months between rented rooms and visits to her parents' friends. Struggles to budget; provokes the first rumours of dependant drinking and loss of faith

1854   Illness and breakdown in Kendal, Westmorland; taken in by the Braithwaite family, who arrange schooling for Robert and Agnes, while Mary moves again, this time to Epsom

1856   Reunited with Livingstone, who returns a national hero from his transcontinental expedition and arrival at the Victoria Falls

1857   Settles with the family in Hadley Green, near London, while Livingstone writes *Missionary Travels and Researches in South Africa*, resigns from the London Missionary Society and is commissioned to lead a government-sponsored expedition to investigate the Zambezi's potential for commercial traffic and colonial settlement

1858   Embarks for the Zambezi delta with her husband and youngest son Oswell on the expedition ship *Pearl*. Discovers she is again pregnant; leaves the expedition at the Cape to travel to Kuruman, where her last child, Anna Mary, is born

1859   Returns to Scotland to be reunited with her other children in Hamilton, where the breach with Livingstone's family has been healed

1859–61   Rents comfortable property in Glasgow, where Robert is attending medical school, finds a tutor for Thomas and begins to restore the children's family life. Questions the purpose and demands of missionary work. News of her criticisms and other social solecisms reaches Livingstone on the Zambezi; he sends for her

1861   Embarks for the Cape

1862   Reunited with Livingstone on the Zambezi. Dies three months later at Shupanga (Chupanga)

Note on African Names

Throughout this narrative I've used the modern or 'common usage' names for places, peoples and individuals, except when quoting contemporary sources, which often use different spellings. The nation which is now Botswana, and much of what is now the Northern Cape of South Africa, were known in the nineteenth century (and well into the twentieth) as Bechuanaland. To David and Mary Livingstone, Robert and Mary Moffat and other Victorians, the people who lived there were the Bechuana, a term no longer in use. Ethnically they are Tswana, their language is Setswana, and citizens of Botswana are called Batswana. Setswana tribal names are composed of a root and the prefix 'Ba' – as in Bakwena (whom Livingstone called the Bakwain), Batawana and Bangwato. This part of southern Africa was also home to the aboriginal Khoikhoi and San, whom Europeans called Bushmen, while the migrations which brought other African tribes and ethnic groups into the region are more fully described in the text.

For simplicity's sake, I've also used the modern place names and tribal names of Mozambique, Malawi and Zambia, except when quoting nineteenth-century chroniclers or discussing them in their colonial context. One curiosity: the Shire River, which inspired Livingstone to call its high hinterland the Shire Highlands, is pronounced 'Shir-ay', and has nothing to do with the 'shires' of the United Kingdom. Shire is almost certainly an English corruption of Chire, as there is no 'sh' combination of consonants in Chichewa, the predominant language of Malawi, the country which the British called Nyasaland.

Foreword

It took Zambia and the Zambezi to send me back to Blantyre and the Clyde. The River Clyde flowed through my childhood and, like most Lanarkshire children of my generation, its definitive hero was not William Wallace, who married on Clydeside, or Robert Owen, the social reformer of New Lanark, or any of the giants of the Industrial Revolution or the early Labour Party. It was David Livingstone, boy bookworm of the cotton mills, saviour of the heathen, champion of the slave; the missionary-explorer who brought moral purpose to epic journeys through the enigmatic land mass of central Africa, and global celebrity to our corner of Scotland.

Livingstone's tenement birthplace was homely and familiar to us. It belonged to the recent past; its counterparts have substantial colonies in the inner cities of Scotland today, and its open, verdant setting remains the perfect venue for Sunday-school picnics and Girl Guide excursions. In a steep cut between the parkland of the David Livingstone Centre and the mature broadleaf of Bothwell Woods, the Clyde makes a last bid to recover its rural glamour before powering into Glasgow. But, in the early nineteenth century, this stretch of river was an engine of industry; a force which employed some 2,000 people in the mills of Blantyre.

The whitewashed Shuttle Row tenement, now the centre's museum, is a remnant of their housing. It was bought, restored and opened in 1929 by public subscription, much of it from the 'saved pennies' of Scottish Sunday-school children. Its most arresting feature is the single room, with its two box beds, in which Livingstone's parents raised five children, much as many African families raise their children in single rooms today.

It is Scotland's National Memorial to its Victorian hero; and, while Shuttle Row remains eloquently humble, the surrounding ground has acquired some accessories of the modern leisure industry: visitor centre, tearoom, book and gift shop, children's play area, 'Explorers' Garden'. The land and buildings are owned by the original David Livingstone Trust but have been managed since 1999 by the National Trust for Scotland; and, while they have become just another recreational destination for secular visitors, the museum is a place of pilgrimage for African Christians.

'Mostly Zambians and Malawians', reports Karen Carruthers, its manager and curator.

This I didn't learn until I started travelling in the African countries where his name – and the name of the Moffat family into which he married – is well known and respected: Zambia, Malawi, Botswana and South Africa. On my early visits, I went mainly to their game reserves to write articles about conservation and safari tourism, but in November 2005 I was back on the Zambezi to cover the 150th anniversary of the explorer's arrival at Mosi-oa-Tunya, 'smoke that thunders'. In a stroke of marketing genius, judging that this stupendous curtain of falling water would make his reputation and stimulate British interest in Africa, he renamed the 300-foot cataract the Victoria Falls.

The Zambians are generous to Livingstone, despite the fact that his compulsive route-finding opened up avenues for more predatory colonial adventurers. If his Blantyre birthplace is the repository of Scotland's tribute to him, then Zambia, where he died, pays its own tributes. Uphill from the Victoria Falls, the town of Livingstone commemorated the anniversary by inviting members of the Livingstone and Moffat families to a day of celebrations. The town also renovated its Livingstone Museum and unveiled not one but two new statues of the explorer, cast by a young sculptor from Lusaka called Nsofwa Bowa. One life-sized model stands outside the museum while the other, a colossus almost forty feet high on its plinth, strikes a questing pose beside the cataract.

Twenty miles upriver is a village called Siankaba, much like any other in rural Zambia, with children, goats and chickens sharing its open spaces, men sitting under the mango tree, women sweeping their yards, nursing their babies, pumping water from the standpipe and grinding maize for the evening meal of *nshima*. Here, I was shown round by a man called Doctor Siloka, who is not a doctor. 'For many years my father worked for a white doctor in the Copper Belt and when I was born he delivered me. So my father called me Doctor.'

White doctors. A small step to the subject of medical missionaries. I told this courteous village elder that I'd just spent three days looking for shoebill storks in Bangweulu, in the remote north-west. This vast wilderness of lake, floodplain and swamp (now more elegantly defined as 'world-class wetland') became an ordeal for Livingstone on his final expedition, two years after he rejected Henry Stanley's invitation to return with him to the United Kingdom. In Bangweulu, in 1873, he got hopelessly lost during his wayward search for the source of the Nile. Weakened by dysentery and malaria, losing blood from ruptured haemorrhoids, he was carried out of the swamps to die at the village of Chitambo, in the district of Ilala.

His heart and other internal organs were buried under a mpundu tree, now gone. I described to Doctor the monument raised on its site; the tall stone pillar was once an obelisk until its top was damaged and replaced by an iron cross. It dates from 1902 and stands alone in a scatter of woodland, as if striving for obscurity. Of the four plaques, the earliest modestly identifies Livingstone as 'traveller' and 'medical missionary'. The most recent was donated by Spanish admirers of Susi and Chuma, the followers who dried and preserved his body with salt and famously carried it over 1,000 miles to the Indian Ocean coast, where it was shipped home for a hero's funeral in Westminster Abbey. But the most moving inscription was added in post-colonial times, on the centenary of his death, when 'after 100 years David Livingstone's spirit and the love of God so animated his friends of all races that they gathered here in Thanksgiving on 1st May 1973, led by Dr Kenneth David Kaunda, President of the Republic of Zambia'.

The year 1973 was also when Tim Jeal's revisionist *Livingstone* was published by William Heinemann. Jeal's book, arguably the definitive biography, and never out of print, takes a challenging view of the character of the explorer and de-sanctifies a reputation which had become almost mythic in the hands of his hagiographers. But Jeal has no doubt that Livingstone's vision and achievements made him a great man.

When I asked Doctor Siloka how today's Zambians viewed the long-dead white man so honoured by their first president, he replied without hesitation. 'A man of God. Zambia is a Christian country because of Dr Livingstone.' And then he recited: 'Born in Blantyre, Scotland, in 1813, sent to Africa in 1841 by the London Missionary Society, married Mary Moffat, daughter of Robert and Mary Moffat of Kuruman, first European to see the Victoria Falls, first European to cross Africa coast to coast, campaigned against slavery.'

I told him he knew more about Livingstone than the average Scot, and he said every Zambian schoolchild was taught his history. 'Some members of his wife's family, the Moffats, now live in Zambia', he added. This I knew. I had just met David Moffat and his wife Christine, who farm north of Lusaka, at the anniversary celebrations; and I'd become aware that an entire tribe of Moffats, descendants of Livingstone's in-laws, has been active and influential in public service, philanthropy, medicine, agriculture and politics in Botswana, Zimbabwe and Zambia from the days when these modern nations had different names and British administrations.

It struck me that Doctor Siloka, like other Africans in this part of the continent, gave equal emphasis to the Moffats' place in Livingstone's story. The pioneer missionary Robert Moffat, his father-in-law, was also a Scot, born humbly at Ormiston in East Lothian. He began his working life as a nursery gardener, learned Latin in his spare time, moved to England and in 1816 had just been accepted for training by the London Missionary Society when he met his future wife: Mary Smith, daughter of his employer at Dukinfield, near Manchester. There followed an enduring love story which crossed an ocean and for half a century survived the chronic hardships and hazards of mission life at the LMS's most remote African station.

There are several biographies of the impressive and charismatic Robert Moffat, who translated the Bible and *Pilgrim's Progress* into Setswana, the language of the Tswana people among whom he lived and worked at Kuruman in what is now the Northern Cape of South Africa. The Moffat Mission, with its orchard and vegetable gardens, thrives today as an ecumenical centre and heritage site. Until his celebrity was overtaken by that of his son-in-law, Moffat was the most famous missionary of his age, when the exotic exploits of evangelists 'among the heathen' were not only admired but also popularly enjoyed for their entertainment value.

There is even a biography of his accomplished, courageous and strong-willed wife. The Scottish writer, painter and co-founder of Voluntary Services Overseas, Mora Dickson (who died in 2002), based her thoughtful book *Beloved Partner* on the letters of 'Mary Moffat of Kuruman'. In it, she describes how the young bride coped magnificently with transplantation from Lancashire to the edge of the Kalahari, eight weeks' journey by ox-wagon from Cape Town, and credits her with much of the mission station's success.

And there is, of course, a mountain of material about David Livingstone, with no apparent limit to the curiosity and imagination of some 100 biographers; not to mention a prodigious archive by Livingstone himself. He was an enthusiastic reporter of his own career. Apart from his journals and books, notably the best-selling *Missionary Travels and Researches in South Africa*, published by John Murray in 1857, he was an obsessive letter-writer. If he were alive today he would surely strive for world domination of the blogosphere. But when I began to explore the literary industry surrounding his life I soon discovered that among all the opinions, theories, claims, counter-claims, myth-making and revisionism of this inexhaustible corpus it is hard to hear the voice of his wife: Mary Moffat Livingstone, first-born child of the Moffats of Kuruman.

Mrs Livingstone is a shadow in the blaze of her husband's sun, a whisper in the thunderclap of his reputation. Yet her own feats as early traveller in uncharted Africa – even if conducted on Livingstone's coat-tails – are unique. She was the first white woman to cross the Kalahari, which she did twice, pregnant, giving birth in the bush on the second journey. She was the first white woman to reach Lake Ngami, in what is now northern Botswana, and the first to travel into the interior as far north as the Chobe River, a major tributary of the Zambezi. She was much more embedded in southern Africa than her husband. She was born there and she died there. He has a tomb in Westminster Abbey. She has an obscure and crumbling grave on the banks of the Zambezi in a destitute region of Mozambique.

She is little more than a note in the margin of an iconic life. She left behind no journal, one maudlin poem and very few letters. She certainly wrote more letters to family and friends, but nobody bothered to conserve them. There is even a suggestion that those written during the unhappiest period of her married life, when her mood was bitter and her faith fragile, were deliberately destroyed to spare the tainting of her husband's reputation. As a result, almost all the substance of this very substantial woman has been filtered through the writings of David Livingstone, his expeditionary companions and his many correspondents and biographers.

Two writers have given brief accounts of her history in its own right. Margaret Forster told her story as an indignant feminist parable in *Good Wives? Mary, Fanny, Jennie and Me, 1845–2001*, Forster's personal analysis of the changing nature of marriage through the partnerships of Mary Livingstone, Fanny Osbourne, Jennie Lee and the author herself, first published by Chatto & Windus in 2001. Another mini-biography appears in Edna Healey's *Wives of Fame*, first published by Sidgwick & Jackson in 1986. Here, Mary features alongside Jenny Marx, wife of Karl, and Emma Darwin, wife of Charles, with Healey reprising the narrative of her Scottish Television documentary *Mrs Livingstone I Presume*, which she wrote and presented in 1982.

But the most sustained and graphic insights into a life-changing period of Mary's life come from Janet Wagner Parsons' *The Livingstones at Kolobeng 1847–1852*. This is an invaluable history of the early years of the Livingstone marriage and the people and events surrounding it. The remnants of the mission station of Kolobeng, now a National Monument, are a few miles from Botswana's modern capital of Gabarone, and the house that Livingstone built above the Kolobeng River was the only settled family home they ever knew.

When she wrote her book, published in 1997 by the Botswana Society and Pula Press, Parsons was living in Botswana, where she spent much time researching missionary-settler history and the European immigrants' relationship with the Tswana people. Her study led to a narrative which she herself says reads like fiction, although its details are as accurate as she could make them. It compellingly recalls the physical and emotional pressures on Mary Livingstone as her husband's wanderlust begins to take over their marriage, and investigates the complex politics of this volatile part of southern Africa in the mid-nineteenth century, when British evangelists, Boer farmers and Tswana tribes co-existed uneasily in the most daunting of environments.

These writers have told me most of what I know about Mary. What I didn't know about her, and about the remote places which shaped her, took hold of my imagination; that, and the image of a lonely grave beside the Zambezi, which – if it were still there – seemed to be her only monument. The only photograph I'd seen was a gloomy black-and-white print in the David Livingstone Centre, clearly old. Mozambique had convulsed since it was taken. The rapid exit of the country's Portuguese colonists was followed by a sixteen-year civil war, and the spot where Mary was buried was at the heart of it.

On one of my visits to Zambia, an ambition took shape. Chiawa is a well-known riverside camp in Lower Zambezi National Park, some fifty miles upriver from Zambia's border with Mozambique. It is owned and run by the Cumings family; and I had become friendly with Grant Cumings, one of the safari industry's leading guides, and his Scottish wife Lynsey. On a moonlit night, we boated out to a sand island in the middle of the Zambezi, where the camp staff built a fire and prepared dinner. There, in this wild and beautiful setting, to the background noises of splashing hippo and whooping hyena, I heard fresh news of Mary Livingstone's grave.

'I've never been to Chupanga, but I've heard the grave is still there', Grant told me. 'The mission which grew up round the site was destroyed during the civil war, and the whole area was heavily mined, but I believe the church has been rebuilt. And the grave is maintained again.'

Maintained by whom? Where exactly was Chupanga, the early Portuguese settlement which was called Shupanga in Livingstone's account of his second Zambezi expedition? How could I get there? These were the questions which plagued me on the flight home from Lusaka and became the impetus for this book. I knew I must get to Mary's grave.

And so the book begins at the end of her life. It is not an orthodox biography or in any way an academic one. Other, better-qualified researchers have exhaustively mined the available sources, and are suitably credited. It is, rather, a journey through her life by way of her own journeys and those I've made in her footsteps in the modern nations of Mozambique, Botswana and South Africa, with detours through Malawi and Swaziland. I am first a journalist, and therefore curious; second a travel writer, and therefore restless. It is both these itches which I have scratched in retelling the story of a woman who became a casualty of her husband's own curiosity and restlessness.

I can't give Mary Livingstone the reflective voice she neglected to leave to history; perhaps only a novelist can do that. But I hope I've found some trace of her ghostly spoor on the lionskin lands of Africa, and caused her to whisper a little more loudly.

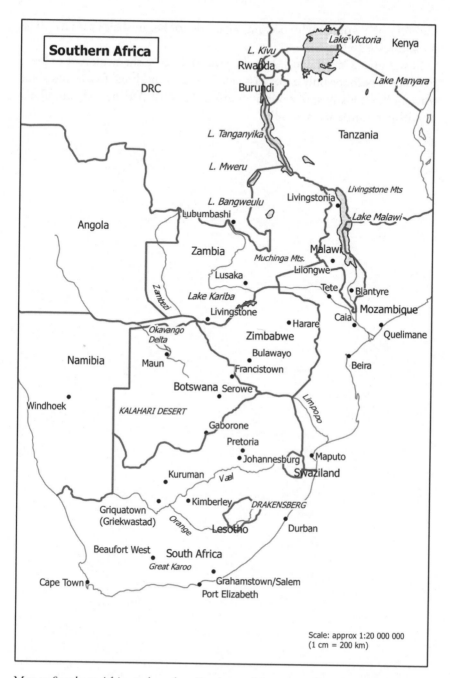

Map 1: Southern Africa today, showing the modern states whose borders were drawn and re-drawn by European colonial powers in the nineteenth century. In 1845, when Mary and David Livingstone were married at Kuruman, in what is now South Africa, the interior north of Kuruman was uncharted.

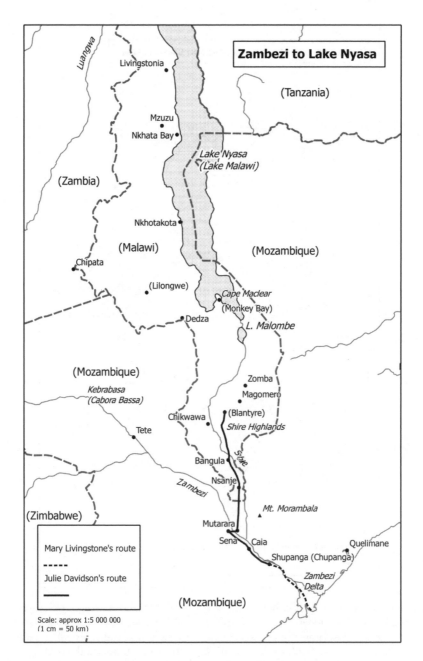

Zambezi to Lake Nyasa

Luangwa

Livingstonia

(Tanzania)

Mzuzu

Nkhata Bay

Lake Nyasa
(Lake Malawi)

(Zambia)

Nkhotakota

(Malawi)

(Mozambique)

Chipata

(Lilongwe)

Cape Maclear
(Monkey Bay)

Dedza

L. Malombe

(Mozambique)

Kebrabasa
(Cabora Bassa)

Zomba

Magomero

Chikwawa

(Blantyre)

Shire Highlands

Tete

Shire

Bangula

Zambezi

Nsanje

(Zimbabwe)

Mt. Morambala

Mutarara

Sena   Caia

Quelimane

Shupanga (Chupanga)

Zambezi
Delta

(Mozambique)

Mary Livingstone's route

- - - - -

Julie Davidson's route

Scale: approx 1:5 000 000
(1 cm = 50 km)

Map 2: The road to Chupanga, with an overview of the Zambezi's relationship
with the Shire Valley and Lake Nyasa, now Lake Malawi. Modern borders are
shown with the modern states and their colonial towns (bracketed). As marked,
Mike Muyafula and I travelled by road to Chupanga from Blantyre, while Mary's
journey up the Zambezi to the place called 'Shupanga' began at the river's delta.

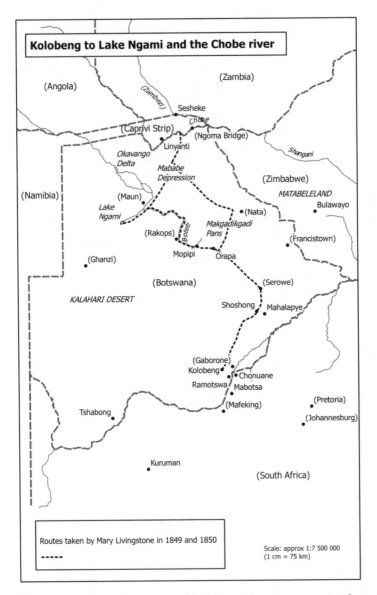

Kolobeng to Lake Ngami and the Chobe river

(Angola)

(Zambia)

(Zambezi)

Sesheke

Chobe

(Caprivi Strip)

(Ngoma Bridge)

Linyanti

Okavango Delta

Mababe Depression

(Zimbabwe)

(Namibia)

(Maun)

MATABELELAND

Lake Ngami

• (Nata)

Bulawayo

(Rakops)

Boteti

Makgadikgadi Pans

(Francistown)

Mopipi

Orapa

(Ghanzi)

(Botswana)

(Serowe)

KALAHARI DESERT

Shoshong

Mahalapye

(Gaborone)

Kolobeng

Chonuane

Ramotswa

Mabotsa

(Mafeking)

(Pretoria)

Tshabong

(Johannesburg)

Kuruman

(South Africa)

Shangani

Routes taken by Mary Livingstone in 1849 and 1850

Scale: approx 1:7 500 000
(1 cm = 75 km)

Map 3: Bechuanaland, now Botswana, at the time of the Livingstones' treks across the Kalahari. The modern national borders are indicated along with the names of the modern states, shown in brackets along with the towns and cities which didn't exist in the mid-nineteenth century. Keith Rampton and I followed the routes marked as closely as possible to Lake Ngami and the south bank of the Chobe, where Mary was left with the wagon camp while Livingstone and William Cotton Oswell crossed the river to Linyanti and continued to the Zambezi at Sesheke. We then crossed the Chobe ourselves into the Caprivi Strip, now part of Namibia, and arrived on the banks of the Zambezi.

Introduction

ALEXANDER MCCALL-SMITH

In 1980 when I was living for a short period in Swaziland, I made a number of trips across what was then the Transvaal to Botswana. My reason for going there was to visit a childhood friend, Howard Moffat, who was then running a small hospital in the village of Mochudi, north of Botswana's capital, Gaborone. I stayed with Howard and his wife, Fiona, for a few days on each of these trips, and it was on one of these occasions that the idea occurred to me of writing about a woman from Botswana who sets up a small business. Many years were to pass before I set pen to paper on that project – seventeen years, to be precise – and when I did eventually write that story I had no idea it would become a rather long-running literary saga, the *No. 1 Ladies' Detective Agency*.

My friend, Howard Moffat, is a member of the same Moffat family whose engagement with Africa is the subject of this remarkable book by Julie Davidson. I had always admired Howard's work, which has been much the same in its concerns and spirit as that of his missionary forebears. I had always taken that view, and yet I found it frustrating that people outside that part of Africa seem quite unaware of what is, by any standards, a most heroic and moving episode in the Western engagement with that continent. I remember, for instance, nominating Howard for a humanitarian award in Scotland and being met with blank and, I'm afraid, indifferent stares from people who had no idea, and, it appeared, little interest in my description of the historical context into which his lifetime's medical work in Botswana fitted. Perhaps it seemed to them that it was all a bit too redolent of a missionary history that many today regard as either embarrassing or even downright harmful.

How differently, though, is the story of David Livingstone viewed in Malawi, as Julie Davidson reveals. If Scotland is largely ignorant of the role that it played in Malawi's history and in the warmth and significance of the relationship, then that is not the case in Malawi itself. Scottish missionaries and Scottish doctors were appreciated there. That is not to say that missionary endeavours have not been arrogant and cultur-ally destructive in many cases, but balance is required in our assessment of their overall effect. Missionaries may have aided colonial penetration and ultimately exploitation, but they also built hospitals and schools and cared for people. Many of them gave their lives for the physical welfare of others. They may have been interested in the souls of their charges, but they were also prepared to go to any lengths to ensure that people were fed, educated and cured of sickness. Not to give that its proper weight in any moral evaluation is, in my view, to allow ideology to obscure reality.

The Moffat family played a crucial role in the nineteenth-century history of east–central and southern Africa. Their story is a dramatic one – it is all about hardship and persistence and determination to relieve suffering. Its principal protagonists are the stuff of great historical saga: Robert Moffat, a man from a simple background who educated himself and then braved immense hardship to establish centres of succour in a part of the continent at the mercy of brutality and disease; David Livingstone, a man who may have been blinkered in his enthusiasms but who fought against slavery and its unimaginable cruelties; and Robert's wife, Mary, and their daughter also Mary, who married Livingstone and who was to die a wretched death because of the path her background and marriage seemed so inexorably to dictate. This book is principally concerned with Mary Livingstone, but the story of the whole family is explored, even to the present generations, still active in Africa.

What sets this account apart from any previous treatments of the life of Mary Livingstone is the way in which Julie Davidson intertwines the story of her subject's life with an account of her travels to the places associated with it. She does this in a most masterly way, depicting the various coun-tries she visits with a highly observant but, most importantly, tolerant eye. In many African countries, the past is not always as evident to the visitor as it is in countries where stone architecture is the rule. Africa is not kind to human buildings – timber succumbs to termites; structures are baked by the sun or washed away; the bush encroaches, covers up. To find vestiges of even the comparatively recent nineteenth-century past, one has to reconstruct from fading and imperfect sources; one has to dig about; one has to listen to voices that are faint and fading; one has to travel down obscure and sometimes dangerous tracks. All of this has been done to great effect here by Julie Davidson, who has created in this remark-able work of historical and geographical reflection a fascinating picture of a remarkable life. I find the resulting story very moving. It is moving because it gets under the skin of a beguiling part of the world that so often claims the hearts of those who engage with it. It is moving, too, because it is sensitive to the spirituality that one finds in that part of Africa and that is so deeply affecting. This book achieves a real understanding of that spirituality without in any way romanticising or sentimentalising it. When she eventually found Mary Livingstone's grave, Julie Davidson laid four small flowers upon it. In this lovely memoir, she lays on that lonely grave more flowers yet.

Alexander McCall Smith

Prologue

Early afternoon in Griquatown, a bump on the far, flat horizons of the
Northern Cape. Main Street is empty but replete with heat. There is shade
to be found in the Mary Moffat Museum; temperate air within its stone
walls, shadows resting in its modest rooms. Out of the shadows comes
the voice of a child, crossing continents and decades in a letter dated New
Year's Day 1869. The address is Ulva Cottage, Hamilton, Scotland.

> Dear Mr Andersen, My name is Anna Mary, last-born of Mary my
> mother, deceased of the desert fever while I was but a 'wee bairn'; I am
> but ten, too young to remember her voice.
>   I do like your fairy tales so much – the tin soldier and the ugly, ugly
> duckling. I would like to go and visit you; when Papa comes home from
> Africa I intend to ask him to take me. I live where he began as a piercer
> of cotton, threading those bales, long enough to join us over six thou-
> sand miles; what with the water-thrust and water-damp.
>   The Clyde is perfect for the manufacture of cloth; without cotton my
> dolly'd have no clothes.
>   I'm sure he will agree. In the New Year.

The New Year came and went, and the visit to Hans Christian Andersen
was never made. But, a few days into his five-year correspondence with
Anna Mary, last-born of Mary Moffat, the Danish writer noted in his
diary that he'd heard from a little girl in Scotland, 'the daughter of Dr
Livingstone, the famous traveller'.

Five more Hogmanays followed without the return of 'Papa'. In June
1871, his daughter confided to the story-teller: 'If you ask me he's forgotten the meaning of his own hearth'. In September 1874, she wrote: 'I did
expect Papa to take me to your Copenhagen. Instead of going the different places I fully intended with Papa, I have been obliged to take the sad
journey to London to see what's left of him buried in Westminster Abbey.'

By then, she was 15. When she was five, Anna Mary met her father for
the first time, and knew him for only a few months before he sailed for

Zanzibar to take up the search for the source of the Nile. When she was not yet two, her mother, tormented by misgivings, left Anna Mary and her siblings in Hamilton to join her husband on the Zambezi, where she died of 'the desert fever', an acute malarial attack, three months after their reunion.

Perhaps the little girl looked for surrogate parents in the painful fairy stories of Hans Christian Andersen; perhaps she instinctively found in 'the tin soldier' the iron man of Africa, the warrior for Christ; and in the 'ugly, ugly duckling' the plain, neglected, unhappy woman who, like his children, became expendable to his vision and ambition.

I

Big Water

'a regular cargo of ladies'

September 2007

'Have you ever hit anything?' I ask Mike Muyafula as we breach the Thyolo Escarpment and sink into the Shire Valley. Here, the pock-marked tar straightens and flattens and the traffic thickens: goats, dogs, bikes, pigs, cows, donkeys, pedestrians; an occasional ramshackle truck doing illegal bus runs, its flatbed loaded with windblown, stoical passengers. This is not my first journey on Malawi's vivacious roads, but it is my most relaxed. Mike seems to have psychic powers of anticipation, reading the mind of every wayward mammal.

'I once hit a goat', he replies, with a trace of shame. 'And goats are hard to hit. They have more road sense than dogs.' His otherwise impeccable record on these anarchic highways has made him a valued driver-guide with Central African Wilderness Safaris, who have put together our itinerary. His mastery of a Land Rover Defender on broken roads and dirt tracks, his solicitous nature, merry smile and easy conversation make him a comfortable companion on our long, cross-border drive to the Zambezi.

Zambezi, Za-mbezi: big water. Africa's fourth-longest river, 2,200 miles from source to delta, begins its expedition to the Indian Ocean in a marsh in north-west Zambia and drains the water systems of most of south-central Africa. It passes through six countries, supports the subsistence farming and fishing of 30 million people, generates hydro-electric power for Zambia, Zimbabwe, Mozambique and South Africa, and maintains a tourist industry in its game-rich national parks. But it has never become a major commercial waterway. It is a volatile river of shifting mudflats and sandbanks with two stupendous geological obstructions to navigation: on the Zambia–Zimbabwe border the Victoria Falls, and in Mozambique the Cabora Bassa rapids, now harnessed by the Cabora Bassa Dam, the fifth largest in the world.

It is a river of no half-measures, benign and tyrannical, remaking itself every rainy season, endowing its dependants with abundant fish and fertile floodplains, destroying their homes and crops with its incontinence. It gives and it takes. It made and destroyed the public reputation of David Livingstone. It was the conduit for his wife's longed-for return to Africa, her birthplace and home, and the source of some rare weeks of happiness. Then it killed her.

I am on my way to a grave, the terminus of a melancholy story, but my mood is cheerful. I have left the grey fag-end of the Scottish summer for the bright skies and blossoms of the southern-hemisphere spring. When Mike picks me up at Chileka International Airport – an amiable, dozy little place despite its international status, earned by a handful of flights to Johannesburg and East Africa – I'm looking forward to my first visit to Malawi's commercial and financial capital: Blantyre, the city in the hills named after the birthplace of David Livingstone by the Scottish churchmen who followed him into the fertile valleys and airy uplands he called the Shire Highlands, because they reminded him of home.

Mary Livingstone never saw these sunny hills, or the strange, square-topped, free-standing mountain of Chiradzulu which threw its shadow over desperate times in their colonial history; or farther north the inland sea which the locals called Nyasa, meaning 'large water', or sometimes Nyinyesi, 'lake of stars'. Her husband favoured Nyasa, and the land of the lake eventually became Nyasaland, the British colony which was reconstituted as the Republic of Malawi in 1964. The lake was renamed Lake Malawi, and the 'lake of stars' is now a marketing slogan for its tourist industry.

As the Shire River spills from this Rift Valley basin and flows south to join the Zambezi some 100 miles from the sea, its hinterland is infused with the history and consequences of the doomed expedition in which Mary played a brief but representative part. Mike and I plan to drive down the Shire Valley and cross the Mozambique border near the town of Nsanje before tackling the formidable obstacle of the Zambezi at Mutarara, where there is one of its few bridges. It would be quicker and less daunting to approach the village where Mary spent the last days of her life from the Indian Ocean coast and the Mozambican port city of Beira. But the route through Malawi is part of her story.

Blantyre glows with the electric blue of flowering jacaranda trees. Most of the post-colonial cities I've seen in East, central and southern Africa have a physical kinship with each other. In their centres, the survivors of colonial architecture – law courts, museums, churches, administrative buildings – crouch stubbornly among the modern monoliths of banks, offices and hotels. In their suburbs, graceful bungalows, charmless low-cost housing, flower-filled gardens, squatters' shacks, air-conditioned shopping malls and unruly markets remain segregated by income, if not race. And, legitimately or otherwise, noisily and brilliantly, the downtown streets, bus stations, taxi ranks and gap sites are claimed by the pavement industries and improvised economies of make-do-and-mend Africa.

Blantyre has all of these and more; not least, at an altitude of over 1,500 feet, an attractive climate and healthy relationship with the generous earth of the Shire Highlands. These were the features which first convinced Livingstone of their potential for British – and therefore Christian – settlement; and today the city fits well into its collar of copper-coloured hills, their late winter bush burnt the colour of autumn bracken on a Trossachs brae. Before we head south, I want a quick look at St Michael and All Angels Church, where the Blantyre Mission was founded by the Church of Scotland in 1876, three years after Livingstone's death.

It was not the first outpost of British evangelism in the new region of Nyasa, where the missionary-explorer had inspired a procession of apostles to follow him up the Shire River. The Kirk was pre-empted by the rival Free Church of Scotland when Robert Laws set up the lakeside mission of Livingstonia, appropriating the revered name. Even earlier, in 1861, as the Zambezi Expedition struggled with its failures, an Anglican mission at Magomero, beneath the hulk of Chiradzulu, lasted barely a year among warring tribes and slaving raids before collapsing in calamity. The Universities Mission to Central Africa (UMCA) was prematurely encouraged into the Shire Highlands by an over-optimistic Livingstone. Its leaders' lives were squandered, and the rash enterprise at Magomero indirectly played a part in the death of Mary Livingstone.

But St Michael and All Angels, the second-oldest building in the country, improvised from local stone without benefit of architect, is the place where the long threads of history linking the two Blantyres are most firmly knotted. Here, Scots of any or no faith (a condition barely comprehended in Malawi) are welcomed with special warmth. And here, I'm greeted with the salute: 'David Livingstone! Dad for Africa!'

The Reverend Harry Ngwale, short, wrinkled and smiley, is not just a disciple of his 'dad for Africa' but also a passionate propagandist for his legacy. As the church's choirmaster, he has escorted his twenty-strong choir, all women, to the Zambian village of Chitambo, where the explorer died. 'It is my dearest wish', he confides, 'to take these ladies to Scotland to sing at the place where he was born.'

Nothing happens fast in Malawi, as in much of Africa. I daren't tell the enthusiastic cleric that my time is short as we amble through the ample grounds of the church and mission, relishing the shade of its venerable trees and stone buildings. 'The first church was mud and thatch.' The Reverend Harry invites me to admire the sturdy structure it became, its untutored design confident yet homely; points out the tablet donated in 1913 by Livingstone's grandchildren on the centenary of his birth; and, when we reach the administration block, flourishes a hand at the ceiling of the 'gallows room'.

'Look up there!' he commands. I lift my eyes obediently to the beam with the iron hooks which, the cheerful choirmaster tells me, once supported chains for the hanging and flogging of miscreants. When the Church of Scotland appointed itself landlord of a huge tract of the highlands, the Reverend Duff Macdonald, the mission's first leader, presided over it like a despot. There was no civil government in Nyasaland at the time, and Macdonald's justice was often dispensed on the dubious evidence of some very intemperate subordinates.

His is a name which still makes the Kirk nervous, and his brutal reputation caused the Assembly of the day to mount an investigation and demand resignations. But he has an apologist in Oliver Ransford, an eloquent chronicler of Malawi's history and of Livingstone's part in it. In his book *Livingstone's Lake*, Ransford argues that Macdonald's only fault was an inability to control his staff, and describes him as 'one of those odd blends of humility, erudition and ill-directed severity which from time to time is seen in clerics of the Protestant Church, especially in Scotland'.

It seems Duff Macdonald enjoyed nothing better than jollying along the annual Sunday-school picnic of his converts; an appealing side to the man, but small comfort to the victims of the impulsive executions and sometimes terminal floggings which tainted the beginnings of this peaceful place. As the Reverend Harry and I debate the morality of these disciplines, Mike Muyafula is too polite to interrupt, but transmits urgency by shifting the keys of the Land Rover from hand to hand. We have much rough ground to cover before dark, and it's already early afternoon. But, before we leave the Blantyre Mission, I ask to see its cemetery, aware that some of its story will be written in shorthand on the gravestones.

Fresh flowers have been placed in water on one small, time-weathered grave, sealed with concrete like many African graves to thwart the investigations of wild animals and feral dogs. The name on the stone is Jocelyn Mary Ross, and its dates are 1956 to 1963. 'We had a delegation from Scotland who wanted to visit Dr Ross's daughter's grave', explains Harry Ngwale. 'They left these flowers.'

Dr Andrew Ross, who died in 2008, was one of Livingstone's biographers and a former principal of New College, Edinburgh University's Faculty of Divinity. As a young minister he spent seven years in Malawi, where his daughter Jocelyn died. The family tragedies of missionary families – perhaps they would call them sacrifices – have a long history. Over

1,700 miles south of Blantyre, near the Botswana capital of Gaborone, is the grave of another mission child: Elizabeth Pyne, infant daughter of David and Mary Livingstone. She was born at the mission station of Kolobeng shortly after the family returned from a gruelling, three-month ox-wagon trek across the Kalahari, and lived for only six weeks. Among the unkempt grass and broken foundations of the Kolobeng site, her grave is marked by a circle of field stones.

March is a chancy month on the Lower Zambezi. The hot, wet summer can lodge in the valley for another month, the air is thick with new dynasties of mosquitoes, and there may yet be more rain, more flooding. In March 1863, David and Mary Livingstone found themselves at a dangerous time of year on a dangerous part of the river: its malarial delta, where they waited to embark two grieving women and their female servants on a ship to Cape Town. The bereaved women were Miss Anne Mackenzie, the elderly unmarried sister of Bishop Mackenzie, leader of the UMCA station at Magomero, and Mrs Henry Burrup, the newly married young wife of one of his recruits. The servants were Miss Mackenzie's housekeeper, Jessie Lennox, and a maid called Sarah, for whom history has neglected to supply a surname.

With Mary Livingstone, they were the 'regular cargo of ladies', as Mary called them, who had sailed from Cape Town to the mouth of the Zambezi in the brig *Hetty Ellen* only two months earlier. Here, Mary was not only reunited with her husband after nearly four years of painful separation, but also returned to the continent of her birth; here, Miss Mackenzie and Mrs Burrup looked forward to their own reunions with brother and husband respectively at Magomero. But by the time they joined the expedition steamship *Pioneer* the Zambezi project was in desperate trouble, the Magomero mission was in disarray, Bishop Mackenzie and Henry Burrup, both mortally ill, were stranded on an island in the Shire River, and Mary Livingstone had less than three months to live.

In September the Shire Valley is smeared with heat haze and the smoke of fires set to clear bush – a tradition which exasperates conservationists but which Malawians, Zambians and other rural Africans find hard to discontinue. Long before they had livestock to graze and crops to grow, their hunter-gatherer ancestors fired the bush to drive game into their spears and flush out hazards like buffalo and lion. This painterly gauze brings its own beauty to our journey, softening the baked landscape and fierce light. On the rim of the Thyolo Escarpment, with the hills of Mozambique and the forests of Majete Wildlife Reserve to the west, Mike pulls off the corkscrew road – Malawi's M1 – to give me a mighty overview of the lowland plains.

On the far edge of a mosaic of fields is a long, pale stain: the Shire River, Livingstone's Zambezi substitute, his second choice for 'God's Highway'. This was the alternative waterway which he judged would bring civilising religion to the pagan interior of Africa, drive out the slavers and import colonies of British administrators, clerics, farmers and traders. These worthy role models (he did not dwell on the possibility of more ruthless immigrants) would then provide the tribes with new economies, discourage their predations on each other and encourage their conversion to Christian worship and practice.

It was, in the context of his time and faith, a noble vision; an aspiration both spiritual and practical which much affected British public opinion, which had become infatuated with the man who was filling vast blanks in the map of Africa and rousing the government to greater action on the abomination of the slave trade. Britain and its Empire had extracted itself from the industry eight years before Livingstone set foot in Africa, but it wasn't until 1836 that its old European ally Portugal, 'after great resistance', declared 'the final and entire abolition of the Portuguese Slave Trade'. Notoriously, the authorities in its African colonies east and west continued to sanction and profit from the trade, while the Omani Arabs of the Swahili coast, among the earliest traffickers, continued to harvest men, women and children from the Congo Basin and the Rift Valley as they harvested tusks from the great elephant herds – without scruple.

Although the government of Lord Palmerston was little interested in new colonies and could see no domestic advantage in Livingstone's ambitions, it agreed to underwrite 'a voyage of discovery upon the Zambesi' to the sum of £5,000; a small but shrewd investment in the popularity of a national hero. But, over a period of six years, the expedition cost £50,000 and a dozen lives, failed to meet its leader's promises and, in the short term, tarnished his reputation.

Less than a year into the 'voyage of discovery', three years before Mary joined it, Livingstone turned his attention to the Shire, forced to accept that the Zambezi could never become a commercial conduit from the Indian Ocean to the tablelands of present-day Zambia. He had, of course, seen the impassable Victoria Falls; and his first choice for a British colony was the high Batoka plateau, to the north of the falls. But he had not seen the rapids of 'Kebrabasa', as he had taken a shortcut across a loop in the river when he charted the Zambezi during his transcontinental journey of 1853–6. And, although he had been advised by reliable sources, Portuguese and indigenous, that this tremendous stretch of cliffs, rocks and boiling water between the Victoria Falls and the Zambezi delta was unnavigable, Livingstone would not be told what he could or couldn't do on a river he believed he'd made his own. He wasted time and resources trying to breach the rapids with the first expedition steamship *Ma-Robert* (named after Mary's Tswana honorific, Mother of Robert, her first-born child) before admitting in his journal: 'This Kebrabasa is what I never expected'.

As with all his frustrated plans, Livingstone then aimed to turn defeat into victory. On New Year's Day 1859, he sailed the *Ma-Robert* into the calm mouth of the Shire River for the first time. Today there are booms across the Shire, and at Kapichira Falls a dam with turbines generating hydro-electricity. At the town of Nsanje, where Mike and I are heading, they have deepened the harbour. Nsanje lies close to the Shire's confluence with the Zambezi, well below the stupendous dam of Cabora Bassa; and there are plans to make it an inland port for landlocked Malawi, with commercial traffic working both rivers to and from the Zambezi delta. Livingstone's dream. Up to a point.[1]

For much of its 300-mile journey from Lake Malawi, the Shire flows through a child's version of Africa: storybook Africa, Tarzan's Africa, its waters thick with crocodile and hippo, its banks dense with Ilala palms, fever trees and – those prehistoric monsters of the arboreal world – baobabs. I first got a taste of its raw nature in Liwonde National Park, between the southern end of the lake and the old colonial capital of Zomba. As I was ferried across the river to Mvuu Camp, a gang of crocodiles was frenziedly spinning the corpse of a hippo, spilling its stomach and intestines into the water. That night, I went to sleep to the unearthly rasp of a green-backed night heron and was wakened by the noise of trees being shredded outside my tent. An enormous shadow brushed the canvas. Through the net window, I saw moonlight gleaming on ivory.

Multi-tasking as it travels south, the river stocks other nature reserves with birds and game and refreshes the fertility of the lowland plains, from

---

1 Nsanje Inland Port was completed and inaugurated in 2010 but is still unused. Malawi's negotiations with Mozambique, which has not yet bought into the project, have faltered, largely because Mozambique remains unconvinced of the navigability of the Zambezi and Shire River waterway.

the cassava plots of subsistence farmers to the cane fields of the Ilovo Sugar Company. As we follow its course, we see nothing but blameless scenes of rural activity: men and women working the land, goats nibbling the verges, cattle waiting thoughtfully by village standpipes, the merchandising of produce on every scale – from wayside children offering unripe mangos and kebabs of barbecued field mice, to expansive markets boisterous with business.

But there remains a wildness about the Shire, and the residue of a dark history. Livingstone soon learned there were obstacles to navigating the river beyond another set of rapids (the Murchison Cataracts, named after his friend Sir Roderick Murchison, one of the founders of the Royal Geographic Society). The euphoria of his first visit, when he began to picture fields planted with cotton and sugar cane, was soon dissipated by evidence that the slave trade was ravaging the valley, with the aggressive Yao, middle men for Arab slavers, preying on the riverside Manganja, who retreated in terror from the *Ma-Robert* and its crew of white strangers.

The Shire Valley was a place of violence and misery, where man-made wretchedness was compounded by endemic malaria. Dr Rowley, one of three survivors of the seven-strong Magomero mission, was to call the Shire 'a river of death', yet word of its high fertile hinterland and a great lake to the north raised Livingstone's spirits and prompted further explorations by boat and on foot. He believed (with some justification, as history, Blantyre and the Ilovo Sugar Company would demonstrate) that he had found his alternative to the Bakota plateau, his colonial promised land. But, as so often with his visionary schemes, there was a high cost. For all his misgivings about the region – and with the minor caveat that they should expect some problems – he assured the ardent organisers of the Anglican mission that the time was right and the Shire Highlands was the place for the first Christian mission station in central Africa.

As the afternoon light deepens, we reach the scattered town of Chikwawa, where we cross the river to its west bank. Near here are the graves of two members of the UMCA. After a bit, the tar surface of the M1 becomes rocky red dirt. The sun is low by the time we reach Bangula, where I ask Mike to point out the confluence of the Shire and the Ruo, one of its tributaries. At this junction, nearly 150 years ago, a rendezvous was planned. Here, 130 miles south-east of Magomero, Bishop Mackenzie and Henry Burrup expected Livingstone to deliver their ladies.

The explorer had unaccountably authorised Miss Mackenzie and Mrs Burrup to join the pioneering mission, despite its unpredictable hazards. (The bishop's sister even brought her piano.) When the clerics arrived for their rendezvous in January 1862, they were already weakened by diarrhoea and a long canoe journey down the Shire in ceaseless rain. As they waited on an island off the mouth of the Ruo, they were further plagued by fever. There was no sign of Livingstone and the 'regular cargo of ladies', who had all been delayed. Three weeks passed, and their health worsened.

The bishop died first; and, with the help of their African followers, Burrup, barely able to walk, buried him on the mainland before being carried back to Magomero, where he, too, died. When news finally reached the Zambezi Expedition's base at Shupanga, Livingstone and his wife escorted the heartbroken bride and the inconsolable sister to the mouth of the Zambezi in the *Pioneer*, which by then had replaced the worn-out *Ma-Robert*. Here, they waited nearly three weeks among the delta's pestilential vapours for a ship bound for Cape Town, by which time Mary Livingstone was well on her way to becoming collateral damage of the Magomero debacle.

Where the Ruo meets the Shire there is little to see except reeds, a pied kingfisher and two sacred ibis. The bishop's grave was unmarked, and the island where he died is now submerged.

It's almost dark by the time we reach Nsanje, a town well outside the comfort zone of Western tourists and well south of the Shire floodplains which attract birders. There are no luxury lodges or hotels in Nsanje, but there are one or two rest houses – the class of basic accommodation used by low-income Malawians, backpackers and the humbler foot soldiers of the great international army of aid and development workers. We're booked into the Sweet Dreams Rest House, three single-storey blocks, like an American motel, arranged around a garden courtyard, with the obligatory mango tree for shade and splashes of bougainvillea and impala blossom. The best rooms, with en-suite bathroom, evening meal and breakfast, cost 1,700 kwacha a night – a sum which would buy, perhaps, a couple of burgers in the West.

Mike is looking a little worried. Central African Wilderness Safaris (CAWS) is an upmarket operation; he is accustomed to transferring clients between high-end lodges and camps, meeting them off private charter flights. He knows my mission is a different kind of adventure – we talked it through on my last visit to Malawi – but in his eyes I'm still an affluent white traveller, slung around with camera, binoculars and too many bags. We meet for supper in the restaurant, where the only other diners are a Dutch couple in the volunteer aid worker's 'uniform' of flip-flops, bead and copper jewellery and Swahili kikois worn like pashminas. 'Is your room all right?' he asks.

'It's absolutely fine', I assure him truthfully, tucking into fish and chips. (The unfilleted fish, baked black as sin with baleful eyes, looks evil but tastes wonderful.) My bed linen is worn but clean, the shower is a concrete cell but delivers hot water, the loo flushes rustily, there are one or two electric cables poking from the ceiling but the lights work; and there's a bright blue mosquito net over my bed, guaranteeing rest beneath its heavenly canopy.

At Nsanje I'm a night's sleep, a border post, a Zambezi bridge and a day's drive away from Mary Livingstone's grave. I've yet to discover that the Zambezi makes nothing easy for travellers. Even today.

2

The Bridge at Mutarara

'a queer piece of furniture'

Frontiers, border posts, the sterile strip of no-man's-land between one nation state and its neighbour, are edgy places, at least in the imagination. They are the nation state in microcosm, a bureaucratic holding-pen where all the most extreme pressures of the territorial imperative come together. Go. Stay. Forward. Back. Pass. Wait. They have their own time zone, which functions independently of the real time of any travel plans. The right piece of paper may add only fifteen minutes to your journey; the wrong one fifteen hours. Factored into the itinerary of our route to the Zambezi is Marka Border Post, a concrete block and swing barrier on the dirt road eighteen miles south of Nsanje. It opens at 8pm, and it is an amiable anti-climax.

'Malawi Revenue Authority: Providing Quality Taxpayer Service in Malawi.' On the bench outside Customs and Excise, two men hunch thoughtfully over a game of mancala, often described as African chess, a board game available to the poorest of players. These men use the regular wooden board pitted with small depressions, and their playing pieces are polished pebbles; but mancala boards can be improvised on the ground, with holes dug for pits, and stones, seeds or cowrie shells deployed as playing pieces. As I climb down from the Land Rover, they give me that stony stare of naked curiosity which often unnerves Western newcomers to Africa. But when I offer them the standard Chichewa greeting *Muli bwanji?* (How are you?), they beam as warmly as if they've been waiting to welcome me. *Ndili bwino, Mama. Kaya inu?* Fine, Mama. And you?

There is a queue of traffic: an ox-cart (evidence of rural prosperity) loaded with excited chickens and two phlegmatic goats; a battered pick-up stacked with plastic-covered mattresses and pots and pans, en route to a trading post. And a taxi-bike, its rear wheel mounted with a cushioned seat, its owner commissioned to transport one adult, two children and their market produce in the following manner: woman passenger on the rear seat, baby on her back, toddler in her lap, basket of vegetables on her head. A journey of fifteen miles will cost her 200 kwacha; a packet of sweets in Europe.

Before Mike disappears into Customs and Excise to submit the vehicle paperwork, I ask him if I can take a picture of the Malawian flag on its pole beside the crash barriers. And, when he nods, I ask him to pose beside it and the notice board of the Malawi Revenue Authority. There are many countries in and beyond the African continent (including Britain) where snapping photos at frontiers is forbidden and may lead to reprimand, camera confiscation, fines or even arrest. But this is Marka, proud ambassador of the back of beyond. Nobody bothers. Twenty minutes later, passports and paperwork stamped, Mike, the Land Rover and I are duly authorised to exit Malawi.

Nor is there much scrutiny at Marka's opposite number on the other side of no-man's-land: the Mozambican border post of Vila Nova de Fronteira. Although the official language of Mozambique is Portuguese, which neither Mike nor I speak, everyone on this side of the border for at least 30 miles also speaks Chichewa, the national language of Malawi. Our path through immigration, visa inspection and payment of frontier tax is smoothed by Mike's courteous exchange of greetings, which I have learned can be helpful with the most forbidding official, and recommend to all visitors to Africa even if they can only manage 'How are you?' in English. But, twenty years earlier, crossing this border would have been a very different experience.

Twenty years earlier, Mozambique's frontiers were fraught with the fall-out from its post-independence civil war, which didn't end until 1992. Portugal was among the last of the European powers to decolonise in Africa, which it did in a hurry in 1975, stripping assets as it went. The backwash from Mozambique's freedom fight was brutal and bitter, not least because it was exacerbated by the destabilising strategies and covert terrorism of South Africa and Rhodesia. When the left-wing party of Frelimo (Front for the Liberation of Mozambique) became the first democratic government of the new republic and launched ambitious programmes of social reform, these two neighbours stoked and provoked internal resistance to a state which they perceived as dangerously Marxist, and which was to become a base for their own militant black nationalists.

The maverick government of Ian Smith's Rhodesia, making its last-ditch stand for white supremacy, set up the guerrilla organisation Renamo, an acronym in Portuguese for Mozambique National Resistance. When the former British colony became Zimbabwe in 1980, the South African Defence Force continued to arm and bankroll Renamo. There followed another twelve years of civil war, during which Renamo (today, more respectably, the main opposition party) became little more than a lawless army of roaming insurgents with a savage reputation. Its war bands supported themselves by pillaging the countryside, recruiting boy soldiers and seeding rural Mozambique with land mines. Government forces could do little to control their activities outside the cities, except plant their own land mines and commit their own atrocities; and Frelimo's social achievements, including thousands of new schools, clinics and hospitals, were reduced to rubble.

Among the casualties were the church, schools and clinic of a riverside village called Chupanga, in the Renamo heartland of Sofala province. In the mid-nineteenth century, Chupanga was known to European travellers as Shupanga: the place where Mary Livingstone died, and the repository of her grave.

The Zambezi Expedition needed a base upstream of the mudflats and mangrove swamps of the river estuary. Some energetic diplomatic activity had persuaded Portugal, well entrenched in the territory it called Zambesia, to authorise Livingstone's government-sponsored expedition and provide some assistance. Britain's Foreign Office gave the explorer an official locus in the colony by arranging his appointment as consul for the port of Quelimane, but the Portuguese drew the line at extending his consular brief to Sena and Tete, their main settlements on the Zambezi. They did, however, offer him the use of a substantial stone house at Shupanga, downstream from both towns but seventy miles upriver from the disease-ridden delta.

Shupanga House was useful for storing supplies and getting out of the rain, although most of the expedition members camped on the river bank or lived on board the boats which came and went during their six years on the Zambezi. Dr John Kirk didn't think much of its site: 'The ground is damp and the atmosphere cold during the morning hours – in fact a more unhealthy place could not well be imagined, damp and shaded with trees, surrounded on the land side by long grass'. This was where Mary Livingstone spent the final hours of her life as her husband and Kirk battled to bring the most acute symptoms of malaria under control. 'I was sent for at 3am', he recorded in his diary for 27 April 1862. 'Found her in a half comatose state. It was impossible to get medicine taken. Blisters would not rise and injections proved unavailing. Steadily coma deepened into perfect insensibility and the skin tinged of a deep yellow ...'

John Kirk, born near Arbroath on the east coast of Scotland, was a snob and a sexist; not unusual prejudices in a Victorian son of the manse.

One of many Scots to make an impact in the service of Britain's African interests, he is best remembered for persuading Sultan Barghash of Zanzibar, where Kirk became British consul in 1870, to close the slave market and outlaw its trade in all the Zanzibari territories. This he did in 1873, the year Livingstone died without knowing that a stake had been driven through the unholy heart of human trafficking on the Swahili coast.

Kirk, then in his twenties, was deeply affected by his time with Livingstone on the Zambezi, the Shire and Lake Nyasa. Among the self-serving accounts of squabbles, jealousies and wayward behaviour in the letters and journals which became the expedition archive, he emerges with credit in every respect except one: he underestimated Mary Livingstone. She did not fit his idea of the wife of a great man. He did not admire the ready way she set about pulling her weight on the cramped *Pioneer*, rolling up her sleeves 'in easy deshabille', without vanity or artifice, to store supplies, cook meals over camp fires and do the laundry on the riverbank. He dismissed her as 'a coarse, vulgar woman ... cut out for rough work'. He also decided she was too fat and 'a queer piece of furniture'.

This queer piece of furniture had been cut out for rough work since the day she was born in a reed hut in the remote bushlands beyond the Orange River. She had crossed the Kalahari twice and won the high regard of the gentleman-explorer William Cotton Oswell, who had first-hand experience of her competence, stoicism and courage. Her own husband called her his 'rib', his 'heroine'. Yet the young John Kirk, with his medical degree from the University of Edinburgh and his observational skills as the expedition botanist, could not detect the stout heart inside the stout body of Livingstone's industrious Ma-Robert.

Mike Muyafula is a good Christian man. There are few educated Malawians unaware that their country's predominant belief system was bequeathed to it by a devout Scot from the cotton mills of Clydeside, but Mike has found his church outside Malawi. On his bush shirt, he wears a star badge on leather mounting with the initials ZCC. I've seen this badge before on the lapels of black Zimbabweans and South Africans, but never had the opportunity to ask what it signifies. On the arid, empty, cheerless road between the Mozambique border and the Zambezi, I get my chance. 'The Zion Christian Church', replies Mike. 'It's based in South Africa. I've been a member for five years, although I come from a family of Roman Catholics. In fact, my brother is a priest.'

Later, Mike tells me why he left the Catholic Church to join the largest indigenous Christian church in Africa, with an estimated 20 million people in its two congregations and long-established headquarters in South Africa's Limpopo province. But, for the moment, I'm more interested in the journey he has made from village boy in the remote north of Malawi to family man with a good job and a modern house in the capital, Lilongwe. Mike is 35, but looks younger. He is short, stocky and lightly moustached, with a guileless smile and warm, attentive eyes. Some faces just have the stamp of goodness on them; Mike's is one of them.

He is Lambya. The Lambya are one of the smaller tribes of the Rift Valley, and their homelands straddle the border of Malawi and Tanzania, where the River Songwe marks the frontier and feeds Lake Malawi. Mike's home village is in the district of Chitipa, on a tongue of land between Zambia and Tanzania. To the south lies the high, heart-stirring tableland of the Nyika Plateau, part of the western escarpment of the Rift Valley, and on its rim is Livingstonia Mission. To the west, plunging into the lake on its Tanzanian side, are the sheer ramparts of the Livingstone Mountains. Mike comes from the land of Livingstone landmarks.

Both mission and mountains owe their names not only to the explorer but also to the perseverance of his followers. Livingstone was dead by the time Robert Laws established Livingstonia, moving sites twice from the malarial lakeside until settling on the healthier plateau nearly 3,000 feet above it. Laws, a doctor of humble origins who was born in the Scottish city of Aberdeen, had been inspired by Livingstone's example since childhood. In October 1875, he and Lieutenant E. D. Young, who had been Livingstone's trusted captain on the *Pioneer*, sailed the first steam vessel that had ever entered an African lake from the Shire River into the shining waters of Nyasa. The moment was marked by the ship's company, who assembled on deck to sing *All Things Bright and Beautiful*.

Laws and Young charted the north end of the lake, which Livingstone had failed to reach, underestimating its length by about 100 miles. (The 'calendar lake', as it's sometimes called, is about 365 miles long and 52 miles at its broadest point.) The two men named its northern bays and landmarks, including the Livingstone Mountains. Their vessel was called the *Ilala*, after the district in present-day Zambia where Livingstone died, and was succeeded by other *Ilala*s. The present incarnation is a veteran ferry built in 1949 at Yarrow's yard at Scotstoun, on the Clyde. The MV *Ilala* was dispatched in pieces by ship, road and rail and reassembled at her home port of Monkey Bay, and has been linking the lake communities from end to end and shore to shore ever since.

She is a glorious relic of the Clyde's imperial reach and may soon be retired. On one of my visits to Malawi, I spent two nights and three days on this sturdy, travel-stained, lop-sided workhorse, celebrated for her wilful temperament, anarchic time-keeping and blithe approach to Health and Safety. I sailed from Monkey Bay at the south end of the lake to Nkhata Bay, on the north-west shore, which is as far as Livingstone got before running out of supplies and running into hostile locals. 'This is the first time I have ever returned without accomplishing all I set out to do', he recorded testily.

He had begun his navigation of the lake in a small gig in September 1861, taking with him his brother Charles and John Kirk, who were among the few members of the increasingly forlorn Zambezi Expedition whom he considered reliable. About the same time Mary Livingstone had embarked on her own voyage from Southampton to Cape Town, where she sailed into Table Bay with a shipboard companion, an aspiring medical missionary whom she had got to know in Scotland. The Reverend James Stewart of the Free Church of Scotland was to cause Mary a certain amount of trouble, and do nothing at all for her posthumous reputation.

The last leg of our journey to the Zambezi takes us through a wedge of the province of Tete, where Livingstone met his nemesis at the rapids of 'Kebrabasa'. We go nowhere near the Cabora Bassa dam. Our road from the border is not long, just over twenty-six miles of deformed dirt, but it is sobering. It has none of the productive bustle of Malawi's roads or sunny salutes of their pedestrians. Although Mozambique has made impressive economic strides since the end of its civil war, Tete's progress, like that of Sofala, was compromised by its support for Renamo in the country's first multi-party elections. When Frelimo was returned to government in 1994 the well-being of these traumatised provinces, which had suffered terribly at the hands of both sides, was not a priority.

The road to Mutarara is waymarked by signs of extreme poverty. Negative signs: neglected fields, few livestock, little activity. The only other vehicle we meet, charging through the dust on its well-sprung chassis, is a Subaru advertising its purpose in giant letters. WFP: World Food Programme. The road is new to Mike, but he has done some homework. 'There is only one trading post between the border and Mutarara', he says. By this, I know he means there is only one place within twenty-six miles where people without any kind of transport can get any kind of supplies; in this case the most basic. The rural trading post is the equivalent of a corner shop on a road with no corners; and, from what we see as we pass the open-fronted shack, the shelves are well-nigh bare.

Just off this dreary road I see, at intervals, families living under canvas. In grubby tents. Depressed-looking people in dismal clothes, like refugees. 'Surely they haven't been living like this since the civil war?' I ask Mike. No. Just since the last catastrophic convulsion of the Zambezi in the year 2000 (there have been lesser ones since), when some 700 people died and half a million were made homeless as the world watched the drowning of the Zambezi and Limpopo valleys on television. Anyone who lives on the Zambezi floodplains is by definition a refugee-in-waiting. Sooner or later, the river will come to get them, their crops and their homes.

We carry our own supplies: water, soft drinks and snacks. By mid-morning, after a pause for elevenses, we've arrived at a curious crossroads. Four dirt roads are staked with a rusty sign with fingers pointing to five destinations: Quelimane, Baue, Malawi, Beira and, twice over, Mutarara. A very old man is propped against the post, exposing his gums in a smile. Ahead, we see the scruffy beginnings of a town and, well beyond it, two free-standing hills, one rounded, one with the profile of a pyramid. Above them, the sky seems paler, as if it has soaked up fresh light. I think I can smell water.

Mike and the ancient wayfarer exchange the time of day for several minutes before I hear a question in Mike's voice. The old man points to one of the Mutarara fingerposts and makes a long speech. Mike looks disappointed. 'He says the bridge is closed between seven and noon, open for only two hours from noon until two, then closed again until dusk.' Simultaneously we look at our watches, and for the first time I begin to wonder about this bridge. I know that bridges are few and far between on the Zambezi, six in total along its length, and if we can't cross at Mutarara it will mean a long, tortuous detour to the bridge at Tete or, backtracking into Malawi, an even longer drive to the Caia ferry, which doesn't run after nightfall.

It's 10am. Mike and I agree we'd better first find our bridge and check out the information supplied by our signpost sage. We jolt into down-town Mutarara, which is very much uptown – a straggle of mud, thatch, cinderblock, corrugated iron, dingy white plaster and terracotta tiles on a long ridge above the Zambezi. The river spreads beneath it, filling the middle distance before the two free-standing hills on the opposite bank – and, although I've seen the Zambezi many times, it never fails to make me catch my breath. We have lively peat-brown torrents in Scotland and quiet chalky streams in England, but we do not do rivers on this scale, with this temperament, with this capacity to deceive. The far bank is hidden behind reed beds and islands planted with crops (which will disappear if not harvested before the rainy season), and only the dimensions of the Dona Ana Bridge give any perspective on its width.

The Dona Ana Bridge. I gasp again. I have been expecting something longer, if lower, than the Victoria Falls Bridge, but nothing with the reach of these forty ironwork spans which stride across the river into the heat haze on the other side. The near bank is a construction site with no apparent access road, only the remnants of an old railway line, denuded of sleepers and choked with prickly pear. While I wait in the Land Rover, Mike holds another conference with a man wearing a tin hat and an air of authority, and returns looking bemused. 'This bridge is actually a railway bridge. It was blown up by Renamo during the civil war. They are repairing it at the moment, but vehicles can cross three times a day.'

It seems we have arrived at a transforming moment in the life of a Zambezi viaduct whose history is as dramatic as its dimensions. The Dona Ana Bridge was the longest railway bridge in Africa when it was built by the Portuguese in 1934; and, although it isn't close to any major road system, its purpose was to link Malawi and the Moatize coal fields of Tete province to the port of Beira.[1] When Renamo soldiers disabled the line in the 1980s, the core structure of the bridge remained sound, and in 1995 American aid money converted it to a single-lane highway for vehicle traffic. In all innocence, we have timed our journey to coincide with the next stage of the Dona Ana's rehabilitation – the restoration of the railway line.

All this I learn later. Meanwhile, we have time to kill as we wait for the lunchtime interval between shifts which will allow us to drive two-and-a-half miles across the Zambezi on a sabotaged railway bridge. A piquant thought; and one which stirs a tremor of apprehension. We drive back to Mutarara's main street, where the only buildings recognisably Western are the dilapidated leftovers of Portugal's colonial past and the functional blocks of Mozambique's needy present: the administrative offices of Mutarara district and the local outstation of World Vision, the Christian NGO. No food stall, no filling station, no market, not even a bottle shop – the African euphemism for bar or off-licence. There is nothing to do but amuse the children by showing them their images on my digital camera, although my presence alone seems entertainment enough.

'Let's drive out of town, Mike. I need to find a bush and mark my territory, as the safari guides say.' My solicitous escort is not satisfied with this request, which is routine in the wilderness, where the guide first

---

1 With the railway line restored, the first train to reach Moatize in two decades arrived on 10 January 2010.

checks your bush for concealed hazards like dozing lion or buffalo. Mike's guiding, however, is confined to highways and national monuments, and the undergrowth is not his idea of a public convenience. 'Let me ask the people at World Vision if you can use their toilet.'

He returns with the key to their privy and the information that the World Vision toilet is at my disposal 'for urine only'. And, not for the first time, my thoughts turn to the Victorian wardrobes of those who knew nothing of easy-care fabrics and lightweight leisurewear: to the drawers, bodices, petticoats and voluminous skirts of the four women who sailed up the Zambezi with Mary Livingstone in the thick heat of summer; how complicated the challenge of their sanitary arrangements; how exacting the demands of their basic functions, from keeping themselves clean to dealing with menstruation in an age of sexual mysteries and body taboos.

They were surrounded by men: 'godless' sailors who pursued the women of the river villages, worldly officers who knew how to behave like gentlemen but must have had their own appetites, and buttoned-up clerics who – with the exception of Livingstone – could only savour their sexuality vicariously. (The Reverend James Stewart, commenting on the mariners' shore excursions, recorded with fascination that 'one woman was abused five times'.) Censored by their own inhibitions, none of these journal-keepers or letter-writers makes much reference to how the female passengers coped with the absence of privacy on the *Pioneer*, although Dr Kirk did observe testily that part of the deck had to be screened off every morning to allow Miss Mackenzie to struggle into her clothes.

Only the Livingstones had the luxury of a cabin; but the overloaded *Pioneer*, which was escorted to Shupanga by three boatloads of bluejackets from HMS *Gorgon*, a Royal Navy cruiser on anti-slaving patrol in the Indian Ocean, listed so badly they couldn't open the portholes. Miss Mackenzie, Mrs Burrup and the two maids camped in a makeshift tent on the deck among furniture for the Magomero mission: not only the piano but also a mahogany wardrobe and handsome set of chairs. The hold and deck space were also crammed with thirty tons of supplies, along with the metal plates and engine parts of the *Lady Nyassa*, the portable steamer on which Livingstone planned to explore the lake. And, somewhere among the bits and pieces of this bizarre cargo, no doubt tolerating her change of circumstances with the resignation of her race, was Miss Mackenzie's pet donkey Kate.

Bishop Mackenzie's sister whined about the heat and mosquitoes, but refused to adapt to the conditions; her fashion accessories of bodice, corset and stays stayed in place. Mrs Burrup was vivacious and popular but also reluctant to surrender drawing-room chic to Zambezi utilitarianism. The maids were dressed more simply, but among the five only Mary Livingstone was as well equipped as any white woman could be to tackle Africa in the raw. Her skin had been weathered by thirty years of strong sun; she valued comfort over appearance and wore loose-fitting dresses which didn't flatter her portly figure but kept it ventilated; her lamentably démodé cotton bonnet protected her head. She was home and at home; and, in one of the few letters where her own voice can be heard (to her London friend Mary Fitch), she judged the Anglicans' expedition extravagant, 'gorged with luxuries regardless of expense'.

Nothing is said of the condition of the 'heads' on the *Pioneer*, although its passengers and crew did have the option of finding their individual bushes on the riverbank during one of the many delays when the boat was grounded on sandbars; not without risk, of course, as the Zambezi then and now has a hefty population of crocodile. Bathing in its waters was impossible for the women, although the men sometimes chanced a plunge; and their piecemeal washing in basins of shared water must have had little impact on accumulated layers of dried sweat and crusted mosquito bites. Bouts of dysentery, or at the very least diarrhoea, compounded the problems of hygiene, and it's no surprise that the manners and tempers of even these disciplined adventurers, devout churchmen and Christian gentlewomen were tested beyond their limits. Accounts of the social dynamics on board the *Pioneer* are, more often than not, catalogues of quarrels, bickering, backstabbing, depression and disillusionment.

These sour moods often settled like clouds of flies on Mary and David Livingstone; Livingstone because he was a poor leader of Europeans, and Mary for the pettiest of reasons. The man who could be so patient and sensitive in his handling of tribal politics was indecisive and short-tempered when managing his expedition colleagues, causing 'constant vacillations, blunders, delays' and displaying 'want of common thought and foresight', according to W. C. Devereux, assistant paymaster of the *Gorgon*.

Devereux was assigned to help Livingstone organise the embarkation of the UMCA party and the mountain of supplies, belongings and dismembered steamship parts, and with the *Gorgon*'s Captain Wilson he travelled on the *Pioneer* as far as Shupanga. He thought highly of the 'kind and motherly' Mary Livingstone, and much appreciated the meals she prepared at their riverside camps, conjuring from iron pots over open fires appetising stews and curries of 'onions, venison ... salt, coconut milk'. But he was not alone in finding fault with her husband's temperament, and noted that he'd 'rarely seen a man so easily led as Dr L'.

Miss Anne Mackenzie, a troublemaker, considered him 'abrupt and ungracious', while the Reverend James Stewart, who had been inspired to come to Africa by the explorer's account of himself in *Missionary Travels*, was soon disaffected. Here was no saintly evangelist and confident adventurer in command of his mission and environment but a harassed middle-aged man capable of dark doubts and sudden rages. But it was to be Livingstone's finer side which asserted itself when Stewart and Mary became the subject of persistent gossip – and what must be the most improbable rumour in the history of scandalmongering. It was whispered that the tall, good-looking young Free Kirk minister and the plain, middle-aged matron had become 'too intimate' on the voyage they shared from Southampton to Cape Town in the summer of 1861 ...

In muscular spate the Zambezi tugs at its banks and bed and turns the colour of clay. But the first time I dipped a nervous toe in the river it was running low and washed clean by the dry winter months. I sat on a sandbank in the shallows while the water folded round my waist like cold silk, and carmine bee-eaters drilled nest-holes in the bank above the waterline. I felt very daring and a little guilty. Crocodile and hippo often cause death and injury among fishermen and villagers, for whom the Zambezi is not only a source of food and income but also a giant laundry and bathroom. With my hosts in Lower Zambezi National Park, I was treating it like a hydrotherapy spa, lounging in the river with beers chilled in its giant cooler.

But blue and benign in the dry season the Zambezi disarms even the locals; as it does at the moment, as Mike and I rumble onto the Dona Ana Bridge. Far below we see women knee-deep in pellucid water, filling plastic buckets and washing clothes, and children splashing on the sandbanks. We have picked up a hitchhiker, a construction worker heading for his home village at the end of his shift. He sits in the back without speaking, which is just as well, as we've left the linguistic land of English and Chichewa and entered that of Portuguese and Sena, the regional language of Sofala province. The sprawling town of Vila de Sena waits at the south end of the bridge, and we take about fifteen minutes to reach it, clanking over trembling timbers and loose boiler plates which have been laid over large 'potholes' in the track.

Mike drives at a sober pace, ignoring the tailgating of the convoy of trucks behind us. I'm conscious that five heavy vehicles and a Land Rover Defender add up to quite a load for an enfeebled bridge, and that my breathing has become a little shallow. When we reach the far side, I ask Mike, 'Were you at all nervous?' He gives me a placid look and shakes his head. There is a still centre to Mike which, in the time I spend with him, only twice shows signs of turbulence: once when he tells me how his young son was almost lost to a neighbourhood witch, and once when we stumble on the scene of a new disaster at a new Zambezi crossing.

3

Missionary Positions

'The great Irish manufactory'

On the African land mass Mozambique is a coastal strip, a ribbon the size of Turkey, with a population of 23 million and a seaboard over 1,500 miles long. With few interruptions its Indian Ocean coast is one long, sugar-white beach and a glittering chain of offshore islands. Some, like Ilha do Moçambique and Ilha do Ibo, were once the home ports of a grievous trade, when Portuguese merchants were the major exporters of slaves to the sugar plantations of France's Indian Ocean islands; others are today's stepping stones to the marine adventures and exotic expectations of the leisure industry.

Before the civil war, white South African and Zimbabwean scuba divers, sailors and blue-water anglers with their snorkelling, paddling, sunbed-lounging families made southern Mozambique their holiday playground. Now they have returned, along with Europeans and other Westerners with weddings and water sports on their minds; and they have begun to push north of the Zambezi into more remote 'paradises'.

The great river separates Mozambique into two distinct topographical regions and for a long time determined the isolation of the more mountainous north. But the beach goes on. And the pristine seaboard of the most northern province, Capo Delgado, is creeping onto the tourist map. I was there in July 2004 to write about conservation and eco-tourism on the low-lying coral islands of the Querimbas, an archipelago stretching 250 miles from Pemba, the provincial capital, to the Rovuma River, which defines Mozambique's border with Tanzania. It was my first trip to Mozambique, and Livingstone and his wife were much on my mind.

Ever since his efforts to navigate the Zambezi beyond Cabora Bassa had been thwarted, the explorer had developed an interest in the Rovuma. Although he had found his way to Lake Nyasa up the Shire River and identified its highlands as the ideal site for a British colony, he remained unconvinced that the Shire was the best conduit to the lake, mainly because the Portuguese, if they chose, could close off the river at its confluence with the Zambezi. The Rovuma debouched into the Indian Ocean and was well beyond the northern limits of Portuguese control. In the months that followed his wife's death, tormented by grief and guilt, Livingstone's interest hardened into a new obsession: he would explore the Rovuma from mouth to source and reveal it as the new highway to Lake Nyasa.

In fact, the river rises east of the lake, and preliminary surveys had shown it to be navigable for only sixty or so miles. But detecting a pattern, the Livingstone biographer Tim Jeal has argued that in moments of crisis the explorer was beyond logic. 'Whenever circumstances had threatened to crush Livingstone in the past, he had fought back by forcing himself to go through with some physically gruelling exploring. Now in his personal misery he would try the same remedy on the Rovuma.' He also forced this remedy on his fellow expeditionaries; and, when the futile excursion into the shallows and shoals of the unobliging river ended after a few weeks, they'd had enough. The Zambezi Expedition was in its death throes.

For its leader its nadir was the dismal ceremony of 27 April 1862, when Mary Livingstone was buried under a baobab tree. Her decline, when it came, was sudden. In the weeks since she'd joined the expedition she was full of energy, often in good spirits, uplifted by the reunion with her husband, perhaps even privately smug that her experience of Africa and her practical usefulness were so superior to that of the sniffy Miss Mackenzie (who disliked her) and the charming if helpless Mrs Burrup. She was even putting on weight – not a common response to the steamy heat of the Zambezi summer, when temperatures climb to nearly 50 degrees, and something which was observed suspiciously by Dr Kirk, who noted she was 'getting very stout', even when their supplies ran low and food was rationed.

The collapse of her health, and of the morale of her companions, came with the tragedies of the UMCA party. The *Pioneer* reached Shupanga at the end of February, but two weeks earlier Captain Wilson of the *Gorgon* and John Kirk had volunteered to take an open boat to the mouth of the Ruo River, where they hoped to reunite Miss Mackenzie with her brother and Mrs Burrup with her husband and set them on their path to Magomero. This gesture was perhaps not as generous as it sounds; both men had become increasingly impatient with the halting progress of the *Pioneer* and the on-board tensions, although their voyage to the Ruo turned out to be just as testing.

When Miss Mackenzie went down with fever, Kirk showed little sympathy for the elderly woman, who was a demanding invalid. Prostrate at the stern, 'she had to get assistance and have herself supported with pillows' every time she changed position; and she refused to wash or change her clothes unless she was shielded by a specially assembled 'bower or shelter'. If the outward journey was demanding, the return journey was desperate.

The open boat conveyed to Shupanga the news of the Magomero disaster, the deaths of Bishop Mackenzie and Henry Burrup, and their emotional debris: two women in a catastrophic state of exhaustion and distress. 'This will hurt us all' was Livingstone's conclusion, thinking of his reputation and his plans for the Shire Highlands. He didn't yet know how much.

Once again, the *Pioneer* headed downriver, this time to make the transfer to the *Gorgon* in reverse. There was nothing else to do for the women of the UMCA but send them to the Cape for a ship home. In his anger and disappointment at the failure of an enterprise which he had so publicly championed, Livingstone could barely tolerate their grief, and even talked of the need 'for better men' within their earshot. It was left to Mary, a seasoned matriarch only too familiar with personal loss, to offer support; to take the young widow in her arms as she sobbed through the night of her first wedding anniversary; to do what she could to comfort both as they waited at the Kongone mouth of the Zambezi delta.

Eventually, the overdue *Gorgon* arrived and the bereaved women were carried silently on board 'on the crossed arms of two bluejackets ... not dead, but next to it, poor Mrs Burrup covered with boils and ulcers'.

Three weeks later, the woman who had tried to ease their distress was herself dead.

There are plenty of descriptions of Mary's death and funeral in the Livingstone literature, but in 2004 I was still far short of up-to-date information on the condition of her grave and how to get there. The David Livingstone Centre in Blantyre had no recent details, although an old photograph showed that long ago the original cairn of stones and wooden cross had been replaced by a tall headstone and brick base. Even the modern researcher's first line of enquiry, the Internet, had little to say about Chupanga. But I did tease out one account of a visit to the grave in the late 1990s, only a few years after the end of the civil war.

Chupanga Mission and its church were in ruins, the surrounding countryside heavily mined and destitute, and the visitors found Mary's grave reclaimed by the bush. They arrived by boat. They were Kingsley Holgate, a well-known South African adventurer and Livingstone enthusiast, his wife Gill and the team he was leading on an expedition from the Zambezi estuary to its source. One of its members, Tony Weaver, reported their landfall at Chupanga 'on a suitably solemn, grey day, a heavy overcast adding a brooding atmosphere to our quest to find and clean up her

[Mary's] grave ... Gill Holgate cleared the undergrowth from the tomb and placed a spray of acacia flowers on the grave.'

I also learned this much: Chupanga is about seventy miles upriver from the Zambezi delta, it lies at the end of nearly forty miles of dirt road near the ferry town of Caia, and 'Shupanga brae', as Livingstone called its sloping riverbank, gave the village enough height to outwit the Zambezi floodwaters. It was the location of a United Nations displacement camp for some 3,000 people who lost their homes and land in the floods of 2000, and it has been used for the same purpose in lesser floods since.

Now here I was in Mozambique, much closer to Mary's grave but still out of reach. It had taken me twenty-four hours to fly from Edinburgh to Pemba by way of London, Nairobi and Dar es Salaam, and in Pemba I was still 500 miles of wild coast and lonely interior north of the Zambezi. I had no time, wherewithal or local knowledge to diverge so radically from a tight itinerary, not to mention the task in hand: the Querimbas Archipelago and its potential for tourism. The task in hand, however, did deliver one of those coincidences which can only be called serendipitous.

Quilalea is so small you can walk round it in half an hour. There's no room for an airstrip, so the luxury lodge on this uninhabited island in the Quilalea Marine Sanctuary is reached either by light aircraft and dhow from its larger neighbour, or more spectacularly by helicopter – which was how I arrived, roaring above a dazzling tapestry of reefs, lagoons and sand islands at 500 feet. The colour of the sea crossed the spectrum from deep indigo to pale aquamarine, and the water was so clear I could spot moving shadows beneath its surface. In July and August, humpback whales migrate through the channels of the Querimbas, but all I saw were shoals of fish sliding between beds of sea grass.

I had hitched the short helicopter ride from Pemba with an American woman working in Mozambique. Spirited, good-looking, independent Michelle Gilardi is a hospitality and catering consultant, and was en route to Quilalea Lodge to devise new menus and relieve the owner-managers for a few weeks. I learned later that she has a high reputation in gastronomic circles and has cooked in some of the world's top restaurants, including La Cirque in New York, but I found her impressive for another reason: the can-do entrepreneurial energy which had brought her to Africa in the first place – initially to Kenya, where she opened one of Nairobi's smartest restaurants, then to Tanzania to explore new ventures, then to Mozambique. (She is still travelling throughout East Africa, troubleshooting in high-end lodges and camps, setting up new kitchens and training staff.)

One night, dinner was served on the tiny beach of the tiny island. When Michelle joined me for coffee, we sat listening to the waves' susurrus and the whispery prowling of ghost crabs, and exchanged histories. She told me that her international career in America, Europe and Africa had made her something of a gypsy, and, although she often returned to her family home in North Carolina, she had little wish for a settled home of her own. I told her I wanted to write a book about another gypsy, Mary Livingstone, and the journeys which defined her life. 'I'm most curious about her grave', I said. 'It's in a village called Chupanga on the Zambezi, near a little town called Caia. Have you heard of it?'

She laughed. 'I drove through Caia just a few weeks ago. I know a family who have a forestry concession near Chupanga and a nice little lodge in the woods. It's just about the only place to stay in those parts. I'm sure the Whites can tell you more about the grave. I'll give you their e-mail address.'

Which is how, three years and many e-mails later, I find myself at the south end of the Dona Ana Bridge on the road to Caia and the village which Livingstone called Shupanga. At last.

Celebrity culture isn't new. The nature of the celebrity's distinction may change, but the imperative to find, admire, identify with and in extreme cases idolise famous role models is wired into the human psyche. When *Missionary Travels and Researches in South Africa* was published by John Murray in 1857, David Livingstone became a national hero. He was fêted by geographers for his epic transcontinental trek from the Atlantic to the Indian Ocean – the first European to have made and recorded such a journey – and he was revered by the devout for its holy purpose, which had taken him into the heart of heathen Africa to save its soul.

The book sold 70,000 copies, lifting its author and his family out of near-penury for the rest of their lives. There will be more to say about Mary's miserable, cash-strapped, peripatetic life in exile while Livingstone's 'two-year' journey to the Atlantic port of Portuguese Loanda, now the Angolan capital of Luanda, turned into a four-year journey across the entire continent. But, for now, she could welcome the security that arrived along with the Royal Geographical Society's gold medal, and, in the most self-effacing way, enjoy her husband's fame.

His achievements were honoured by similar bodies in mainland Europe; various cities scrambled to offer him their freedom; Oxford University awarded him an honorary degree; and Queen Victoria asked to meet the man who had given her name to his most phenomenal geographical 'discovery'. There followed months of lectures and public appearances – the kind of book tour which would be the envy of today's most successful writers – and, in an age when the visual image was in its photographic infancy, Livingstone was often recognised in the streets of London.

In Scotland, meanwhile, one young man and one little boy were so fiercely inspired by his example that it shaped the rest of their lives. The child was Robert Laws, effectively the founding father of the Christian church in Nyasaland. In his book *Livingstone's Lake*, Oliver Ransford identifies Laws as the perfect exemplar of 'our idea of what a Victorian missionary should be. To begin with, his background is exactly right. He came from humble stock. His father was a cabinet-maker living in Aberdeen, and an Elder of the Kirk; his mother died of consumption when he was two, and the little boy's earliest recollection was of being lifted up to see her lying in her coffin.'

From an early age, Robert's nightly prayer was precise and specific. 'Oh God, send me to the Makololo.' (The Makololo tribe, confined in shrinking territory between the Chobe and Zambezi rivers, were Livingstone's hosts at their capital Linyanti on his first journey to the Zambezi, and succeeded the Tswana as promising candidates for conversion.) He grew up at a time when Scotland was flushed with pride at the fame of its lad o' pairts and gripped with evangelical fervour. Much as a boy today might want to be a rock musician or a professional footballer, Robert wanted to be a medical missionary. When he sailed into Lake Nyasa in 1875, two years after Livingstone's death, he was living his dream; and, in his leadership of the Livingstonia mission at Cape Maclear and its subsequent locations, he had the resourcefulness, humanity, tenacity and courage to turn it into reality.

'For the next half century', Ransford writes, 'Laws laboured beside the lake and competes with two other doctors – Livingstone and Banda – for the distinction of being its most potent single human influence.' This judgement was made in 1967, three years after colonial Nyasaland became the Republic of Malawi under its first president, Hastings Banda. Today's Malawians may think otherwise.

The young man who was also galvanised by the legend which Livingstone was fast becoming was James Stewart, the humourless, socially awkward but physically glamorous cleric who is remembered as much for his fantasy role as Mary's putative paramour as for his seminal role in the founding of Livingstonia. Stewart's background was radical, his personality repressed; he was the son of a farmer who had walked away from the established Church of Scotland in the Disruption of 1843, and from his youth he was convinced that God and the Free Kirk had plans for him.

For eleven years he studied theology and medicine at the universities of St Andrews and Edinburgh; and, when *Missionary Travels* was published, he fell upon its contents like a new gospel, whose apostle was the missionary-explorer who came to obsess him. Was it a divine hand which led him to the apostle's wife, who was living in a rented house in Glasgow with her five children while Livingstone battled the rapids of 'Kebrabasa' and all the other frustrations of the Zambezi? Or was the Reverend James Stewart conducted to her door by a power more temporal – his own calculation that through Mary Livingstone lay access to her husband?

They met when she was looking for a tutor for her second son, 10-year-old Thomas, called Tom. Stewart was recommended for the position, and a friendship was born. He was 30, she was 40. He was over six feet tall, well built, with handsome features lurking beneath a full beard and thick auburn hair. She was short, overweight and sallow, with a long nose and heavy brows. He was insecure, emotionally stunted, unfamiliar with women. (Both his mother and much-loved stepmother died at an early age.) She was lonely, ill-at-ease in Scotland, missing the husband who had left her once again for a mistress more exotic and alluring than any human one.

For all the disparity in their age and appearance, and for all the moral obligations of their faith, it is just conceivable that the bereft circumstances of this odd couple might have created the conditions for romance. At any rate, that's how it looked to fellow passengers by the time Stewart and Mary sailed into Table Bay in August 1861.

When Mary arrived at the Cape nearly three years after her husband and his mixed bag of government-sponsored expeditionaries had launched their Zambezi adventure, it was her second attempt to join the expedition. Her first was in 1858. When the Colonial Office steamship *Pearl* left Birkenhead on a wintry day in March, it had on board not only the expedition boat *Ma-Robert* but also Ma-Robert herself. Despite opposition and concern from family, friends and supporters, Livingstone had decided that his wife could not be left alone in the United Kingdom. Without him, she was wretched and vulnerable, couldn't manage money, was tempted to drink too much and became increasingly embittered. It isn't fanciful to speculate that, if the explorer had failed to return from his march across Africa between 1853 and 1856, her dismal, nomadic life in Scotland and

England might have spiralled ever downwards into serious debt, chronic alcoholism and permanent loss of faith – of which more to come.

Even if the prospect of returning to Africa didn't excite Mary – which it did – it was not in her character to defy her husband. But it greatly pained and troubled her to leave behind three of their four surviving children, now living in Scotland with Livingstone's family in the Clydeside town of Hamilton. The youngest, six-year-old Oswell, who had been born on Mary's second trek across the Kalahari Desert, was inexplicably permitted to join the ship's company.

Why take their youngest child, potentially the most defenceless against the deadly diseases of the Zambezi Valley? Perhaps because this ambitious project was expected to last several years, and their parents didn't want to interrupt the education of his elder siblings, Robert, Agnes and Tom; perhaps because his father, in the impulsive mood inspired by the prospect of more African exploration, considered it a bracing adventure for the boy; perhaps because both parents had plenty of experience of taking young children on long journeys into the unknown. Or perhaps to console the mother, the presence of one child being better than none.

As it turned out, the expedition ended at Cape Town for both mother and child. The chronic queasiness and vomiting which had afflicted Mary on the five-week voyage were not just the result of rough seas. 'The great Irish manufactory', as Livingstone merrily called her frequent pregnancies, as if they had nothing to do with him, had renewed production. Now Mary was required to have intimate experience of young Dr Kirk, who would never become a friend, whose account of her in his journal is at best negative and at worst sneering. It was John Kirk, as the expedition's medical adviser, who diagnosed her seventh pregnancy, which followed fast on the miscarriage she'd had only months earlier. This development – unexpected but hardly unlikely, given the Livingstones' reproductive history – was something of 'a hindrance', according to her husband.

There was now no question of Mary and Oswell continuing to the Zambezi. Heartsick and tearful, she waved off the *Pearl* as it left for the delta, then resigned herself to the long ox-wagon trek to her parents' mission at Kuruman, in the distant bushlands beyond the Orange River. By happy chance, Robert and Mary Moffat happened to be in Cape Town to meet a ship bringing home another daughter, Jane. And, although Livingstone wrote extravagantly, as he often did when parting from his wife, that this new separation was 'like tearing the heart out of one', he was thus absolved of the responsibility of escorting her to Kuruman or finding another solution to a problem he described as 'a great trial to me'.

It was more of a trial to Mary. She was six months pregnant by the time the party left for the north, and their three-month journey was stalked by one misfortune after another: heavy rain, sickness, bogged-down wagons, dying oxen. Six days after they finally arrived at Kuruman, her last child, Anna Mary, was born. The following spring Mary said goodbye to her mother and father, whom she would never see again, and took Oswell and the new baby back to Scotland to join their brothers and sister. But not for long. Anna Mary was only 18 months old when Mary, as she wrote to her friend Mrs Fitch, was urged by Livingstone to 'embrace the first opportunity to come out'. And, when she left Southampton in July 1861, she was again in the company of a medical missionary, this time the Reverend James Stewart.

The voyage out consolidated their friendship but was also to end it. Stewart had secured funds from the Free Church of Scotland to open an 'industrial station' in central Africa. The church's plan was to develop land for cotton production – something for which Livingstone claimed the flat valley of the lower Shire was ideal – and his eager disciple seized upon this commission as the perfect excuse for joining the Zambezi Expedition. Better still, he had already earned the good opinion of his hero's wife and would have her company on the journey out. He was not to know that an existing member of the expedition had highly imaginative suspicions about the couple which, when they arrived in Cape Town, he had already circulated as rumours.

The engineer George Rae had been dispatched to the United Kingdom to organise the building of a portable steamer to explore Lake Nyasa. The profile of Rae which emerges from history is almost a caricature of the dour Scots engineer in every respect except one: he was not a man of few words. He was a gossip and mischief-maker. When he met them in Glasgow it was he who decided that Mary's relationship with Stewart was improper; and it has to be said they had also given their shipboard companions some grounds for speculation. Not only did they spend hours together on the moonlit deck, locked in conversation about their respective hopes and fears, but Stewart was also known to visit Mary's cabin regularly, often at night.

Mary wasn't looking for romance; emotional comfort, certainly. Mr Stewart was 'kind and attentive', she wrote to Mrs Fitch; 'he will not allow me to mope'. But she also needed something more radically sustaining. She was in torment. The wrench of leaving her children, particularly the toddler Anna Mary, caused her great anguish and overwhelmed any pleasant thoughts of reunion with her husband and Africa. 'My dear baby, how my heart yearns for her, I miss her so much.' Her consumption of brandy went up but wasn't much help, inducing moods of near-hysteria and guilt-ridden nightmares. It was then that she sent for James Stewart, who, with his medical training, tranquillised her with the Victorians' opiate of choice: laudanum.

The 'kind and attentive' cleric soon tired of Mary's feverish emergencies, which included requests to borrow money (she maintained the common-place fiction that her expensive brandy habit eased her seasickness). He began to record unflattering observations in his journal. Some are almost certainly exaggerated: he later claimed that she drank so heavily 'as to be utterly besotted at times'; but, if this were true, he was the only witness to these excesses. Other remarks describe the mood-swings of a woman who was obviously depressed, possibly menopausal but also well outside the experience of the unsophisticated young man. He talks without insight of her 'queer and disagreeable moods', adding the gratuitous insult 'dull, dumpy and discontented'.

For all that, Mary's spirits rose when they reached Cape Town, and James Stewart allowed her to show him the sights. He still needed her.

For Mike and me the surprise is Caia. This undistinguished town has only one claim on the attention of drivers travelling between the road systems of southern Mozambique, northern Mozambique and eastern Malawi: its elderly ferry service.[1] After the Dona Ana Bridge was blown up, the Caia ferry became the only crossing point on the Zambezi between the Indian Ocean and the provincial capital of Tete, some 200 miles upriver. Throughout the 1990s, only one boat plied the fifteen-minute crossing; and, although a second was added later, queues of trucks can last not just hours but days, at the expense of any perishable goods – which is why we have avoided the ferry on our journey from Blantyre.

The Dona Ana Bridge deposits us at Vila de Sena, once a fortified out-post of early Portuguese colonists. From there we follow the route of three parallel transport systems: a well-graded gravel road, the forlorn track and listing telegraph poles of the disabled railway line, and the river itself. Looking to the north bank we see a widening of water where the Shire River empties into the Zambezi; but the tall reeds, flat littoral and slug-gish flow make this key junction in the history of the Zambezi Expedition unremarkable. We might have missed the confluence of the two rivers

---

1 The ferries stopped running on 1 August 2009, after carrying their last passen-ger, Mozambique's President Armando Guebuza, from Chimuara on the north bank to Caia on the south, to inaugurate the new bridge.

altogether if it weren't for the towering landmark of Mount Morambala where, after the Magomero disaster, the Anglicans made another short-lived attempt to establish a mission, before retreating to Zanzibar. Here their replacement leader, Bishop Tozer – another victim of Livingstone's impulsive optimism and blithe disregard of potential obstacles – denounced these traits with the judgement that they made him 'a very dangerous man'.

By now it's late afternoon and there are few people about; but after nearly forty miles of empty road we arrive on the outskirts of Caia to find monumental change under way. The town roars with activity. The mightiest monsters of the construction industry have colonised the riverbank, titanic piles have been driven into the water, there are men in hard hats everywhere, and the ferries and dug-out canoes are sharing the river with dredgers, workboats and floating cranes.

We are in at the delivery of a new Zambezi bridge, only the seventh to be built across the 2,200-mile waterway in over 100 years – since the days when Cecil Rhodes imagined 'the spray of the falls over the train carriages' on a bridge downriver from the Victoria Falls. This project began as an ambition when Mozambique became independent in 1975, got started with the access roads five years later, was mothballed during the civil war and finally got under way in March 2006. Eighteen months later it looks as though it still has a long way to go, and over the next two days we get quite intimate with the vital statistics of this prodigious infant. We also find that the Zambezi, as ever, exacts a toll from those who challenge its obstacles.

For the moment, as we negotiate the workings of its approach road and find the tar highway to the port city of Beira, five hours' drive to the south, we have our sights set on the penultimate leg of our journey. We are only half an hour from the track through Catapu forest to M'phingwe Lodge, the 'nice little lodge in the woods', as Michelle Gilardi described it. Waiting there, I hope, is a woman called Gaia Allison: another link in the chain of contacts tugging me towards the grave of Mary Livingstone.

4

Flowers for the Grave

'Our love did not die with the honeymoon'

The priest has invited us to lunch. Gaia Allison has done the ground-work for my visit to Chupanga Mission, and we've only just met. Already, I'm slightly in awe of Gaia. I sense she has a special talent for getting things done, sorting things out. I've met her kind before, people who live and work in some of the most problematic corners of the world. What's more, although she's the daughter of an English father and Italian mother, with a home in Cumbria, she was born in Zambia and spent her early life in Tanzania. It's my fancy that Europeans raised in Africa inherit a gene of competence lost to their kin in the urban West, where we pick up telephones to fix our cars, plumb our washing machines and mend our fences; where we have surrendered our resourcefulness to those who make a living from our helplessness.

But Gaia's competence extends beyond the practical. Within a year of arriving in Mozambique, she had taught herself Portuguese; another lan-guage added to the several she speaks, just like that. At the rustic bar of M'phingwe Lodge, where we reward ourselves for our successful rendez-vous with chilled bottles of Manica, Mozambique's excellent lager, she tells me what *m'phingwe* means. 'It's the Sena name for the African black-wood, one of the most valuable hardwoods in Catapu forest.'

Gaia knows her timber. She has an MSc in forestry from the University of Oxford, and it's her interest in forestry which has made her familiar with Catapu, nearly 100 square miles of miombo woodland where every hardwood tree logged is replaced by four new ones. (Catapu is one of the few indigenous forests in southern Africa to be certified by the Forest Stewardship Council, the non-governmental, not-for-profit organisation which promotes the responsible management of forests worldwide.) But she has other credentials too, and they've been put to use in some of the world's poorest countries. Her experience in international development has taken her to Bolivia, Nepal and now Mozambique, where she goes by the picturesque title of 'livelihoods adviser'.

Based in Beira, funded by Danish development aid, her role with the provincial government takes her all over the battered province to assess and investigate 'alternative livelihood opportunities' for the near-destitute people of Sofala. She's often alone on the road, spending time in isolated villages, teasing out personal histories from men and women still trauma-tised by the atrocities of the civil war; talking over plans and possibilities with elders, chiefs, teachers, health workers and – often the most enduring voice of their communities – parish priests. This is how she first came to Chupanga, visited the mission, saw the scruffy cemetery, the crumbling tomb, the famous name, and had an idea.

We've been e-mailing each other for over a year, put in touch by Graeme White, the contact passed to me by Michelle Gilardi on Quilalea. The White family, immigrants from Zimbabwe, are partners in TCT Dalmann, the company which holds the lease on Catapu. Graeme runs the business operation from their factory in Beira, where a workforce of local crafts-men turns rare panga panga and mutondo hardwoods into hand-made furniture, while his father, James Anthony (known as Ant), manages the forest and its on-site sawmill. M'phingwe Lodge, simple timber cabins with a small restaurant and bar, is an eco-sideline. Its guests are mainly parties of birders, long-distance travellers and, since work started on the new bridge at Caia, middle management and engineers.

Although Gaia's wide-ranging brief is to explore income-generating ideas and land-rights issues for people displaced by war or flood, it also touches on tourism, which is edging back into an interior which had an unhealthy reputation even after the war ended. Sofala, like other rural provinces at the heart of the conflict, was seeded with land mines; and the area around Mount Gorongosa, much of it part of Mozambique's most magnificent protected wilderness, was brutally damaged in other ways. In 1983, the Chitengo headquarters of Gorongosa National Park was attacked by Renamo rebels, who kidnapped several staff and two foreign scientists; and, from then on, the park saw some of the fiercest battles, including hand-to-hand fighting. It was closed and abandoned, its roads and buildings destroyed by bombing. For nine years until the end of the war, Renamo controlled Gorongosa district, co-opting or coercing many of the locals into their forces and predating on others.

People and wildlife shared the suffering. The park's large-mammal population took dreadful losses as both Frelimo and Renamo slaughtered hundreds of elephants to sell their ivory to buy arms and supplies. It was also open season for the plains game – buffalo, zebra and wildebeest, shot in their thousands for bush meat – while the big cats were targeted for sport or died of starvation when their prey disappeared. The park also became a refuge for starving villagers who hunted at will to feed them-selves. When the war ended in 1992, widespread hunting continued for another two years, by which time most of the large-mammal population had been reduced by 90 per cent. Only the birds survived well.

To a surprising number of South Africans, the great weight of land north of the Limpopo River is another continent. I once stayed at a camp in Ndumo Game Reserve in KwaZulu-Natal, near the Mozambican border. The reserve looks across a floodplain into Mozambique and is famous for its variety of bird species, logged at 430. There, I shared a game drive with two friendly, middle-aged women from Johannesburg who were dedicated birders. They were well-educated Afrikaners who ran their own marketing and PR company, and they were keen to talk (or whisper) as we waited patiently for the reappearance of a shy gorgeous bush shrike. They wanted to know which other South African reserves I knew; and I confessed that this was my first visit to their country. As for birds, I told them I'd only started taking an interest in them since I'd spent time in Zambia and the Luangwa Valley, which also claims over 400 species.

'That's really interesting!' they enthused. 'Zambia, you say? Do you know, we've never been to Africa ...'

But South Africans do go, have always gone, to Mozambique. Except during the civil war. It's an idiocy of that war – of so many wars – that the country which bankrolled one side and prolonged the hostilities is again sending its citizens there to enjoy themselves; not just to the beaches and historic coastal cities, but increasingly to its interior, to shoot game if they are hunters, to shoot pictures if they are photographers, or just to enjoy the wildlife. They and other tourists are now returning to Gorongosa, where the land mines have been cleared and roads reopened. An ambitious recovery programme launched by the Mozambique government and the Carr Foundation, a US not-for-profit organisation, is steadily restocking the park; the big mammals are back; new camps are opening, and the lodge and public campsite at Chitengo have been restored and upgraded. Gorongosa, 2,500 square miles of prime wilderness, is easily reached by road from Beira and its airport, and its main gate is only three hours' drive from Chupanga.

This is Gaia's idea: when tourists have exhausted their interest in wildlife, send them on a 'heritage trail' – to the grave of Mary Livingstone.

The Cape is an incomparable landfall. As early as 1598 Sir Francis Drake, that supreme mariner, called it 'a most stately thing and the fairest Cape we saw in the circumference of the Earth'. But sailing into Simon's Bay or Table Bay seems to have become so routine for those who commuted between the ports of the United Kingdom and the nineteenth-century colony that its spectacle is seldom mentioned. When he first arrived in 1841, Livingstone, in a letter to his sisters, did make a passing reference to 'lofty Table Mountain with its beautiful table cloth of fleecy clouds', but, for Robert and Mary Moffat and their family – and most especially for their daughter Mary – Cape Town came to represent not scenic splendour but the functional terminus of too many painful leave-takings and too few welcome returns.

Today it is southern Africa's most visited city. Unless they are cruise-ship passengers, most travellers arrive by air, rail or road, but it's still possible to get some idea of what it must have been like to make that early landfall by taking the tourist catamaran across the great sweep of Table Bay to Robben Island, now a UNESCO World Heritage Site. This is not, of course, the main reason why people visit the scrubby slab of rock which was once the prison of Nelson Mandela and other activists of the anti-apartheid struggle. But it is a bonus of the five-mile crossing and an accessible way to see the city and its context from the sea.

From this perspective, Cape Town seems not so much a city as a natural wonder, where even today the human imprint is incidental. The swooping motorways, the high-rises of City Bowl, the spanking new football stadium at Green Point are overwhelmed by Table Mountain; not just the familiar flat profile of its summit but also the striking outriders of Lion's Head and Devil's Peak, its frieze of stupendous buttresses, the Twelve Apostles, and the ridges and slopes which reach deep into the city's heart. It doesn't take too much imagination to strip away the suburbs and modern infrastructure and to sense something of the joy and relief which must have brightened the final approach of Mary Livingstone to the land of her birth.

What was the city like in the mid-nineteenth century? It had been a port of great significance to the British Empire since Britain snatched the Cape from the Dutch at the turn of the century; and its commercial and civic architecture, assertively Victorian in contrast to the graceful Cape Dutch style of the earlier colonists, dominated the waterfront. But it still didn't have a decent harbour. The Atlantic seaboard of the Cape Peninsula is notoriously exposed to tempests, but the British colonial government had long been reluctant to meet the cost of a safe berth for its maritime traffic and had sanctioned only piecemeal developments, like a lighthouse in 1823 and an inadequate jetty in 1832.

The 'Cape of Storms' continued to send ships to the bottom of Table Bay. But, when Mary and Stewart landed on 1 August 1861, a new harbour and major dock – now the 'heritage' showcase of the Victoria and Albert Waterfront and ferry terminal for Robben Island – was finally under construction. The first batch of rocks for the breakwater had been tipped into the bay by Prince Albert, the teenage son of Queen Victoria, only a year earlier, after Lloyd's insurance company took the decision to refuse cover for ships which risked anchoring there.

What other sights did Mary show Stewart as they strolled around Grand Parade, the great esplanade beside the Castle of Good Hope, South Africa's oldest building? Some of the grid of the modern centre was already in place, although swathes of nineteenth-century architecture have been lost to redevelopment. When Mary first knew Cape Town as a teenager, there were still remnants of the network of channels, ditches and sluices which gave it the sobriquet Little Amsterdam, but by 1850 the last of these canals had been filled in and the handsome thoroughfare of Adderley Street built on its conduit.

Then, as now, Adderley Street ran north from the Company Gardens towards the sea, although today its route to the foreshore is blocked by an unlovable highway system and Cape Town International Conference Centre. Almost certainly, Mary would have included it in her tour, if only because the Company Gardens have a history as picturesque as their setting. The gardens pre-date the Castle of Good Hope, and were the nursery which gave birth to the original Dutch settlement at the Cape. They were laid out in 1652 to cultivate fresh produce for the ships of the Dutch East India Company as they travelled between the Netherlands and the archipelago which is now Indonesia, and were given over to botanical horticulture at the end of the seventeenth century, when a growing elite of immigrants created a demand for civic aesthetics.

There would also be more personal reasons for Mary's interest in this area. Just north of the Company Gardens, on Wale Street, is St George's Cathedral, a rallying point for the anti-apartheid struggle and the place where Desmond Tutu was enthroned as South Africa's first black archbishop. (In 1989, Archbishop Tutu led 30,000 people from the cathedral to Grand Parade and City Hall, where one ringing sentence of his speech became fixed in the rhetoric of democratic South Africa: 'We are the rainbow people'.) Although the foundation stone of the present Victorian Gothic building wasn't laid until 1901, the cathedral succeeded Cape Town's first Anglican church, also St George's.

Here, on 27 December 1819, Robert Moffat of Ormiston, East Lothian, recent recruit of the London Missionary Society, married Mary Smith of Dukinfield, Lancashire, newly arrived from Portsmouth on the sailing ship *British Colony*. Shortly afterwards, the newlyweds left the town for an unusual honeymoon – a seven-week, 800-mile ox-wagon trek to the mission station at Griquatown, to begin the lifetime's partnership which was to leave a dynasty of public-spirited Moffats in Africa. Their first child, a daughter, was born in Griquatown on 12 April 1821. Forty years later, as she continued to enjoy the company of a handsome escort on the boulevards of Cape Town, the daughter's character was being sorely traduced.

Another golden morning, every tree trembling with birdsong. If I were a serious birder an African pitta would be a huge bonus on the road to Chupanga. This colourful little migrant is a 'special' of the Catapu woodland, rarely seen on its seasonal visits, and on the way to breakfast I spend a few minutes scanning the branches. But I'm not a serious birder, just someone who takes delight in the bountiful variety of Africa's birds, beguiled as much by their names as their looks. Scarlet-chested sunbird, lilac-breasted roller, carmine bee-eater, pink-throated twinspot – names as beautiful as their owners. Scribbled in my notebook are my three Catapu spots to date: scimitar-billed hoopoe, paradise flycatcher and fork-tailed drongo. All are common residents, but I have special affection for the noisy, impertinent drongo, as it was the first small African bird I learned to identify. (Not very difficult. It looks like a male blackbird without the yellow bill and with a deeply forked tail.)

The birds are a distraction, something to divert my attention from the flutter in my midriff as Mike, Gaia and I climb into the Land Rover. I'm on the last lap, over three years and 6,000 miles from the day I first made up my mind to reach Mary's grave. Ant White waves us off. 'Don't forget to take a good look at that new altar in the church', he instructs. 'I paid for it! I was raised a good Catholic boy, and when the priest comes to call I pee in my pants.' Back on the Beira–Caia highway, the rusty sign to the Chupanga turn-off is soon upon us. 'That name means nothing to passers-by,' says Gaia, 'but Livingstone's name does. What we need is a visitor attraction sign pointing the way to a historic monument. Mary Moffat Livingstone's Grave.'

We tunnel into trees on the dirt road. Baboons and bush buck skitter in and out of the forest, which Gaia tells me is no longer Catapu but a hunting concession: the insecure home of buffalo, leopard, kudu, sable and other trophy antelope. 'The forest's all miombo around here, isn't it?' I ask. I'm trying to improve my grasp of African vegetation, and know that dense miombo woodland with its spreading canopy is typical of moist savanna areas like the Zambezi hinterland. It is difficult to penetrate, which gives the men with guns something of a challenge.

My personal forest favourite is the open woodland of the mopane tree, much loved by elephant and found all over the drier savannas of south-central Africa. Mopane is easy to recognise; its delicate leaves are perfect replicas of butterfly wings, and the mopane worm is an important source of protein for thousands of Africans. The worm is actually the caterpillar of the emperor moth, which deposits its eggs on the host tree to guarantee the larvae an unlimited supply of leaves when they hatch. But, before they can complete their metamorphosis, huge numbers of caterpillars are collected to be smoked or dried; traditionally by women and children, although these days they are also harvested commercially and canned in brine or tomato sauce.

The only mopane worms I've eaten were sold as crunchy snacks scooped into paper cones in African markets. They would have benefited from a little salt, when they might have passed for pork scratchings.

Gaia's mobile phone rings. It is Padre Medard Biembe Bakamba of the Congregation of the Sacred Hearts, the church which reopened Chupanga Mission in 1995. Gaia concludes a brief conversation in Portuguese, then tells us: 'It seems he can't give us lunch after all. His cook is ill. But he has asked the oldest man in the village to join us in the mission grounds. Apparently he knows a bit about Shupanga House, where Mary died.'

I'm suddenly seized by a sense that we're unprepared, and remember a promise I made to Tim Jeal, the Livingstone biographer who first sparked my interest in Mary. A month earlier, I'd met him at the Edinburgh International Book Festival, where he was talking about his new biography of Henry Morton Stanley. When I told him about my upcoming journey to Mary's grave, he asked: 'Lay a flower for me'.

'We must find flowers', I insist. 'Flowers for the grave.' Not as easy as it sounds in the bush, even in spring. All around us, the trees are draped in fiery veils of flame creeper, but they are too high to reach. Then, as Mike slows the Land Rover to let us look at three white-backed vultures snacking on a corpse too mangled to identify, we spot some large vermilion blossoms on a shrub. They look a bit like hibiscus. '*Femandoa Magnifica*, I think', says Gaia. 'But I don't know their common name.'

I jump down and pick four blossoms, one for each of us and one for Tim Jeal. Soon we reach a crossroads, another junction of lumpy dirt and rocks exposed by the rains. It's the back road to Inhaminga, the town which was once a major railway junction and the engineering headquarters of the Mozambican railway system built by the Portuguese. Much of the network was blown up by Renamo and is slowly being rebuilt. Gaia has told us Inhaminga is a 'creepy sort of place, like a cemetery for derelict railway carriages and old engines'. Now she suggests we take a look at it after we've been to Chupanga. 'We can get some snacks there to keep us going, and maybe pay a visit to Africa wa Yesu. That's the mission which did its best to look after Mary's grave before Chupanga Mission reopened.'

Within an hour, the forest begins to thin and open into a flat swathe of baked earth and dry grass with a scatter of trees and shrubs, a doum palm or two and a conspicuous baobab. Among them saunters the usual village welcoming committee of goats and chickens. A tall metal road sign, one post wildly askew, tells us we've arrived at Chupanga. An effort has been made to give its approach some presence. We drive along a rudimentary avenue of young mango trees, each ringed with whitewashed stones, passing an encampment of marquees with the letters UN stencilled on their weathered canvas. 'A feeding centre', explains Gaia. 'There are still a lot of displaced people around from the last floods.'

Then we see the river, its near shore hidden below the slope of 'Shupanga brae', its far side reaching into a smoky blue vacuum. A small flotilla of canoes is at work midstream. We pass a sprawl of mud and thatch, a cluster of roofless, windowless, cinderblock buildings, and steer towards a steeple and belfry. Rising above the bleached elephant grass and dingy colours of neglect is the restored church, its walls brilliant with fresh white plaster trimmed with blue facings. Shades of paradise. Its newness, its stainlessness are arresting; it looks like a totem of redemption. Whatever I may think of the agenda of the Congregation of the Sacred Hearts, who have made the recovery of the church a priority, I am moved by its pristine assertiveness. For all I know, it may do more for the morale and well-being of Chupanga village than any number of welfare programmes.

Gaia leads the way purposefully towards the graveyard. Broken walls, dilapidated gate, scorched earth where the undergrowth has been burnt back; a spread of modest headstones and nameless home-made crosses. The cemetery is still in use. Fresh earth is piled before one wooden cross, and plastic flowers have been placed before it in a bucket. Some of the oldest headstones have English inscriptions which speak of other travellers stricken down in the service of saving souls; or maybe just because they fell in love with a missionary. Young Catherine Cameron, for example, 'beloved wife of John McIlwain, Blantyre Mission'. She died of fever some 200 miles from Blantyre, in 1887. She was 21. What was her story?

It isn't hard to find the centrepiece of Chupanga cemetery. It's clear that Mary's grave became the prompt for subsequent funerals at this level spot overlooking the river, and that a graveyard grew up round it well before the Jesuit mission was founded in 1895. Mary's tomb has indeed the stature of a historic monument, even if its tiered base is cracked and its tall iron headstone disfigured with smoke.

HERE REPOSE THE MORTAL REMAINS OF

MARY MOFFAT

THE BELOVED WIFE OF DOCTOR LIVINGSTONE

IN HUMBLE HOPE

OF A JOYFUL RESURRECTION

BY OUR SAVIOUR JESUS CHRIST

SHE DIED

IN SHUPANGA HOUSE

27TH APRIL, 1862

AGED 41 YEARS

On the other side of the headstone, the inscription is repeated in Portuguese. I place our four blossoms at its foot. I'm not a practising Christian, and it would be false to say a Christian prayer, but how can the moment be anything other than intense, even solemn? We are all silenced by it. 'Poor Mary lies on Shupanga Brae', Livingstone reflected, when he had come to terms with a loss which was not only profound but which also seemed to take him by surprise, as if he thought his wife as invincible as he believed himself to be. Then he added, in archaic Scots: 'and beeks fornent the sun'.

And basks in the sun: a strange way to describe the eternal rest of the woman he sincerely loved and – not always a contradiction – regularly abandoned. There is both wistfulness and envy in the remark, as if he wished he, too, could bask for ever in the sun of Africa.

Our own morning sun climbs higher. There is no shade in the graveyard, which was once refreshed by the canopy of a baobab tree. Mary's funeral has been described many times. Her life ended an hour before sunset on the evening of 17 April, five days after her forty-first birthday, and the burial arrangements involved two of the men who had caused her most hurt: the engineer George Rae, who was required to nail together a makeshift coffin because the ship's carpenter was ill; and the Reverend James Stewart, whom Livingstone asked to conduct the service – a request which showed the least petty side of his nature. He had complete faith in his wife. When the distressed Mary told him about the Cape's slanders on her and Stewart, he dismissed them as 'madness', 'nonsensical' and 'tittle-tattle'.

When she arrived back in Cape Town for what was to be the last time, Mary was 'most cordially received' by its colonial community, some of whom she barely knew but for whom she was, by association, a celebrity. The warmth of their welcome surprised her; but the shipboard gossip had been disembarked with Livingstone's wife, and her very public perambulations with James Stewart did nothing to subdue its contagion. Mary lacked the kind of worldly imagination that looks for scandal where none exists; her experience of men was limited and generally pragmatic; in their early life together in Africa her relationship with her husband was a working partnership (though she was always the junior partner) for all that it had its share of sexual passion and romantic love. She had no instinct for flirtation and no inkling that her friendship with the equally unworldly Free Kirk cleric could be perceived as anything other than innocent. When the blundering Stewart complained to her that vulgar tongues were accusing them of being 'too intimate', she was not only shocked but also furious. She left his company abruptly, he recorded, 'without bidding goodnight'.

But not for long, even though the canard followed them to Durban, where they were to wait for the little brig *Hetty Ellen*, bringing George Rae and the forty sections of the *Lady Nyassa*, and then travel on to the Zambezi with the UMCA party. There was already friction between the High Church Anglicans and Stewart, whose extreme Presbyterianism was something to be mistrusted and whose gauche manners and shabby clothes, in their view, were evidence of inferiority. Mary was also a disappointment to snobbish, priggish Miss Mackenzie – 'that old hag' as Stewart later described her. The bishop's sister considered Mary socially unqualified to be the wife of an exemplary churchman and national hero, relished the rumours of impropriety and lost no time in dispensing them to anyone who would listen.

The reappearance of George Rae didn't help; to the whiff of sexual scandal he added a conspiracy theory, proposing that James Stewart was a bogus churchman, a trader in disguise and up to no good. As a result, the Anglicans refused to sail with their brother-in-Christ, and only Mary's authority and written intervention secured his passage. For all the humiliation of the gossip, they still needed each other. A dependency had developed. Although Mary was staying with her brother Robert and his wife, she continued to receive Stewart's calls. They took more strolls together, this time along the beaches of the Durban waterfront, sometimes after sunset when, according to Stewart, 'fireflies gleamed through the trees ... the air was filled with all the murmur of insect life'. But there were also more outbursts of irritation; and when he was wakened one night and summoned to the Moffats' house to treat another of Mary's mysterious crises – possibly a panic attack – he was privately disgruntled. The episode, which as usual he treated with laudanum, caused him emotions he was 'not disposed to chronicle'.

Elsewhere he is less reticent, and his journal is punctuated with references to Mary's 'queer fits' and moodiness. In this fractious atmosphere, two days before Christmas, the cargo of ladies and their companions finally set sail for the Zambezi delta. Four weeks later, on 31 January 1862, the *Hetty Ellen* and HMS *Gorgon*, with the *Pioneer* in tow, came within signalling distance of each other at the river's mouth. 'I have a steamship in the brig', flagged the *Gorgon*. 'Wife on board.' On the *Pioneer*, Livingstone replied: 'Accept my best thanks'. The Livingstones were reunited. Even Stewart was moved by Mary's emotion as the ships approached each other; and, when the transfers were made and the couple embraced, he was stirred to observe: 'All the troubles and work of many years seemed compensated for in the romance of this morning'.

Husband and wife hadn't seen each other for nearly four years. Later the new widower remarked on this when he wrote to tell Mrs Fitch of the death of 'My beloved partner whom I loved and treasured so much for eighteen years ... Our love did not die with the honeymoon, though that was spent in hard work in the Bechuana country, and the last three months after an unexpected separation of four years were as pleasant as any I had spent in her society ...'

The baobab is a sacred tree, an extraordinary tree, once seen never forgotten. The bulbous trunk, with a girth which can measure upwards of 80 feet, looks more like a titanic tuber than a column of timber, and the spray of stumpy branches which tops it off looks more like roots. And so it is called 'the upside-down tree', with a suitable fable to explain its origins. When the Great Spirit created the world it gave each animal a tree of its own, reserving the baobab for the hyena. Not best pleased with its peculiar gift the hyena (always the bad guy in African stories) threw it down in disgust, and it landed the wrong way up. But for all their bizarre appearance these giants are honoured for their size and antiquity. In rural Africa trees are a resource often turned into firewood, but the baobab survives, some individuals for over 1,000 years, for two reasons: it is a repository of myth and legend, believed by many Africans to be the home of their spirit ancestors; and, more prosaically, its wood doesn't burn well.

Dr John Kirk, that other unfriendly shipmate, supervised the preparation of Mary's grave. A deep pit was dug beneath the tree; and at 1pm on the 18th, under a sullen sky heavy with heat, four sailors carried the coffin to its side. Livingstone was supported by his brother Charles, who couldn't help noticing the flocks of birds in the baobab branches, 'and some pretty canaries ... singing sweetly in the adjoining trees'. The Portuguese military stationed at Shupanga offered to fire a farewell salute, but Livingstone, although appreciative, refused the gesture. That night the sailors kept guard over the grave, which, until a stone cairn could be raised over it, risked being disturbed by scavenging animals.

Nobody has ever doubted that Livingstone's grief for Mary was anything but real and terrible; that it humbled him, made him a gentler, less intemperate person. To her father, Robert Moffat, he wrote: 'I loved her when you gave her over to my charge, and the longer I lived with her, the better I liked her'. Mary's tragedy was that he didn't live with her for very long. They had been married eighteen years, but half that time was spent apart.

The baobab is long gone. I've found no record of when it fell or was felled (the Portuguese had no cultural attachment to baobabs, which decay fast when they die), but in the photograph of the grave in the David Livingstone Centre the present tomb, which replaced the cairn and wooden cross, is overhung by a tree which is no baobab. Now even that lesser tree has gone, but we do find the remnants of a massive stump, maybe fifteen feet across. Unless, improbably, Mary's bones were disinterred and reburied in a new position under their new tomb, the baobab's canopy must have cast quite a shadow; the stump is at least ten yards from her grave.

'Bom dia!' We are hailed from the cemetery gate by a tall, athletic figure wearing a white T-shirt, baseball cap and sunglasses. He has a sunny smile and a warm handshake. I suppose I was expecting someone grave and grizzled in cassock and biretta, and it takes me a moment to grasp that this cheerful young man is Gaia's contact at Chupanga Mission: Padre Medard, the priest who is keen to co-operate in any plan which will bring more visitors to the grave, where they might be encouraged to contribute to the upkeep of the cemetery and even make a donation to the mission.

Padre Medard may not be able to provide lunch, but he has placed a small table and several chairs under a cashew tree near the church. To this effort we contribute our bottled water, and here we are joined by Antonio Loli John: frail, soft-spoken, tenderly courteous, his eyes milky behind thick glasses, his meagre body propped by a walking-stick. In a land where 100,000 people died in the civil war, where the average life expectancy is 38, Senhor John is not just a survivor but an ancient. He is 81, the oldest man in Chupanga, and he has something startling to tell us. It seems probable that Mary Livingstone breathed her last in a slave holding-pen.

5

The House of the Spirit

'My dearie, my dearie, you are going to leave me'

Shupanga House was still standing when the African historian and medical man Oliver Ransford argued, provocatively but plausibly, that in middle age, if not earlier, Livingstone showed all the symptoms of manic depression, or bipolar disorder as the condition is now called. *David Livingstone: The Dark Interior* was published in 1978. In it, Ransford describes a single-storey house with a tiled roof 'lying before a semi-circle of high bush, and facing across a sloping lawn onto the Zambezi'. It was still standing twenty years later, although, like the rest of the infrastructure of Chupanga Mission, it was broken, abandoned and buried in undergrowth.

The mission was once among the largest and most important in southern Africa. Several members of the present Mozambique government were educated at Chupanga. In its pomp, its community was nearly 400 strong, it maintained seminaries for boys and girls, mixed day schools, a maternity clinic, an old-folks' home and a vocational workshop. These were once housed in the concrete shells we have seen near the church. As the Archdiocese of Beira began to audit its resources in the aftermath of the civil war, it looked at the thick stone walls of Shupanga House and saw a contribution to the restoration of the mission. The Sena Sugar Company, major employers downriver at Marromeu, were replanting their cane fields and firing up their mill again. They needed all the building material they could lay their hands on for a new road. The house was demolished and its stone sold.

This we are told by Padre Medard as we sit beneath the cashew tree, with Gaia translating the priest's Portuguese (we later learn he is from French-speaking Burkina Faso) and Antonio Loli John patiently waiting to show us the site of Mary Livingstone's death. Before he gets the chance, there is an interruption to our quiet, slow-moving morning, in which the only distraction has been an outburst of alarm from the mission's pen of guinea fowl when they spot a prospecting raptor. A Toyota Land Cruiser towing a motor boat on a trailer roars up to the graveyard wall, and two middle-aged white men jump out. One is short and square, the other tall and bulky, and they're both wearing bush clothes. They wave salutes at us before disappearing into the cemetery.

Padre Medard gives a knowing smile. He has already explained that Mary's grave does attract the occasional passing tourist. For the best of reasons, the mission tried to exploit this by padlocking the graveyard gate, printing information leaflets in Portuguese, Sena and English, keeping them in the church with the key, and inviting visitors to pay a small entrance charge when they collected a leaflet and the key. But most people just bypassed the church and stepped through the gaps in the cemetery wall, so he and his colleagues gave up.

Gaia Allison has in mind something more formal for the Mary Livingstone 'heritage trail': all-weather signs at the Chupanga turn-off on the highway, more signs directing visitors to an information centre in the church itself, fixed storyboards with photographs, and a modest admission charge to see them and the grave. The mission is keen to co-operate, but its overburdened income has an overwhelming priority: education for girls. Otherwise, says Padre Medard, their status remains low, their rights minimal, they get married off at 12 or 13 and risk early HIV infection.

'Let's hear what these guys think about putting this place on the map', suggests Gaia, hailing the two visitors as they reappear. They are friendly and are happy to join us beneath the cashew tree. The stocky man, Brian Mullins, is a hunting guide and safari operator from Grahamstown, in the Eastern Cape of South Africa; his lofty companion, Bryce Martin, is a client from Seattle, on the US north-west coast. Their private safari has brought them to a camp site in Coutada 12, the hunting concession we passed through on the way to Chupanga; and the men have done business there to the satisfaction of both.

Bryce has shot a buffalo, an old bull aged 13 or thereabouts. Veteran bulls which have passed their breeding prime leave the herd, often turn cranky and become dangerous animals to hunt in dense bush. 'Did him a favour. He had decayed teeth and a torn lip.' Bryce has also bagged a sable antelope whose spectacular scimitar horns are destined for his Seattle wall, but while boating on the Zambezi the hunters saw so few hippo that they chose to leave them alone.

Now they are doing a bit of sightseeing. 'When I'm in this area, I always bring clients to see Mary's grave', says Brian. 'We've got history, her and me.' Africa may be a vast continent, but sometimes it feels like a small country. Unexpectedly, out of the bush, comes another connection with Mary's past: a link to the schoolgirl years she spent in the Eastern Cape, in the village of Salem near Grahamstown. 'I grew up on stories of Livingstone's wife', explains the cheery shooter. 'I went to Salem Academy, which had its roots in Mr Matthews' Methodist school, where she boarded. Salem is only about twelve miles from Grahamstown. It's a kind of blink-and-you'll-miss-it village, but very pretty.'

Little is known about this shadowy spell in Mary's early life, but it represented the first of many long separations from those close to her and, perhaps, helped mature the stoicism which was expected of missionary families, and which she showed in later life. At the age of nine, she was sent with her younger sister Ann to a well-regarded, firmly religious but inexpensive school in what was a new and vulnerable village.

Salem was in a troubled area, settled by farmers lured to the Eastern Cape by the British to act as human buffers between the Cape Colony and the territories of the Xhosa. Unlike the hunter-gatherer San and pastoralist Khoikhoi people, whom the Bantu-speaking Xhosa had themselves displaced, the Xhosa were settled farmers – and very much in competition for land with the European immigrants. For 100 years from the late eighteenth century, they fought a series of frontier wars against Boer and British expansionism. One of their chiefs, Maquana Nxele, was imprisoned on Robben Island, setting a precedent for its role as a corral for political prisoners resisting white domination.

Britain's strategy for colonising this intermittent war zone was peremptory. Potential settlers were shipped out from the United Kingdom and into Port Elizabeth with the promise of land, transferred by ox-wagon to the interior and left to fend for themselves. Those who built the first cottages at Salem arrived in 1820, and among them was their local hero, Richard Gush. A Devon carpenter, he was a devout Quaker who, in 1834, rode out unarmed to negotiate with Xhosa who were besieging the village. When he asked them what they wanted, they replied that they were hungry. He rode back to Salem and returned with bread, potatoes, tomatoes, tobacco and some pocket knives. The Xhosa withdrew their siege.

Gush built Salem's first church. Only then did he raise a house for his family, who had been living in a cave during their first seven years in South Africa. The colonists found much of the allocated land hopeless for crops and inhospitable to cattle, but they have become lionised in Anglo–South African history as 'the 1820 Settlers'.

By the time Mary arrived at her new school in 1830, many had retreated into rural redoubts like Salem and the nearby centre of Grahamstown, which twenty years earlier had been the headquarters of Colonel John

Graham, leader of an expeditionary force against the Xhosa. Today it is among the best-preserved colonial towns in the Eastern Cape, with an annual arts festival which is the largest in Africa and, it's claimed, second only in size to Edinburgh's international arts festival. The descendants of the 1820 Settlers still regard Grahamstown as the unofficial capital of English-speaking South Africa.

It was Ma-Mary's idea that her two young daughters should be educated at the Reverend William Shaw's 'Wesleyan establishment' at Salem. Robert Moffat's redoubtable wife, known throughout the region by her Tswana honorific (which celebrates the name of the first-born, boy or girl), was already the mother of four and soon to be pregnant again. She was heavily committed to her Kuruman duties, which became even more onerous when Moffat was absent on diplomatic missions to warring tribes, and felt she couldn't do justice to her daughters' schooling at home. She had happy memories of her own boarding-school days – at an evangelical Moravian church near Manchester – and the reputation of Salem's pioneer teacher, William Henry Matthews, was high. Matthews, the eastern colony's first teacher, was an autodidact who served as a soldier in the Napoleonic Wars and spent some time in a French jail. Here he was allowed to attend night school, and here he learned to speak French.

He opened his first school in Salem in a borrowed cottage; and, before Salem Academy got a home of its own with a boarding house, he conducted his classes in the east end of the Reverend Shaw's church. (The beautiful, panelled yellowwood division between the two areas is in immaculate condition today.) To Mary Moffat senior, the separation from her young daughters was 'a new form of trial', but she consoled herself with the thought that Salem was close enough to allow her to visit them. Perhaps every two or three years.

The ox-wagon journey took six weeks. They would have travelled south from Kuruman past the buried treasure later disinterred in the diamond mines of Kimberley. They would have crossed the Orange River and skirted the edge of the Great Karoo, the high, seasonal desert which the Khoisan call the Great Place of Nothing. They would have passed through the foothills of the Sneeuberg Mountains, at the northern limit of the Cape frontier, to reach the handsome Dutch town of Graaff-Reinet, an important station on the road from Port Elizabeth to the interior. For all the heartbreak of the coming separation and the apprehensions of the uprooted children, they would have been uplifted by the physical splendours of their route.

It was the southern-hemisphere winter, and perhaps the little girls saw their first snow on the Sneeuberg, the Snow Mountains. As they crossed the Plains of Camdeboo and steered towards Grahamstown, where they arrived on 1 August, they would have navigated through a sea of springbok. Until the end of the nineteenth century the springbok migrations of southern Africa were among the wonders of the natural world. The herds were millions-strong, miles wide and deep, the largest processions of mammals ever witnessed; and when they flowed round Graaff-Reinet the dust took two weeks to settle. Hunting and fences have since done for these mighty assemblies of antelope, which provided protein for the pot for every traveller who knew how to shoot. To the Moffats, it would be unimaginable that one day their numbers throughout southern Africa would be reduced to a few hundred thousand.

Ma-Mary made this journey again only twice in the six years the girls spent at the self-styled 'Athens of South Africa'. Their affectionate father, who would have been quite content to have them remain at Kuruman, didn't see them again until Ann was 14 and Mary 15, when they were sent with their brother Robert to a new school in Cape Town. In her book *Wives of Fame*, Edna Healey maintains that Mary was 'happy enough' at the Salem school but offers little evidence for this sanguine claim, contrarily adding that she was often lodged during the holidays with unwilling hosts, was on the receiving end of hostility from settler families who called mission children 'white Africans' (an insult in those days) and, shy by nature, 'learned at an early age to set her face to hide her feelings'.

The sun has almost cleared the steeple of Chupanga church. We have lingered too long beneath the cashew tree talking to the safari guide and his client. We have told them of the difficulty of maintaining the churchyard, and how the local method of clearing undergrowth – burning it – is damaging the gravestones. We have explained that the mission has no money to install the information boards we would all like to see in the church, no money to pay for direction signs or any of the literature which would help to promote a heritage trail. 'What we need', announces Gaia, 'is a Mary Livingstone Fighting Fund.' Whereupon Bryce Martin, the trophy-hunter from Seattle whose day job is 'real estate', puts his hand in the pocket of his bush shirt, pulls out some notes and without fuss hands a $100 bill to Padre Medard. 'Let me make the first contribution', he says quietly, turning away from the priest's gasp of thanks.

Not for the first time, as we wave the two men off in their Land Cruiser, do I find myself touched by the easy generosity of an American.

Antonio Loli John is beginning to feel the heat, but takes the lead as we file through the long grass towards the river and a tangle of trees and shrubs. The bush has not entirely reclaimed the foundations of Shupanga House, and the Sena Sugar Company hasn't entirely plundered all its stones. We find more than rubble: chunks of wall three feet thick, a fragment of gable netted in roots and creepers. Just for a moment Senhor John hesitates before using his stick to lever himself over what might have been a threshold. '*La casa di spirito*', he says. The house of the spirit; the haunted house. He was afraid to go near it when he was a child. Nobody would live in it. Everyone in Chupanga knew that it had a cruel past and was possessed by the unquiet souls of the dead.

With the help of Gaia's Portuguese, I probe the old man's memory. What was the house like? It had very thick walls and very small windows and only one door. Like a jail. He had asked his father what it was used for, and was told that, in the old days, slaves were held in the house until they were fetched by boats to take them down the river. Did the ghost of Mary Livingstone haunt the house? No. The ghosts of slaves.

And that's all he can tell us. Somewhere in the mouldering files of an obscure Portuguese archive there may be records, even audits of the human goods passed down the Zambezi to the slave markets of Ilha do Moçambique and Ilha do Ibo. There may even be mentions of a holding-pen at Shupanga, which was a major commercial centre in the nineteenth century. When the local Portuguese eventually abandoned their clandestine interests in slaving, Shupanga House took on the function of a self-catering guesthouse for legitimate traders moving up and down the river. But if any of the member-chroniclers of the Zambezi expedition had any idea that the old, unfurnished building placed at their disposal had once been put to more miserable use, none of them mentioned it.

There is no reason to distrust oral history. Antonio Loli John's testimony is credible, given the persistence of the trade in Portugal's colonies long after their mother nation declared it illegal in 1836, and given the river's well-documented role as a slaving route to the coast. Perhaps Livingstone and his companions suspected but chose to ignore the dark history of Shupanga House; perhaps they felt it simply didn't matter. By the time she was carried from a tent on the riverbank the stricken woman needed more than the cooler air and minimal comfort of a bare stone house. Only dimly conscious of her surroundings, she was unlikely to be disturbed by its tainted past. She was beyond recovery.

Mary had been ill for a week. On the journey back from the delta it seemed, for the first time, as if the suffocating heat of the valley and the depressed mood on the *Pioneer* were beginning to sap her health and spirits. John Kirk observed that she looked sallow, and diagnosed 'indiscretions', hinting waspishly that she had 'undermined' her own health by drinking too much and succumbing to anxiety over the gossip which still blighted her relationship with Stewart. Mary had also gained weight since she first joined the expedition – 'getting very stout', as Dr Kirk put it – and his recurring interest in this may well amount to veiled speculation that she was again pregnant. It was by no means improbable. But on 21 April, while approaching Shupanga, she developed a fever which her husband had no difficulty in identifying as malarial. The fever refused to retreat before his administration of heavy doses of quinine – his 'rousers', as he called the pills. Livingstone was among the first tropical travellers to demonstrate the potency of quinine in trouncing some strains of malaria.

Not this time. By 24 April, Mary was supine and suffering in the riverbank tent, vomiting so persistently that she couldn't keep any medicine down. Two days later, she was moved to an improvised bed of mattress and tea chests in Shupanga House, where James Stewart had been living while the Livingstones escorted Miss Mackenzie and Mrs Burrup downriver. Her husband's efforts to save her became ever more desperate. He and Kirk tried everything in their repertoire – treatments almost as distressing as her symptoms, from poultices on her calves, her stomach and her neck to the invasion of an enema. By now she was badly jaundiced and delirious, her final hours further tormented by delusions about her children. She muttered worries about Robert, the eldest, a troubled teenager who was becoming wayward. And, as she approached the tipping point of her life, she imagined Agnes in mortal danger on the edge of a cliff. 'See! Agnes is falling over a precipice!' On the 27th, she became semi-conscious and, as the day wore on, comatose.

Livingstone had his own agonies. He knew he was failing to save his wife – but, worse, he feared he was failing to save her soul. Mary's faith had been challenged by her years alone in the UK, when the certainties of her childhood and early life were eaten away by misery and bitterness. She was known to have made damaging remarks about the lot of missionary wives – one of the more urgent reasons her husband had decided to keep her by his side on this expedition – and when they were reunited he worked hard to reinstate the beliefs he had always assumed they shared.

She had confessed doubts in her letters to him (among those which have been lost, either accidentally or intentionally) and in their weeks together on the Zambezi she aired them again. He was painfully aware that only 'God's will' and 'God's work' justified the sacrifices he had not so much asked of her but imposed upon her. His response to her scepticism was to read the Bible and study its lessons with her, and pray long into the night to smooth out the kinks so perversely warping her faith. Mary had seldom expressed such deviance from her husband's beliefs, and he preferred to describe this new independence of thought as 'a gloomy, desponding state'.

Now she was dying. When she lost the power to swallow and became more deeply unconscious, the iron man of Africa began to cry. At 6pm, he asked James Stewart to join Kirk and himself at her bedside. Stewart had been Mary's friend but had grown to dislike her, and in his journal he seems to suggest she was faking the severity of her illness even as she was carried into Shupanga House. He was also disillusioned with her husband. But even he was moved when he found that 'the man who had faced so many deaths, and braved so many dangers, was now utterly broken down and weeping like a child'. The three men knelt and prayed as her breathing faltered, Livingstone frantically concerned for her afterlife to the end. To the Protestant missionary, it seemed every bit as crucial that she affirm her faith as if he and Mary had been raised in the Catholic Church and she must have the last rites.

What happened in the closing moments of her life is ambiguous. Livingstone himself recorded that he bent over his wife and pleaded: 'My dearie, my dearie, you are going to leave me. Are you resting on Jesus?'

In her book *Good Wives?* Margaret Forster judges that there was 'something grotesque about the scene, in his asking such a question of a woman who was barely breathing and hadn't spoken for the last twenty-four hours, but to him it was a matter of damnation or salvation'. The quinine had deafened her, and he had no way of knowing whether she could hear him, but the distraught husband convinced himself that she not only understood the question but also answered it. To his youngest son Oswell, he wrote that she 'looked up towards Heaven thoughtfully. I think it meant yes.'

She looked up towards Heaven thoughtfully? I've always been tempted to read this signal differently. Could it be that, badgered beyond endurance, Mary simply rolled her eyes to the skies in the time-honoured manner of long-suffering wives everywhere? We'll never know.

The evangelical imperative is still vigorous in the province of Sofala. Chupanga Mission is rising from the ashes with the help of a global church founded on the secular backwash of the French Revolution. On Christmas Day 1800, Father Pierre Coudrin, of the Diocese of Poitiers, and 'the Good Mother Henriette Aymer', who had spent time in prison for hiding a priest, both dedicated themselves to 'reparation' in defiance of the Revolution's godless zealots. In 1817, the Congregation of the Sacred Hearts was approved by Pope Pius VII. They have been active ever since in Europe, the USA and, today, most widely in the developing world.

Ninety minutes' drive away is a younger, more local engine of evangelism, although it, too, has an international dimension. Afrika wa Yesu, which in Sena means Africa for Jesus, was also born out of revolution. Its founders, Rod and Ellie Hein, are a Zimbabwean couple of remarkable courage and commitment. Their mission work in northern and central Mozambique during the most savage years of the civil war was driven by the kind of proselytising fervour and unquestioning faith which makes me feel queasy; but after reading Ellie Hein's book *Beyond the Shadow* I have nothing but respect for their tolerance of danger and hardship. The author's prose may read like an over-excited Pentecostalist tract, but the story it tells is both horrifying and inspiring. The Heins' pastoral support and practical help for the broken people of Renamo's heartland brought them close to the rebel commanders, and they have been credited with facilitating the negotiations which led to the 1992 Peace Accord brokered in Rome by the United Nations.

I never get to meet them. They are both in Zimbabwe when we pay our brief visit to Afrika wa Yesu's headquarters, established on the outskirts of Inhaminga when the war ended. But in its pleasant garden compound of ginger-coloured buildings we're warmly received by a young Romanian woman, one of the 'multi-national, multi-gifted power team from six nations' whose purpose is 'winning souls'. Although the mission is non-denominational the Heins' tireless fund-raising in the USA reaps a predictable harvest from American evangelicals; and at Inhaminga and the northern port of Nacala (a Muslim area, where 'souls are being won for Jesus Christ') Afrika wa Yesu now runs residential Bible colleges to inspire and train Mozambican disciples. To an agnostic like me, its more valuable programmes are those which offer emergency relief, primary health care, including a mobile dental clinic, and vocational training for young men. At Inhaminga it also runs the 'House of Hope' – a school which provides over 100 local children with daily meals along with rations of spiritual teaching and supplementary education.

If a town as forlorn as the capital of Cheringoma district can be *en fête* then Inhaminga is *en fête* when we arrive in its centre in the early afternoon. It's the president's birthday, therefore a public holiday, and the main street is busy with idling men who would otherwise be working. Our Land Rover and white faces soon draw a small crowd of children and youths, and Mike decides he should stay with the vehicle while Gaia and I go in search of a shop to buy cold drinks and snacks. Breakfast was seven hours ago. As we cross the road, a group of men, cheerfully drunk, spill out of a bottle shop and block our way with a barrage of questions in Portuguese and Sena. They mean no harm, but Gaia swats them aside by will and presence alone. There is something of the Valkyrie about Gaia, who is tall and powerfully built with a cascade of thick flaxen hair. She commands attention wherever she goes.

We eat biscuits and drink Coca Cola standing on the pavement. Soon, we realise we're being watched by a boy of about ten. He is barefoot and skinny in torn, too-big shorts and filthy T-shirt, and he perches on one leg like a stork, staring with an unblinking intensity impossible to ignore. It's rare for African children not to return smiles, but this one just stares. His eyes follow every biscuit Gaia takes from the packet, every gulp I swig from my bottle of Coke, but he says nothing. Inhaminga is not a tourist town. He hasn't learned to beg. 'He looks hungry', says Gaia, holding out the second packet of biscuits. He hesitates before taking it slowly, as if scared it will be snatched away. When I offer him a Coca Cola, he is barely able to trust the evidence of the moment. At last he smiles as his hand closes round the curvaceous bottle with the script that even the illiterate can read. The ultimate totem of Western potency is in his grasp.

We take some more supplies back to the Land Rover for Mike, then set off to see the sights of Inhaminga. When Rod and Ellie Hein arrived in 1992, the Peace Accord was only months old. They found a shattered town and a traumatised people, their numbers swelled by thousands of starving refugees from the countryside, who had heard that UN food aid was on its way. Inhaminga was once a handsome colonial town, a cathedral town endowed with flower-filled gardens and amenities to meet the expectations of a key workforce – the Portuguese managers and engineers who ran the workshops of Mozambique's railways. The Heins found its infrastructure destroyed and its population fearful, unconvinced the war was over. It had been badly bombed; there were atrocities on both sides; they were shown mass graves. But it still had a decent airstrip, one of the few in the region big enough to be used by UN cargo planes; and, although damaged, its 'beautiful twin-towered Catholic cathedral' was largely intact.

In her book Ellie Hein describes how they stood on the steps of the town's old colonial hotel and 'made a new commitment to God'. A crowd gathered before them as their mission team sang and the Heins preached. 'Now prophesy to this town of Inhaminga. You see all the devastation, no vehicles moving, everything broken down and destroyed. The day is coming when you will see the walls being rebuilt, vehicles will travel again down these roads, shops will open and the market place will be full of food ... Yes, Lord, these bones shall live. We shall help make this town live.'

Today, Inhaminga does indeed live, and they have played a part in its resurrection. But it remains a melancholy place, haunted by the ghosts of the privileged people who abandoned Mozambique on its independence, taking their assets with them, or fled the town when war arrived. But the colonists couldn't pack up the locomotives and carriages of the Caminhos de Ferro de Moçambique, many still rusting on their useless rails,[1] or their splendid recreational facilities. We visit their remnants: an Olympic-size swimming pool hoarding a puddle of dirty water, with three teenage boys horsing around in its cracked cavity; an empty paddling pool with a chute where children once slid down a concrete elephant's trunk; seatless swings and seized-up roundabouts. The skeletons of fun and games, dressed with mad gaiety in flowering creepers. But the soccer pitch is still in use, though scrubby, and the complex of solid if unlovely railway houses is inhabited again.

Afrika wa Jesu's compound, which is about three miles out of town, was built close to the runway where Rod Hein could land the Cessna 206 which had a vital role in their aid work during and after the civil war. Chupanga Mission had been destroyed by Frelimo in their drive against the Renamo rebels of the Gorongosa region, and was deserted and in ruins when the Heins paid their first visit to Mary's grave. According to Ant White at M'phingwe Lodge they can take the credit for retrieving it from sub-Saharan Africa's most tenacious colonist: tropical vegetation. 'I know that Rod took some time to find the grave, it was so overgrown', we are told by Simona Caba, who has recently arrived from Transylvania. Gentle, slender Simona, who has huge bright eyes, offers us tea and puts herself to some trouble to find a mission newsletter in which the Heins describe their restoration work at Chupanga. It is dated June 2006, and they write:

---

1 Inhaminga today has recovered its railway and station. The track, wrenched from its bed by the bare hands of Renamo rebels, has been restored; and the line from Beira reopened in 2009.

A few years ago we came to see the grave, in awe of the sacrifice and incredible work carried out in Africa by her famous husband. We found it overgrown and in disrepair, and have visited several times to restore it. The last time we were here we replaced the gold bracelet of a child that had become exposed as time wore off the top of a corner pillar where someone (perhaps David Livingstone himself?) had placed it and covered it with cement. Grief gripping his heart he wrote to Oswell his son: 'With many tears running down my cheeks I have to tell you that poor dearly beloved Mama died last night about seven o'clock ... she loved you dearly and often spoke of you and all the family, especially little Baby.' Did someone bring out the bracelet from the arm of little baby when they brought out the head plate for the grave from England?

The child's bracelet is a new mystery. It certainly wasn't put there by 'David Livingstone himself'. The cairn and cross raised over the grave in 1862 were replaced by the existing tomb long after he left the Zambezi, although I've yet to find out when. On the metal plate attached to the base are the words 'With Respect and Admiration from the Livingstones of Africa', but there's no date. It seems likely that these family members – and I've still to discover who they were – cemented the bracelet in the corner pillar, and it's possible it did indeed belong to Anna Mary, 'little Baby', by then an adult. Whatever the answers, the Heins' account of their activities at the grave has given me more questions to ask when I get back to Scotland.

6

Lost Tribes

'Oh no, you must always be as playful'

Every marriage has its secret rooms. The more mature the marriage, the more numerous the rooms. Who can ever look at the public façade of a long partnership and speculate with confidence on its internal workings? For all Livingstone's effusive praise for his wife in his letters and journals, and for all the emotional hunger in Mary's few surviving words about her husband, it would be easy to assume that the quotidian life of their union was a plain, workmanlike business, enlivened only by bouts of sexual activity which produced regular pregnancies more reliably than any harvest dependent on the seasonal rains of Africa. But, after Mary died, in the eloquence of his grief, Livingstone opened one or two windows on the private chambers of their relationship; none more surprising than the room where they kept their sense of fun.

It was never the custom of Victorians to smile for the camera when they were introduced to the new technology of portrait photography. It's no surprise that Livingstone looks stern and humourless in all the familiar images he has left to history; but he had a droll turn of phrase and could relish the comic. There is, however, an arresting grimness about Mary in the only photograph where she appears alone and in close focus. It's the least flattering image of a woman who is plain in all her photographs, but who looks coarse-featured in this one. Oliver Ransford unkindly likens her to the Queen of Spades. It was taken when she was in her late thirties, and there's something ambiguous about her expression. The eyes, beneath heavy brows, might be resentful or merely tired; the mouth, beneath a long nose, might be bitter or merely resigned.

It's well nigh impossible to believe that the woman in this picture, which illustrates her brief biography in Scotland's David Livingstone Centre, has any trace of frivolity or skittishness in her nature. But it seems she did, and it seems that she and Livingstone often shared a spirit of playfulness. When Livingstone wrote to their friend Mrs Fitch to tell her of Mary's death and to reflect that 'the last three months after an unexpected separation of four years have been as pleasant as any I have spent in her society', his remark was credible enough, given that he was quite capable of obscuring the tragedies of Magomero and the UMCA women with the black cloud of his own tragedy. And, despite the frustrations of the *Pioneer*'s halting progress up the Zambezi when it first collected its 'cargo of ladies', in those early weeks the mood on board was not always one of unrelieved fractiousness.

There was much to interest the newcomers to Africa, even if they flinched from the nudity of riverbank villagers and deplored the lascivious behaviour of their escort of bluejackets. And there was much to comfort and exhilarate Mary in the return to her native land, whose sights and sounds would reach back through her years of loneliness to the early days of her marriage. The Zambezi Valley is greener and wetter than the semi-arid Kalahari bushlands where the Livingstones had their only settled home, but they share many of the same sensations; especially at night, when the land releases the heat of the sun, and the air smells of earth and woodsmoke and something more elusive; something ancient and enduring and charged with expectation. It seems to come from the womb of the world, the ancestral belly which formed and carried the human race and grew us from infancy until we marched out of Africa to colonise the rest of the planet.

Perhaps Mrs Burrup, Miss Mackenzie, her housekeeper Jessie Lennox, and Sarah, the maid with no surname, trembled at the night noises of the bush: the furtive rustles in the undergrowth and sinister splashes in the water, the alarm barks of baboons, the knowing whoop of hyenas, the heart-stopping challenge of lions, whose great, groaning roars can travel five miles. Perhaps even the ambient orchestra of cicadas and tree frogs unnerved them. But, to Mary, they would be night music; a welcome distraction from sleep, which was too often plagued by agonising dreams about her faraway children.

Then there were the dinner parties; surprisingly merry evenings in the *Pioneer*'s cramped saloon, the men drinking beer, the women drinking punch made by the *Gorgon* officers, with Livingstone as host, entertaining his ill-assorted, socially disparate guests with anecdotes about his travels. One night, his dog, a demented old bulldog called Log, fell through the cabin skylight and landed on the table, causing not so much fright as hilarity. And, when the *Pioneer* cleared the mangroves and mudflats of the delta and entered the Zambezi's main channel, the shifting landscape became less oppressive, with the riverine forest opening onto palm savanna. As the air cooled towards sunset, husband and wife took long walks on these grasslands, seizing the chance to be alone, while those who could shoot seized the chance to hunt. The shore excursions did much to relieve shipboard tensions and even involved horseplay, some of it childish; on one occasion, Livingstone and the officers ambushed the ladies by jumping out of a thicket, roaring like lions.

As he describes the last weeks he spent with his wife, the explorer's reflections are an anthology of guilt, regret, anguish, nostalgia and fearful piety. He remains concerned for Mary's soul. 'My heart smites me', he declares in his journal, lamenting that he 'did not talk seriously' about her doubts 'and many things beside'. To Ma-Mary, his mother-in-law, with whom he had long had a prickly relationship, he opens his heart as never before with the humility of a penitent. 'This unlooked for bereavement quite crushes and takes the heart out of me. Everything else that happened in my career only made the mind rise to overcome it. But this takes away all my strength. If you knew how I loved and trusted her you may realise my loss ... There are regrets which will follow me to my dying day. If I had done so and so etc. etc. ...' To Mary's brother John, he admits: 'I had got so into the habit of feeling her to be part of myself I did not fear but she would hold out'.

To his son Oswell, he gives the pitiful details of her last moments, perhaps too intimately and comprehensively to console the eight-year-old. 'She saw me shedding many tears in prospect of parting with my dear companion of eighteen years, and must have known that her bodily case was hopeless. She answered my kisses up to within half an hour of her departure. It was only after we had commended her soul to Him who himself passed through the gate of death, that she took no notice of me. She was then breathing with her mouth a little open, shut it quietly and breathed no more.'

And to Lady Murchison, wife of his friend Sir Roderick Murchison of the Royal Geographic Society, he gave Mary the eulogy denied by the nature of her funeral – and largely denied by history: 'At Kolobeng she managed all the household affairs by native servants of her own training, made bread, butter and all the clothes of the family; taught her children most carefully; kept also an infant and sewing school – by far the most popular and best attended we had. It was a fine sight to see her day by day walking quarter of a mile to the town, no matter how broiling the sun, to impart instructions to the heathen Bakwains. Ma-Robert's name is known throughout all that country and 1,800 miles beyond ... A brave, good woman was she.'

Too much, too late? In all his correspondence, Livingstone emphasises and repeats his description of Mary as his 'dear' or 'faithful' companion of eighteen years. She was companion to him, and he to her, for only nine of them; and even these were interrupted for months at a time. Perhaps the long separations during those eighteen years were the preservative that kept their relationship fresh, with every reunion a honeymoon and each child a honeymoon baby. That there was some joy and laughter in their marriage is startlingly demonstrated by what, to my mind, is his least florid, most affecting tribute to his wife. In his journal he recalls how, shortly before she became ill, they shared some light-hearted moment which made him remark: 'We old bodies ought now to be more sober'. And how the morose woman of the Blantyre photograph replied: 'Oh no, you must always be as playful ... I would not like you to be as grave as some folk I have seen ...'

A lost tribe. The white people of Africa, the Europeans who may have been there for five or six generations know, if they have any imagination, that they remain guests in the lands of their birth. Once I was told by the wife of a farmer in northern Kenya: 'If you live in Africa, you live with a suitcase packed'. It is a metaphorical suitcase, kept at the back of a cupboard in the mind, ready to be pulled out at short notice. 'Yet where do we go?' reflected this woman, who still has family in the United Kingdom, who sent her children to St Andrews University and holds exhibitions of her delicate wildlife watercolours in the galleries of Edinburgh. She is third-generation Kenyan – and in the semi-wilderness of the high Laikipia plateau, on the great ranches where Boran cattle and red Maasai sheep co-exist with lion and leopard, in the turning of the cycle of seasonal extremes, where rain is never inconvenient and sunshine never frivolous, she has mislaid her British compass. 'We don't belong in the UK. We've lost the habit of being British, yet we don't belong in Kenya.'

The lost tribe, most of them, remain hugely privileged when measured against the economic standards of their host countries, but work harder and harder to be good guests. And if the day comes when they do feel themselves unwelcome they load up their packed suitcases and leave their homes, and the countries which they call home, to find another niche in the continental land mass, which many find impossible to quit. They don't have the genes of the Kikuyu or Xhosa or Shona, but an old fever runs in their blood like a virus transmitted from generation to generation. The French call it *mal d'Afrique*, an infection which only troubles them when they lose for ever their handhold on the parental body of Africa, progenitor of us all. Its symptoms are not mere homesickness, more a form of separation anxiety.

You don't even have to be born in Africa to pick it up. On his rare visits home, David Livingstone pined for Africa as he never pined for Scotland – as he never ached for the fields of Lanarkshire, where he first took an interest in natural history, or the hills of Argyll, where he had his roots. (His grandfather, Neil, was a dispossessed crofter from Ulva, a small island off the west coast of Mull, in the Inner Hebrides, and like many Highland migrants moved to the Clyde Valley to find work in the power-houses of the industrial age.) Scotland had become more of a sentimental idea, and in his books and journals he would tap into his memories of home to describe the African landscape, sometimes to implausible effect. 'Coming down the Zouga', he wrote in *Missionary Travels*, 'we had time to look at its banks. They are very beautiful, and resemble in many parts the river Clyde above Glasgow.' Only if you clear the wild fig trees and camelthorn, replace the pale sand of the Zouga river valley with the dark soil of Clydeside and replant its banks with alder, elm and ash.

But, for all this fanciful nostalgia, there is little in his attitude to Scotland which compares with the passion and poetry of his feeling for Africa. He was in thrall to its uncharted interior; and the death of his wife, whose even more acute *mal d'Afrique* almost destroyed her during her exile in Britain, did nothing to diminish its hold on him. Nor did the ignominious collapse of the Zambezi Expedition three years later, nor the motherless children who hadn't seen their father for six years, nor the incongruous adventures and sorry death of his son Robert (of which more to come). Even 'little Baby', Anna Mary, whom he had never met, didn't have the power to release him from its spell. He returned to the United Kingdom for only a year; long enough to make financial and domestic arrangements for his family and – more importantly – accept a commission from the Royal Geographic Society.

On offer was the opportunity to win the most coveted prize in European geographical exploration. An earlier RGS expedition led by Henry Burton and John Speke had left unresolved their conflicting evidence on the source of the Nile, and the prospect of picking up this challenge restored Livingstone to jubilant spirits. 'The mere animal pleasure of travelling in a wild unexplored country is very great', he wrote euphorically. 'When on lands of a couple of thousand feet elevation, brisk exercise imparts elasticity to the muscles, fresh and healthy blood circulates through the brain, the mind works well, the eye is clear, the step is firm.' In the summer of 1865, he left the United Kingdom for the last time to begin the eight-year journey which was to redeem his reputation, secure his place among the immortals of Westminster Abbey, make the career of his most effective hagiographer, Henry Morton Stanley, and end in agony in a mud-and-thatch hut on the edge of the Bangweulu swamps. All without finding the headwaters of the Nile.

The White family of Catapu belong to the lost tribe of Zimbabwe. The day and its encounters have left me dusty and drained, but when Mike, Gaia and I return to M'phingwe Lodge around sunset we are restored by the bustle at the bar. There are newcomers: an environmentalist on the road to the northern city of Nampula, a party from the construction company building the new bridge at Caia – and Pat White, Ant's wife, who shares her time between their home and business in Beira and the lodge.

As she soon tells me, Pat was born a Scot. When she was five, her parents left the Aberdeenshire village of Hatton for a new life in the British colony of Rhodesia. She has been married to Ant White for over forty years. If the early years of every marriage are a form of adventure, hers were a cliff-hanger. In the 1970s, at the height of the Rhodesian Bush War, she rarely saw her husband. He had joined the Selous Scouts, the elite special-forces regiment of the Rhodesian Army, which practised ruthless tactics of counter-insurgency.

Pat is a comely blonde woman who must be heading for 60 but doesn't look it. Neither does Ant, who is whip-lean and handsome, with little grey in his dark hair. But there is something old about his eyes, although they are still bright; something scoured and empty in their blue gaze, as if they've been stripped clean of a retinal storehouse of images. The Selous Scouts, by their own charter, were directed to pursue 'the clandestine elimination of terrorists/terrorism both within and without the country'.

As the military arms of Rhodesia's black nationalist movements, Zanu and Zapu, waged war on Britain's rebel colony, which had unilaterally declared itself independent in 1965, the Scouts met violence with violence, dirty tricks with dirty tricks. In the deep bush of Rhodesia, Zambia, Botswana and Mozambique, their small undercover teams, many of them black, penetrated insurgent-controlled territory, often operating independently for weeks at a time, sometimes passing themselves off as enemy guerrillas. Their numbers were not large: an active core of 500 grew to around 1,000 through their policy of 'turning terrorists' – recruiting captives to their own ranks. But they were tough, superfit men expert in bushcraft, sabotage and unorthodox manoeuvres, and between 1973 and 1980 they were responsible for 68 per cent of insurgent casualties. One of their last operations was the attempted assassination of the Zapu leader Joshua Nkomo, who was based in Zambia.

The Scouts were a mixed-race volunteer unit whose seventeen-day selection course was so rigorous that on one occasion only fourteen of 126 applicants were accepted. They took their name from Frederick Courtney Selous, the Victorian explorer, professional hunter and soldier who became the right-hand man of Cecil John Rhodes as that predatory adventurer campaigned to annex to the British Empire his territorial claims in what is now Zimbabwe. Selous was also the most celebrated big-game hunter of his day, but turned conservationist when he saw how the indiscriminate safaris of fashionable trophy-hunting were devastating elephant populations. His name was bequeathed to Africa's single largest wildlife reserve, the Selous Game Reserve in Tanzania, where he was killed by a German sniper during the First World War. He had rejoined the British Army at the age of 64 to fight in its East Africa war.

A hugely romantic figure in the British colonial pantheon, Selous was inspired in his London youth by the Africa literature of David Livingstone, and was himself the inspiration for Allan Quatermain in H. Rider Haggard's novel *King Solomon's Mines*. He was the perfect role model for the young white Rhodesians of the Scouts, who were encouraged to grow long, unkempt beards which earned them the nickname 'Armpits with Eyeballs'. On the regimental association website, there is a picture of Ant White looking very young indeed, despite the shaggy beard; and another of Captain Anthony White, beard now trimmed, in a roll-call of those who won military honours. It was taken in 1979, during the regiment's last full operational year. When Zanu and Robert Mugabe were elected to the first government of independent Zimbabwe in 1980, 'it became abundantly clear that the controversial Selous Scouts had no place in the new order'. The force was disbanded, and many of its members moved to South Africa, where they were welcomed into the South African Defence Force, then busy helping Renamo rebels fight Frelimo. Another bush war.

Among those who left for South Africa was Ant White, whose beard is long gone. When I ask him how he spent the years between leaving Zimbabwe and settling in Mozambique, he gives an odd little smile. 'I was a soldier.' A career soldier? 'Yes.' The monosyllabic reply discourages further inquisitiveness, and I return our conversation to David and Mary Livingstone. 'You know, they spent only half their married life together, and they were married for eighteen years.' Ant shrugs. 'I can do better than that. I've been married forty-two years, and I reckon I've been away from my wife for more than half that time.' Then he tells me about the people who looked after Mary's grave in the aftermath of the civil war: Afrika wa Jesu, and an Irish priest called Father Eamonn who was based at Chupanga Mission for a time but returned to Ireland. Ant himself contributed handsomely to the restoration of the church, funding its new altar. The least charitable of his neighbours gossip that the altar is penance for a sinful past.

I ask Pat White what she'd been doing in South Africa before she joined Ant in Beira. 'I had a business making rechargeable torches.' She is happy to talk about the challenge of life in rural Sofala only ten years earlier. 'That road between Beira and Caia was dirt. There was no electricity in Caia, there was no filling station, there wasn't even a market. Initially, we built M'phingwe Lodge as a camp for the engineers working on the new highway. At night we lived by candlelight and paraffin lamps like everyone in Caia – or those who could afford them. And we had to bring everything: kitchen equipment, furniture, bedding, food, drink from Beira. Now that the pylons have come down from the hydro-electric plant at Cabora Bassa life has got a lot easier.'

Cabora Bassa, Kebrabasa, Livingstone's nemesis. Today, it powers the national grid of Mozambique and beyond.

The lost tribe of David Livingstone made their way to the Lanarkshire town of Hamilton in the autumn of 1852, when a two-storey cottage opened its door to a short, hefty young woman towing a rabble of children. She had a swarthy complexion and tired dark eyes, she was dressed unfashionably in loose-waisted clothes, and when she spoke her accent was neither English nor Scottish. There was something outlandish about the children, three boys and a girl all aged under six, the youngest of whom was Oswell, nicknamed Zouga, born on the banks of the Zouga river less than a year earlier. They lapsed into speech which sounded gibberish to the people of Burnbank Road. With some apprehension, Neil and Agnes Livingstone welcomed the daughter-in-law and grandchildren they had never met, recently uprooted from their home on the doorstep of the Kalahari.

Ingraham Cottage, which the Livingstones renamed Ulva Cottage in tribute to their Hebridean roots, is still there, now plain number 17. It has a plaque on the wall which claims it was David Livingstone's home 'from 1862 until his death on 1st May 1873'. It may have been his house, but it was never his home. He stayed there only briefly, on two occasions: in

1857, when he, Mary and the children visited his mother and sisters after his return from his coast-to-coast trek across Africa (his father died as he was sailing home); and in 1864, during his last visit to the United Kingdom after Mary's death.

His wife's visit was also short-lived. In the mid-nineteenth century, the purlieus of Burnbank Road would have been rural, even beautiful; but not to the eye of Mary Livingstone, compelled to leave the brilliant spaces and infinite skies of her homeland as she entered the unhappiest years of her life.

Perhaps the global army of multi-national workers who mine the earth's resources or build its new infrastructure is also a lost tribe. It is certainly a nomadic one. 'Meet the *chef grande* of our new bridge.' The group from the construction company has finished dinner and returned to the bar, where Pat White introduces me to the big, affable Dutchman who is project manager. Johannes Heins does have a home, but not in the Netherlands; in Rio de Janeiro, where he has a Brazilian wife who is currently keeping him company in the air-conditioned purpose-built village (with swimming pool) raised for the engineers and managers. Johannes is rarely in Rio. He travels the world building bridges. His special skill is building very long bridges: three in Nigeria, four in the USA, and the second bridge over the Bosphorus. The Caia bridge will be nearly a mile and a half long.

'Come and see how we're getting on.' He invites us all to the site the next morning, with the added lure of 'the best cappuccino and espresso in Mozambique' in their village restaurant. Ant is too busy to leave his sawmill, but Gaia, Mike, Pat and I accept with enthusiasm.

The bridge is at an early stage, but the rudiments of its scale, with the high flyover of its southern approach in place, already look impressive. Despite Johannes's explanations and statistics – 'it will have twenty-nine spans, with the central span cantilevered, and we're aiming for a target of two spans a month' – I can make little sense of the prodigious activity around us, but feel its controlled power: the measured movements of the monster equipment, the slow but steady straddling of the river in giant steps, the hot, hard labour of the black workforce who don't live in an air-conditioned prefabricated village with swimming pool. Near the midstream pontoon, where drills are pounding the Zambezi bedrock, the fishermen of Caia throw their nets from dug-out canoes, as they've done for centuries. To their forebears, the puffing *Pioneer*, on its sorties up and down the Zambezi, must have seemed an equally dramatic harbinger of transformation.

The coffee lives up to its reputation. When we take our leave of the hospitable Johannes and his friendly wife and colleagues, our little party goes its separate ways in its separate vehicles. Gaia is driving back to Beira, Pat has shopping to do in Caia, and Mike and I decide to take a look at the famous Caia ferry. Ignoring the rising colossus which will soon make it obsolete, the ramshackle craft idles by the riverbank, waiting to embark the ramshackle trucks which provender the isolated interior of the northern provinces. But, when the main north–south highway takes its first leap over the Zambezi, the road will open up a whole new economy.

The river, as ever, exacts its own toll. As we drive back to M'phingwe, we come upon a disaster. Mike brakes. Just off the highway, operated by a sub-contractor, is the site of the silos which mix the cement for the bridge's piles. One towering cylinder has partially collapsed, sending heaps of masonry and cement crashing to the ground. The accident has just happened. Urgent figures heave rubble, fight dust; stretchers appear; a klaxon sounds; vehicles speed.

Mike pulls the Land Rover onto the verge, not to gape but to pray. 'Please God, please God', gasps calm, capable Mike, eyes closed, chin on chest, chest heaving. 'Please God no-one has died. Please God no-one has died.' I'm almost as shocked by his distress, shaken by the intensity of his prayer, as I am by the sudden rupture of our golden, easy-going afternoon. When he recovers himself, there's nothing we can do but drive on.

Industrial accidents and their fatalities are only too commonplace in the developing world. They rarely make more than down-the-page domestic stories. We are the bush telegraph which brings the news to M'phingwe Lodge, in its secluded forest glade, but we hear no more details before we begin our journey back to Malawi next morning. It takes Gaia Allison and an e-mail, three weeks later, to let me know that five construction workers died beneath the fractured cement silo, beside the great Zambezi river and the makings of its seventh bridge.[1]

'Do you think', I ask Mike, 'that we've time for another visit to the grave if we leave early enough? No meetings, no interviews, just us?'

---

1 The Armando Guebuza Bridge was completed in early 2009. Its length, almost 1½ miles, makes it the second-longest bridge in Africa. It strengthens the coastal road network which links Kenya, Tanzania, Mozambique and South Africa.

'For sure. If we get held up at the border we can stay at Nsanje for another night.'

It's Sunday. We thank the Whites for their help and say goodbye. An hour later, the Land Rover is bumping towards the white pointer of the steeple at Chupanga. Mike lets me walk alone to the tomb, where our offering of bush blossoms has shrivelled and turned black. I clear them away, silently revisiting some lines of doggerel which I can't get out of my head. Livingstone was the subject of a clumsy poem his wife wrote in 1856 to welcome him back from the transcontinental journey which made him a celebrity. As poetry, *A Hundred Thousand Welcomes* is banal, but its sentiments are so charged with pain and pleading that they become touching. 'How did I live without you all those long long years of woe? It seems as if t'would kill me to be parted from you now ... You'll never part me, darling, there's a promise in your eye; I may tend you while I'm living, you will watch me when I die.'

The promise in Livingstone's eye was not kept. He *did* part from her again, over the first years of the Zambezi Expedition. But he also watched her when she died. I take a last, long look round. The Zambezi is peaceful under puffs of cottonwool cloud, the guinea fowl gossip softly in their pen, the exuberant sound of African hymns spills from the church, where good Padre Medard is taking the service. Not a bad place in which to spend eternity.

We retrace our steps. The journey is uneventful for me, but not for Mike. Back on the highway, we pass the scene of yesterday's accident, negotiate Caia and crunch onto the gravel road to Vila de Sena and the Dona Ana Bridge. We aim to reach it by noon, when we will again be able to cross during the lunchtime change of shifts. On the way, Mike remarks that he's looking forward to getting a signal from his phone, as we've both been out of range of our mobile networks. 'I'd like to phone my wife about the new baby. It's due today.'

'Mike! Why didn't you tell me? We must get you home as quickly as possible. Let's not overnight at Nsanje. Let's bash on to Blantyre.'

He looks doubtful. 'It will be dark before we arrive.' His employers at CAWS urge their drivers to get their clients to their destinations before sunset. Road travel in much of sub-Saharan Africa is more dangerous at night, although not usually for the lurid reasons so relished by Western media outlets. Car crashes may be less dramatic than car-jackings, armed robberies or terrorist ambushes, but car accidents are much more common than these rare catastrophes. In countries where poor road surfaces, casual vehicle maintenance and unlicensed drivers create their own form of anarchy, the accident rate soars after dark, when some vehicles have no tail lights, others only one headlight, and pedestrians and domestic animals are hard to see. But I have complete faith in Mike's driving skills.

I had asked about his family on our drive south, and knew there was a fourth child on the way. Ever sensitive to the interests of his clients, Mike has chosen not to distract me with the imminence of this milestone in his personal life. Now that we've accomplished our mission, he's prepared to tell me more. He hopes the new baby will be a girl, but most of all he hopes it will be healthy and that his wife will recover well – the anxieties of any prospective father, given an edge more critical by his own accident of birth in one of the poorest countries in the world. 'It is in God's hands', he adds. I'm tempted to disagree, but have too much respect for the faith that sustains so many struggling people in Africa.

By Malawian standards, Mike is not struggling too hard, although he can only afford a few bricks at a time to raise a wall round his garden 'so we can keep chickens which won't get stolen'. He and his wife Ruthie, childhood sweethearts whose families were able to keep them in secondary education, have made steady economic progress since they left the rural north for Lilongwe. Mike, who speaks five local languages as well as English, arrived at his job with the safari operator by way of a tobacco company and a car-hire business, and Ruthie is a teacher in a state primary school. They have their own modern house, much of it hand-built by Mike, with room for themselves, their three children and Mike's niece, whom he is putting through school. Since settling there they have had only one grave worry: the episode of the neighbourhood witch.

When Mike mentions the witch his hands tighten on the steering wheel, and a light tremor runs across my scalp. Suddenly, we have left the familiar world of family, home and work with its universal resonances, and entered the parallel universe of African belief systems. He reaches the story by way of my questions about the Zion Christian Church and why he joined it, setting aside the worship of his Catholic upbringing. 'They helped me. They helped me save Wachisa from the witch.'

Mike becomes so agitated as he tells this story that he stammers over the detail, but here is its gist: Wachisa is the eldest of Mike's three sons, now aged 10. His real name is Michael, but he picked up his nickname, which means 'messy', when he was a toddler. He began having what we in the West would call 'behavioural problems' when he was six, and also developed a bad case of ringworm which no amount of medication was able to cure. He fell behind with his school work, and, unknown to his parents, took to visiting the home of a local woman, whom Mike later learned had a sinister reputation. Wachisa told them he had not been happy in her company but felt compelled to continue his visits until his parents put a stop to them.

'Some people from the Zion Christians prayed with us, and soon the spell was broken. Wachisa is fine now: no ringworm, no bad behaviour, doing well at school.'

I don't know what to say. Eventually, I ask what happened to the witch.

'Some neighbours wanted to burn her house, but I reported her to the police. She went to prison.'

A century and more after Kuruman and Kolobeng, Livingstonia and Blantyre, witches and the power of darkness still co-exist with Jesus Christ and the power of prayer – just as they do in many places where ancient beliefs and traditions are embedded in the cultural psyche; as they did in pre-Enlightenment Europe, and still do in some of Europe's more remote corners. No contradiction there to the rational mind. Witchcraft deals in the supernatural, and so does religious faith, and there are punitive aspects to both. After all, when Livingstone and his fellow missionaries exhorted 'the heathen' to reject their pagan gods, they urged them to commit to an equally invisible spirit world, to a God so implacable that if Mary Livingstone lost her faith she would also lose her place in Heaven.

I don't pursue these thoughts with Mike, who falls silent for a while. As the temperature rises and the hot miles grind by, we clear the two potential obstacles to our smooth passage back to Malawi – the railway bridge and the border – and reach Nsanje by mid-afternoon. There, we recover our mobile-phone signals and make a brief stop at the Sweet Dreams Rest House to buy more water. Mike makes the call to Lilongwe while I'm using its washroom; and, when I rejoin him his face is glowing with good news. 'The baby was born yesterday. My wife is already home and they are both well. I have another son.'

We leave the Shire Valley as the sun sets and climb the Thyolo Escarpment into the vast, spangled canopy of the African night. It's after eight by the time we reach Blantyre, where Mike's office has booked a room for me at Ryalls Hotel. He has a sister in Blantyre with whom he will spend the night, and as he hands me over to the booming welcome of the massive, gold-braided doorman at Ryalls I feel I'm losing something. But there will be time tomorrow, when Mike drives me to the airport, to say proper goodbyes and wish him safely home to Lilongwe and his new son.

Ryalls is in Blantyre's central business district, but it isn't as formulaic as I expect. It is the city's oldest hotel, although it has been much expanded and modernised. Along with its bit of history, it has a big flower-filled garden, and reception staff who are tenderly patient with this weary, travel-dazed woman who is so unprepared to be reclaimed by the world of international hospitality that she takes several minutes to produce her passport and complete the registration form.

I won't deny there is some relief in succumbing to a pleasant, air-conditioned room where I can pad bare-footed into the bathroom without checking for scorpions or snakes and don't need to shake moths or spiders or flying ants from a mosquito net; where I read the room-service menu, although I'm too tired to eat, and open the mini-bar, although I don't need a nightcap, by way of reconnecting with my own parallel universe.

I've been on the road for fourteen bone-shaking hours and am fit for nothing but bath and bed. I even ignore the television with its twenty-four-hour news channels, although many years of mainstream journalism have hard-wired me to keep in touch with global news. But there is work to be done before I sleep. My bush sandals have left my feet ingrained with dust. It takes a long soak, some fierce scrubbing and a power shower to extract the grime from my toenails and the crevices of my heels and toes. How did the Victorian travellers keep themselves clean? As the last of the powdered earth of Mozambique swirls down the plughole, I feel another twinge of loss. I'm already missing the birdsong of the Catapu forest, missing the great river and, for all its sorrowful history, missing the bright space of Shupanga brae, where Mary Livingstone beeks fornent the sun.

7

A Brief Detour to the Realm of the Great She-Elephant

'I like waggon [sic] travelling better than I expected'

September 2008

I've been invited to attend a royal birthday party in Swaziland. But first I must revisit Lanarkshire, and Livingstone's Scottish home. When his parents moved from their Shuttle Row tenement in Blantyre to a cottage in nearby Hamilton, they came up in the world. The house was much larger and more comfortable, and Hamilton itself has long been a place of some aspiration. Once the county town of Lanarkshire and seat of the Dukes of Hamilton, it has a fine rising site on a southern flank of the Clyde Valley. Like some of its neighbouring towns, it entered the industrial age on a coal-mining economy; but it always managed to keep a stately distance from the pitheads. When the mines closed a century later, Hamilton diversified into light and service industries; and, in the early 1970s, as Scotland planned the reorganisation of its local government, Lanarkshire councillors voted themselves the ambitious new administrative buildings which are now the headquarters of South Lanarkshire Council.

Their high-rise offices and grandiose plaza with improbably blue 'water feature' make a useful landmark in Almada Street. They are not far from its junction with Burnbank Road, where three nineteenth-century cottages are wedged between a garage and a red sandstone tenement with a fish-and-chip restaurant on the ground floor. The forecourt of number 17, the 'Livingstone house', is used as a parking bay for second-hand cars. Further down Burnbank Road is a hotel which used to be called the Zambezi Hotel.

Much of the lower Clyde Valley is cluttered with sprawls of piecemeal housing, industrial units, leisure centres and retail parks wrapped around with motorway; the urban overspill which attends the river's progress into Glasgow. But, from Almada Street and Burnbank Road, you can still be surprised by a clean line of hills to the north: the Campsie Fells, and beyond them the summit of Ben Lomond. Hills have a lot in common, a universal kinship, whatever their geological history. Sometimes when I've been travelling in Africa I've come upon hills which make me believe, in a slippage of time and place, that I'm back in Scotland. Did Mary Livingstone ever lift her eyes to the Campsies, losing their fresh summer pelt of bracken and grass to the rusty mane of autumn, and believe for a moment she was back in the lionskin lands beyond the Cape?

When his hunger for exploration began to consume him and Livingstone made the decision to send his wife and children 'home' to the United Kingdom, he persuaded his employers, the London Missionary Society, to maintain them. It was his intention that, with an LMS stipend, Mary would find lodgings near his parents and sister in Lanarkshire. There she would have the support of his family; there she would find schools for volatile Robert, sweet-natured Agnes, sickly Tom and, in time, the infant Oswell, and supervise their education. (The reputation of Scotland's state education system was still among the highest in Europe.) There she would learn to budget her meagre income – no small challenge for a woman whose housekeeping currency had been beads and barter – and there she would exchange the demanding but straightforward stewardship of a bush home for the greater comfort but more complicated management of a Victorian household.

In practice, her introduction to Scotland and her in-laws was calamitous. Livingstone's lost tribe arrived in October as northern Europe entered the darkest time of the year, with little more than six hours of daylight in the Clyde Valley. Never unchallenging at the best of times, the Scottish winter of 1852 was exceptionally wet and cold; but, before long, a chill more bitter had settled on Mary's relationship with her husband's family. She spent only three months in Hamilton, where, after leaving Burnbank Road for Almada Street, she changed her address twice. In January, without leaving a forwarding address, she left abruptly on the backwash of a mysterious quarrel with the senior Livingstones.

The rupture, her restlessness and her anxious letters to the LMS about money were the first symptoms of a depressive condition which almost crushed her over the next four years. Livingstone's 'heroine', his 'rib', 'the best spoke in the wheel', calm, uncomplaining Ma-Robert, the 'brave, good woman' whose name was known and honoured throughout southern Africa, was brought to the edge of disintegration by a combination of two circumstances: her isolation in a foreign land which required unfamiliar qualities of resourcefulness, where she was unequipped for the fast-moving complexities of the new industrial age and untutored in the nuances of its social structures; and the absence of a husband on whom her emotional dependence was almost pathological, and whose adventure in central Africa, as he tramped from coast to coast, was beginning to look like abandonment.

Blantyre is only four miles from Hamilton. Mary was to return to her husband's home neighbourhood in 1859, and her children were again to live with his family, but she has left few footprints in the Clyde Valley. Ulva Cottage, now 17 Burnbank Road, remains; but the two cottages she rented in Almada Street have gone, while nothing of her unhappy time in Lanarkshire – and little of her life elsewhere – is on public display in the Shuttle Row museum at the David Livingstone Centre. 'All the more reason', I e-mail Gaia Allison, 'why we should aim for some kind of permanent exhibition in Chupanga church.' The Blantyre museum's curator, Karen Carruthers, is enthusiastic and promises all the help she can give in the way of material. But there is no money from her employers to take Mary's story to Mozambique. The DLC managers, the National Trust for Scotland, are engaged in a chronic struggle to fund and develop their existing properties.

So far, I've been moving between the bleakest milestones on Mary's landscape; but there were sunnier spots in her childhood and early marriage, even if the remote interior was always fertile ground for crises and her life there interrupted by years spent in places not of her choosing. I must now travel to her beginnings: to her birthplace at Griquatown, her parents' mission at Kuruman, and to Kolobeng, the only settled home of her marriage. I must find a way of getting to South Africa's emptiest and least visited province, the Northern Cape, and to the remnants of Kolobeng, over the border in Botswana.

Just as I'm calculating costs (high) and computing logistics (time-consuming) there is another collision of timely coincidences. The tourism department of the Kingdom of Swaziland, a rare survivor of the world's absolute monarchies, invites me and some colleagues from the travel press to a double celebration: the fortieth birthday of King Mswati III and the fortieth anniversary of Swazi independence. Almost simultaneously, I'm contacted by a Johannesburg safari operator who has read my account of the visit to Chupanga in the magazine *Travel Africa* and who offers to drive me to Griquatown, Kuruman and Kolobeng – destinations which he has been investigating for a 'Livingstone Trail' safari.

The Swazi invitation will get me to Johannesburg. The tiny state, smaller than Wales, is locked into the South African land mass between the north-east provinces of Mpumalanga and KwaZulu-Natal and the Mozambique border, and is only thirty minutes by air from Oliver Tambo International Airport. In 1968, 'the peaceable kingdom of Swaziland' peaceably shed its status as a British protectorate. Despite the disapproval of its big neighbours, the two republics for whom democracy is a recent novelty, it claims to cherish its identity as an authentic African monarchy, although it does have its dissidents.

It is never hard to interest the press in the Swaziland anomaly and all the traditions which go with it. Ceremony is the cornerstone of its tourist industry, although the two great annual festivals of the Incwala, or 'first fruits', and the Umhlanga, or Reed Dance, have symbolic power far beyond mere visitor attractions. They are rituals which confirm the right of the royal dynasty to govern a population of just over a million – a supreme authority shared by the king and the queen mother, who is known as the Great She-Elephant.

The Incwala, which welcomes the first crops of the new season, is a male festival, the most sacred in the Swazi calendar, and involves several weeks of dancing in the Royal Kraal, where the king is among the chief performers. Of more tantalising interest to Western visitors is the Reed Dance, where thousands of bare-breasted teenage girls and young women convene to honour the king and queen mother and celebrate the beauty of their own bodies. The dancers must be 'unbetrothed', therefore virgins; an improbable status for many of them these days. Controversially, this all-female festival is said to offer the monarch the opportunity to expand his household of wives. The 'cattle market' reputation of the Reed Dance is regularly denounced by the feminists of southern Africa.

With commissions for magazine and newspaper features secured, I accept the invitation to the '40-40', as the organisers call the double anniversary, and accept the offer from Keith Rampton of Explorer Safaris. We make a plan to rendezvous when our party returns to Johannesburg. Keith tells me he has allowed 'four days, five max' for our journey to the roots of Mary Livingstone; and, for added value, he has built into our itinerary the obscure mission sites of Mabotsa and Chonuane, each of which had a role in her transition from missionary daughter to missionary wife.

The bereft wife and harried mother who arrived in Hamilton in 1852 was not without some experience of the United Kingdom. Between the ages of 18 and 22, Mary spent four years in England in very different circumstances, surrounded and supported by the large Moffat family while her father toured the country, enrapturing the devout with the passion of his oratory and captivating audiences with the striking looks and compelling presence which turned him into the LMS's most valuable fund-raiser and recruiting officer for Africa. There, he claimed, 'a thousand campfires' beckoned those who would bring a more vivifying light to transform its dark interior.

Among the listeners who took him at his word was a gauche, gruff young Scottish doctor who had recently completed his theological training with the LMS – an organisation chosen, as he later explained, 'because it sends neither episcopacy, nor Presbyterianism, nor independency, but the gospel of Christ to the heathen'. David Livingstone was so inspired by Moffat's eloquence that he abandoned a plan to go to China and persuaded the society to send him instead to Kuruman.

It's just possible that Livingstone met his future wife during this period, as her father often spoke at the Aldergate Street boarding house where young missionaries lodged before taking up their overseas postings. If so, there is no record that either made any impression on the other. With characteristic obstinacy, Livingstone had chosen to ignore the universal truth that every missionary needed a wife by letting slip the one romantic possibility which came his way after he left Scotland. Mary, it seems, did receive some interest from a cousin 'but watched without apparent reaction as her only marriage prospect appeared and disappeared'.

The purpose of Robert Moffat's visit to England, which turned into an unexpectedly long sabbatical, was not to undertake an evangelical tour but to commission a printer. All the family were taken by surprise when he was besieged by invitations to speak and preach. By 1839, the former gardener from East Lothian had achieved a towering reputation as Kuruman's founder and patriarch, and his diplomatic skills and fearlessness also made him an influential figure in intertribal politics and sometimes mediator between Boer and Tswana. He was often away from home, leaving the domestic management of the mission to his wife and, occasionally, his eldest child. Mary, still in her early teens, was once required to make the long journey from her Salem school to help her mother through a difficult pregnancy, before being returned to her studies.

By 1839, Moffat had also found time to complete his ground-breaking task of translating the New Testament into Setswana. He first sought to have his manuscript printed in Cape Town, where Mary was now training to be a teacher. By all accounts a loving father, he had seen his first-born child only once since she was ten. It was his resourceful wife who had supervised the transfer of their three eldest children from their Wesleyan school to further education in Cape Town. With their younger siblings, she trekked again from Kuruman to Salem, crossing the Orange River in a perilous flood, collected the three pupils and embarked them on a ship from Port Elizabeth. Before they sailed, Mary, now 15, was violently ill with some unspecified ailment and had to be carried on a chair to the shallows and lifted on board the vessel's lighter. But she 'bore it well', her mother recorded, before enduring eleven days of stormy weather on the voyage to the Cape.

In her account of this episode, Edna Healey speculates that Mary's illness was the first of a series which might have been psychosomatic. Janet Wagner Parsons, author of *The Livingstones at Kolobeng 1847–1852*, disputes this but has few doubts that six years of exile from Kuruman and separation from her parents altered Mary's character. The 'carefree, vivacious' child of the mission station was educated 'at great cost to her happiness, and the experience left its mark in the form of a stubborn, unnatural self-reliance and a tendency to hide all her feelings'.

By the time she arrived in England, uprooted again when Robert Moffat found that Cape Town didn't have the facilities to print his Setswana manuscript, she was 'self-contained and shy'. She never stopped missing Africa, where her earliest childhood companion had been a Khoisan orphan; and, behind the shield of her reserve, she seems to have cherished few personal expectations, accepting that her destiny held little but unremitting hard work and grave responsibilities. The demands of mission life, to which she would return, and the family tragedy as they left the Cape for the three-month voyage to London, had already made that clear.

It was twenty years since Mary Smith of Dukinfield had left Lancashire for Africa to marry a man she hadn't seen for three years but with utter certainty knew she loved. Since then, she had borne eight children: four boys and four girls. One of each had died in infancy, not unusual by Victorian standards; and, given the isolation and hazards of her children's birthplace, the losses might well have been more. At 43, she was again heavily pregnant when the family arrived in Cape Town; but she was eager to introduce the young Moffats to her former homeland and her surviving parent, their grandfather, and expose them to some experience of its culture. She made no objection to the haste with which her husband, desperate to see his Setswana manuscript in print, booked passage for them all on the first available ship.

It was a sorry craft: a small, cramped troopship en route from China, its cabins and hold stinking with the effluence of human and animal bodies. There was an epidemic of measles in Cape Town and measles on board. The children were all ill when they embarked; the worst afflicted was six-year-old Jamie, a gifted boy who had a special place in his mother's heart. As they wallowed at anchor in Table Bay, their misery was compounded by seasickness. What followed next was harrowingly instructive to the young Mary, perhaps even a vision of her grim future. As Ma-Mary went into labour, she continued to nurse and comfort the younger children with Mary's help until she gave birth to a daughter, underweight and feeble. It seemed unlikely the baby would survive the conditions on the diseased ship; and the mother's attention was in any case divided in the most tormented way.

Jamie was suffering, slipping in and out of consciousness, calling for his mother, and was laid beside her on her bunk. Nursing the new baby with one arm, she cradled the boy in her other. In her biography *Beloved Partner*, based on the letters of Mary Moffat of Kuruman, Mora Dickson describes a scene which might have come straight from the Old Testament. 'Mary, watching in anguish while this beloved child grew closer and closer to death, saw no sin in praying that, if she had to suffer a loss, it should be the puny baby that might be taken. But the prayer was not answered. The baby lived and two days after her birth Jamie died and was buried in Table Bay. The next day, in a terrible storm, they sailed for home.'

'Home' was never home for her eldest child and namesake. Mary Livingstone's first encounter with the United Kingdom may have been less traumatic than her second, but she was never at ease there. When the Moffats finally began making plans to return to Africa early in 1843, the younger Mary took it upon herself to organise the packing of an alpine range of baggage, including new equipment and many other donations for the mission. Her enthusiasm was urgent.

Already waiting at Kuruman, eager to start his new career in advance of the Moffats' return, was the man who would be the instrument of her next, more damaging exile.

The purple-crested lourie has plumage too gorgeous for its own good. A large, long-tailed, fruit-eating bird of the forest and bushveld, not only is its crest purple but its primary feathers are crimson. It flaunts the colours of emperors and kings, and pays the price. For ceremonial occasions, Swaziland's royal heads are crowned with halos of crimson lourie feathers, while most of the local leopard population have donated a huge wardrobe of pelts to the uniform of the nation's warriors. 'Colourful' is a tired old word in the lexicon of travel writing, but it won't lie down and die in Somhlolo stadium on the occasion of the biggest party in Swaziland for forty years.

Colourful but controversial. The national stadium in the eZulwini Valley has been refurbished for the event, and the sunlit fields beneath the twin peaks of Sheba's Breasts (the legendary site of King Solomon's mines, according to H. Rider Haggard) are filled with the temporary camps of Reed Dancers. The Reed Dance festival ended six days earlier with the record participation of 60,000 maidens, all of whom have been commanded by King Mswati III to hang around for his birthday and contribute to the spectacle. This costs money. The official budget for the '40-40' is £1.4 million. Most of the regional media, including those from South Africa, are critical of such profligacy in a country which, for all its good infrastructure and pleasant, well-furnished capital, has dire rural poverty and the highest rate of HIV/AIDS in Africa. In the streets of Mbabane, all-singing, all-dancing trade unionists demonstrate against this royal extravagance.

But the party goes on, and those among the population who can make their way to the Somhlolo stadium for its climax of speeches, dedications, brass bands, Swazi drumming, precision marching, tribal dances, ceremonial dress and undress have been promised free lunch. In a few days' time, if all goes to plan, I will again pick up the trail of Mary Livingstone, whose birthplace is only about 500 miles to the west as the purple-crested lourie flies. Meanwhile, with my British colleagues, I've been accredited a place in the press enclosure – a prime site at the edge of the arena beneath the royal box, perfectly positioned to watch nine African heads of state and other VIPs pull up in the shiny new fleet of BMWs bought for the occasion.

Here, we are also well placed to see the entrance of the Great She-Elephant, the queen mother, slow-moving and well fed, her personal limousine bearing a golden elephant on its chassis, her face bearing an expression which might be arthritic discomfort or might be bad temper; and to observe that all the royal women – the unmarried princesses bare-breasted, tapping on mobile phones – have accessorised their traditional dress with designer handbags, sunglasses and shoes. The king's thirteen wives have just returned from a shopping trip to Dubai.

Polygamy was the most troubling and troublesome of the practices challenged by nineteenth-century missionaries. Livingstone's one enduring convert, the clever and impressive Sechele, chief of the Bakwena, struggled with the instruction from his new Christian deity to return all but his senior wife to their fathers' kraals; a desperate humiliation for the women, who were not well received by their disgraced families. Sechele found it hard to be monogamous, as do men in every culture. When he took to visiting one of his rejected wives, she became pregnant and the lapse was exposed. Livingstone felt obliged to ban him from communion for three months; but Sechele's spiritual tutor was not without imagination. In his early days among the Tswana, he sometimes asked himself if the Christian mission was right to interfere so radically in social systems which had their own rationale and equilibrium.

As for Mary, some of these young women were her only female friends at Kolobeng. She had grown up with the Tswana, and spoke their language 'like a native', as her husband mentioned without irony. Her private thoughts on the bewildering banishment of the chief's wives are not on record, but her mother, Ma-Mary, did observe in one of her letters that Mary was not the most pious of her children.

In modern Swaziland polygamous culture co-exists with the Christian church; not so very different from the position of Roman Catholics who are happy to ignore papal instruction on contraception, even abortion. The king's unknown number of children has also been lavishly equipped for the double celebration. Royal births, such triumphant occasions in other monarchies, are never announced in Swaziland, perhaps because a growing number of dissidents resent the style in which the royal juniors are raised.

There are few, if any, apostates at the birthday party. A whole-hearted cheer goes up as King Mswati arrives to tour the stadium and greet his subjects. A burly, good-looking man whose naked 40-year-old torso is a little loose around the midriff and pectorals, he could well blame an English public-school education for his expensive tastes – because they owe nothing to genes. His revered father, King Sobhuza II, was sage, modest, progressive and frugal in everything except his appetite for wives (he had seventy). He it was who sent Mswati to Sherborne and negotiated independence from an unresisting British government. Until he died in 1981, he was the world's longest-serving monarch.

For all the brilliance of the royal wardrobes, for all the drama of leopard loin skins, cowhide shields and flourishing assegais as the Swazi regiments jog into the stadium, it's the men in suits who interest me most. As they step from their individual BMWs and mount the stair to the royal box, I have a rare opportunity to see at close quarters many of the most powerful men south of the Sahara; to hear their reception from the Swazi crowd, watch their body language as they greet each other, some with warm embraces, others with cool handshakes, and to be reminded of something the West chooses to ignore, or only grudgingly accepts: our villains may be Africa's heroes, and vice versa. Some of these Big Men are a bit of both. Some deserve to be wholly admired.

The presidents of Botswana, Madagascar, Malawi, Mozambique, Namibia, Rwanda, Tanzania, Uganda and Zimbabwe take their seats. There are a few notable absences. Zambia's president is gravely ill, and Kenya's president is dealing with the tense aftermath of a disputed general election. But the most conspicuous absentee is South Africa's Jacob Zuma, who is Zulu and therefore ethnic kin to the Swazi king (and, by the way, a fellow polygamist). South Africa is represented merely by its first minister, which is perhaps Zuma's way of making a statement about democracy.

Some of the heads of state are identified for me by the regional reporters in the press enclosure. Others I recognise, as they have been in government for quite some time. Yoweri Museveni of Uganda always wears a broad-brimmed bush hat with his formal suits. Bingu wa Mutharika[1] of Malawi has often stared down at me from the walls of border posts and airport terminals. Here comes tall, slender, scholarly-looking Paul Kagame of Rwanda, whose deft policies of reconciliation (now under strain) helped to rebuild his country after the 1994 genocide. And the man with light skin is Ian Khama of Botswana, whose mother was English and white and whose father, Sir Seretse Khama, was the founding father of the modern nation; an exceptional statesman who presided over the transition of his country from the British Protectorate of Bechuanaland to the Republic of Botswana.

Not without painful difficulties. Seretse Khama was paramount chief of the eminent Bangwato tribe, and his 'interracial' marriage to Ruth Williams, whom he met while studying at the Bar in London, drew censure from his family and tribal elders – and a disgraceful response from the British. In the early 1950s, to appease the apartheid regime of South Africa, whose cheap gold and uranium the UK needed in the impoverished post-war years, both Labour and Conservative governments conspired to have Khama deposed and exiled from his own country. The couple were popular with the Batswana, however; and, when they were later allowed to return, Khama led the movement for independence. In 1966 he became Botswana's first president, setting the template for the stable, well-run, prospering democracy it remains today. The Livingstones would recognise the spirit of Sechele in this luminary of the Batswana.

Here comes a man whose stiff-legged walk and calm smile of self-belief make him more familiar than any other statesman. If the sky were a roof it would be raised by the roar of approval for Robert Mugabe as he steps from his limousine. The unrepentant tyrant of our former British colony

---

1 President Mutharika died in April 2012 and was succeeded by Joyce Banda, southern Africa's first female head of state.

is no such thing to the Swazi crowd. At the very least, he is an international celebrity, an elder statesman of African nationalism who suffered and triumphed in its liberation struggle; at the very most, for those who remember the tenacity of white supremacism in this region of the continent, he is their irreproachable champion.

The birth of Mary Livingstone in Griquatown nearly killed her mother. I don't know what to expect of Griquatown, although I've briefed myself on its place in the early history of South Africa, when the first European settlers introduced new genes to its tribal peoples, many of whom were also colonists – pastoralists from the great Bantu migrations which rolled down from the north in successive waves from about 2,000 years ago. They brought with them their long-horned Nguni cattle and their fat-tailed sheep and gradually displaced the Khoisan, the collective name for the ethnic group Khoikhoi and San, the aboriginal people of south-west Africa. (The Stone Age culture of the Khoisan can be traced back nearly 30,000 years in the astonishing vitality of their rock art.) The Bantu immigrants pushed the hunter-gatherer San deep into the Kalahari, where they later became known to Europeans as Bushmen; and the Bantu evicted the Khoikhoi, who had themselves become pastoralists, from the best grazing land. Then came the Dutch. They arrived in the seventeenth century, most of their early colonists male and single. By the eighteenth century, southern Africa had a sizeable population of people whose genes, in various combinations, were European, Khoi, Bantu and later Asian, with a small contribution from the San.

The Dutch called them Baastards, a name which became a source of defiant pride for the mixed-race population. They were inevitably disadvantaged, usually despised by both European and indigenous communities and often demonised. But they had their uses. The Dutch trained the men to ride and shoot, conscripting them into fast-moving paramilitary units to help repress insurgencies among the San and Khoikhoi. By the time the British annexed the Cape at the beginning of the nineteenth century, this policy had created a skilled and opportunistic Dutch-speaking people who increasingly looked for an independent stake in the lands of their birth, and whose bands of horsemen were harassing the indigenous tribes along the Orange River. Enter the London Missionary Society. They naturally found the name 'Baastard' offensive and persuaded them to adopt a name taken from the nomadic Chaguriqua tribe, who were among their number. They became Griqua, but their 'offensive' name lives on in the Baster people of Namibia, who have similar origins.

The Griqua were also encouraged to establish settlements north of the Orange River; and there remains today, west of Kimberley, a large region of the Northern Cape called Griqualand West, where we are heading. By 1820, when Robert and Mary Moffat arrived two months after their wedding in Cape Town, Griquatown was the interior headquarters of the LMS's African outreach. The Moffats spent five years between it and Lattakoo, a failing, drought-stricken mission station even farther north, before a new site in the well-watered Kuruman valley was negotiated with the local chief, and the missionary couple could start doing the ground-work (in more ways than one) for the station which was to become an enduring model of its kind.

Did Mary Moffat, raised in a devout, newly middle-class Lancashire household where servants did all the heavy work, where her domestic duties were largely supervisory or decorative, ever ask herself if romantic love and the saving of souls were sufficient rewards for those early days? Her letters home, no doubt self-censored for her parents' peace of mind, are rarely other than cheerful even when describing hardships and hazards to test the toughest of pioneers – which is what the Moffats were. (Mary's mother grieved deeply for her faraway daughter, believing she was lost to her for ever. And so it proved: Mrs Smith died before they could be re-united on the Moffats' trip home twenty years later.)

Her first impressions on her seven-week, 800-mile 'honeymoon' to Griquatown have the wonder of novelty. From Beaufort West, 350 miles north of Cape Town, she wrote home: 'when I consider the manner in which we live, just eating and sleeping when it is convenient, I am truly astonished ... I like waggon travelling better than I expected ... We have seen no beasts of prey ... M saw the footmarks of one about a mile from where we outspanned one day; and at the farmhouse we saw last week we were informed that sixty lions had been killed in six years in that neigh-bourhood. At that farm we saw two tame ostriches, which to our great surprise devoured pebble stones like bread.'

Ma-Mary was always to enjoy the slowly shifting landscape and sense of freedom which came with trekking, as long as the weather was dry and the open road without danger or obstacle; not always the case. Even during later journeys with her small children, she maintained her pleasure in daily travel 'of eight or twelve hours on an average, riding about three and a half miles an hour ... If there are children they play on the bed or lie asleep.' Today's members of the Caravan Club will fully appreciate how she enjoyed being 'mistress of a compact small home on wheels', even if the trekker's counterpart of the Swift Charisma was hauled by twelve temperamental oxen driven by 'Hottentots'. (There is no such tribe as Hottentot; this name, now proscribed as derogatory, was given by the Cape colonists to the Khoisan in imitation of how their languages sounded to European ears.) The design of the ox-wagon had been perfected by Dutch settlers; and its micro-efficiency is comprehensively described by Mora Dickson in *Beloved Partner*.

> There was a forechest across the front, forming the driver's seat, in which were kept supplies of tea, coffee, rice, etc. in canisters and bags. Across the back was an afterchest filled with bulk stores, from which the forechest was replenished weekly. Lining either side were smaller chests for crockery and utensils; at the back of the forechest room for trunks containing the clothes. Over the space in the centre there was a stretcher on which the mattress went and under which numerous boxes and containers were packed away. During the day a moveable back was put up to make a seat and a small table could be let down from one of the sides. Underneath the wagon itself were slung the pots and pans, and round the sides sailcloth bags held provisions.

Keith Rampton and I travel more lightly to Griquatown.

8

Lion's Den Fountain

'She had no choices, only situations'

We are driving beneath an ice-blue vault in the last vestiges of starlight. Behind us, a rusty rim of sunrise lies along the high, rolling northern suburbs of Johannesburg, their gardens stocked with trees, blossoms, guard dogs, lizards, swimming pools, hadeda ibises, night watchmen, barbecue patios, sunbirds, sunbeds and advanced security systems. 'This highway takes us past Soweto', announces Keith Rampton, who knows I am new to everything in the South African metropolis except its hub airport. I've flown in and out of Oliver Tambo a dozen times but I've never spent a night in Johannesburg until now, when I've been welcomed into the Ramptons' attractive family home in Fourways. In an early letter home, Ma-Mary wrote: 'I have never met so much hospitality in my life as I have witnessed in Africa, though the Dutch are considered fond of saving'.

Nor have I; and the Ramptons aren't even South African, never mind Afrikaans. Keith is from a village near Basingstoke in Hampshire; his wife Caroline is another member of the lost tribe of white Zimbabweans, although she met and married Keith in England. They moved to South Africa with their two children in 1990, as the apartheid system entered the early stages of its reluctant retreat and Keith took on a management role in the IT industry. In 1990, Nelson Mandela was released from prison to open talks with the Nationalist Party's F. W. De Klerk. More political prisoners were released, repressive laws were repealed, and the armed struggle of the African National Congress was suspended. But it took three more years of tense negotiation and internal conflict, with the threat of civil war always present, before the date was set for the first multi-party election and Mandela was able to tell his country that 'the countdown to democracy has begun'.

As we cruise towards the N12 in Keith's well-sprung, deeply cushioned, air-conditioned Land Rover Defender, a luxury version of the workhorse which took me from Blantyre to Chupanga, he tells me there is a price to pay for their comfortable life in Johannesburg, where he and Caroline have recently become self-employed. 'We live in a chronic condition of low-grade stress. Not work, but crime. Keeping alert, being wary becomes a way of life, but it takes its toll.'

I have tiptoed around the subject of Johannesburg's infamous reputation, the enduring taint of the brutal years of apartheid, the persistence of inequity, the hobbling progress – and lack of it – of democratic government. Few locals want to hear the opinions of drive-through visitors, often delivered in the form of unsympathetic judgements – 'It's payback time, isn't it?' – or simple pieties. As we pass the roofs of Soweto, I crane my neck. Its homes and infrastructure are still contained by the walls which turned black townships into ghettoes and white properties into gated communities. I remind myself that Soweto has become Johannesburg's leading tourist attraction with its own prospering economy, and resist mentioning that most of South Africa's crime is 'black on black'. Better to stick to safer topics: is it Keith's high blood pressure, the medical evidence of his stress, which has caused him to 'jump ship from corporate life', as he puts it, to set up his own off-road vehicle-hire and safari business?

Not really. Keith began his working life as Land Rover Man and wants to end it that way. In England, he studied motor-vehicle engineering at Farnborough College of Technology and spent five years with a Land Rover dealership before moving into electronics; and his loyalty to the marque is absolute. He has just turned 50 – a prompt in many lives, children grown up, wife launching her own career in 'change management', steering the employees of multi-nationals through the workplace insecurities which come with restructuring. The family has always travelled for pleasure through the cross-border semi-wildernesses of southern Africa, on- and off-road, camping in the remote bush, confident that nothing can go wrong with a Land Rover which Keith can't fix. To this, add a sturdy presence, a cheerful personality, a national guiding qualification, a course in snake-handling, and the kind of practical competence which builds campfires, raises tents, cooks braais and cures biltong – and Explorer Safaris was under way.

'The amazing thing', he adds, 'is that I discovered that no other safari operator was using that name – just as I was developing a passion for the history of the African explorers, Livingstone, Stanley, Burton, Speke and all the rest. And as we're here in South Africa and close to Botswana, where his expeditions began, it seemed logical to start with Livingstone.'

We are doing each other favours. The business is new, and very dependent on its Land Rover self-drive division, which Keith runs with a partner. But he himself wants to be on the road. I am his first passenger on one section of his infant 'Livingstone Trail', and he has done an impressive amount of research, contacted curators and clerics at the various sites on our route and identified guest farms where we (and his future clients) can stay. It is my good fortune that, although our present itinerary is limited to the places which shaped the early life of Mary Livingstone, Keith is also keen to plan a trip across the Kalahari to Lake Ngami, and on to the Chobe River – the journeys she made with Livingstone before he dispatched his family to Scotland.

Meantime, I serve the purpose of a trial run from Johannesburg to Griquatown, Kuruman, Kolobeng, Mabotsa and Chonuane, although this is not the route which would have been followed by the Moffats and their fellow missionaries. The Missionary Road to the interior took a north-east trajectory from Cape Town to avoid the worst desert conditions of the Great Karoo, passing through Beaufort West at the northern limit of the settled colony. Johannesburg didn't exist. As we drive south-west through the province of Gauteng, we drive along a reef of gold, the Witwatersrand, and mark its multi-national signposts: AngloGold Ashanti, Harmony Gold, still digging. Gauteng means 'place of gold' in the Sotho language, and it was gold which turned an expanse of high, empty veld north of the Vaal River – the Transvaal – into Johannesburg. The first plot of land was auctioned in 1886.

There is another treasure trove on our road to Griquatown, although its riches have been exhaustively plundered: Kimberley, capital of the Northern Cape. It was once the most advanced city in the southern hemisphere, with libraries, trams and electric lights before any other. Its diamonds made fortunes, caused conflict, launched the hegemony of De Beers in the South African industry and inspired the fantasies of Cecil Rhodes, who sought to stamp Britain on Africa 'from Cape to Cairo'. Today, its Big Hole is 800 feet of emptiness, the rock sweated out by pick and shovel between 1866 and 1914 in an extended rush of money-lust. With the Kimberley Mine Museum, the Big Hole is the city's pre-eminent visitor attraction; but we don't have time for more than a brief tour of the migratory Old Town, whose historic buildings were moved piecemeal from the city centre to clear space for commercial development.

Since we left Johannesburg before dawn, we have covered over 280 miles of the well-surfaced N12, tracing the border between North West Province and the Free State; passing Bloemhof Dam, a spill point for irrigation, where flamingoes stalk the shallows of the reservoir; skirting the massive grain-silo plant at Christiana; slowly dropping some 1,500 feet from fertile highveld to dusty thornveld as we approach the border of the Northern Cape; eating on the road, sustained by fruit, water, vacuum mugs of coffee and – Keith's speciality – mini-sausage rolls. Now we must drive another 100 miles or so on a lesser road to Griquatown, where we hope to meet the curator of the Mary Moffat Museum in the early afternoon.

Kimberley lies near the confluence of the Orange and Vaal rivers, which have an epic role in South Africa's history and a pivotal place in its modern agriculture, power and water supplies. The Orange River is the country's longest. It rises in the Lesotho Highlands and meanders 1,300 miles westwards before debouching into the Atlantic, where it forms part of the border with Namibia. It is the only major water system to pass through the seasonal deserts of the Great Karoo, the Kalahari and the Namib, although in years of drought it sometimes fails to reach the sea.

The Vaal is its largest tributary, travelling almost 700 miles from its source in the Drakensberg, marking the borders between Mpumalanga, Gauteng and North West Province to the north and the Free State to the south, before joining the Orange River in the Northern Cape. The alluvial deposits of both have been mined for diamonds; but, long before the first stone was found, these waterways often frustrated the Moffats in their to-ing and fro-ing between Kuruman and the Cape. When the rivers were in spate, there was nothing to be done but wait until their floodwaters subsided – and that could take a month.

Once, while Ma-Mary with some of her family and a queue of other travellers waited by the Vaal River in gruelling heat, news arrived that David Livingstone had reached the west coast of Africa: 'A wonder to the world', his mother-in-law commented acidly. She was more interested in reaching the north bank of the Vaal, where her husband waited to escort her to Kuruman; and it was agreed to attempt a crossing. 'The water was still high and the rush of currents under the waggons formidable', writes Mora Dickson. 'Deeper and deeper they sank until the foremost stuck in mid-stream, and not all the shrieks and yells, whips and bullying of the drivers could make the demented oxen move it one inch further. Night was coming on, so it was arranged to carry the women and children over on the shoulders of the men and abandon the waggons till morning.'

The Vaal River lies quietly in its channel as we speed over its pre-cast concrete bridge.

The girl who would become Mary Livingstone was born in a reed hut near the only source of permanent water in Griquatown. Her parents' future was as yet unmapped, as the London Missionary Society was undecided where to place them, and they had already spent months in similar insecurity farther north at Lattakoo, where they lived in the vestry of the mud-and-thatch church with their wagon still unloaded. At Griquatown, according to Mora Dickson, they were ministering to 'a community of half-breed European, Hottentot, Bushman, Bechuana, with whom they did not feel wholly in sympathy'. At Lattakoo, there was an indigenous community with a receptive and well-intentioned chief, and it seems clear that the Moffats felt their mission lay not with the Griqua but with the Tswana, whom they called Bechuana.

Griquatown, however, did serve as an introduction to the domestic challenge of mission life and the resourcefulness it demanded. Mary Moffat registered her disapproval of the established layout of mission houses, with their separate kitchens at the rear (a traditional arrangement in African homes). She vowed to do things differently when she had a home of her own, objecting that the isolated kitchen and storeroom encouraged thieving: 'If one turn one's back, perhaps half of the food has gone and spoons, knife, fork or whatever lies about is away'. She was also doubtful about doing laundry by beating clothes on stones in the river; and her obliging husband promised he would make her tubs when they were settled. He had already made her sieves for flour, corn and meal and built her a brick oven – as Livingstone was later to observe, missionaries must be jacks-of-all-trades – and she learned to make soap and candles from the melted fat of the sheep which was slaughtered weekly to feed the missionary families.

She accepted much, however – even, after some resistance, the local custom of sealing earth floors with cow dung, the most effective method of laying dust and defeating flies and jiggers. The dung was renewed every week and smoothed into a shiny skin, and soon she was inspecting her 'fine clear green cow-dung floors with as much complacency as the best scoured'. The floors of many rural homes in Africa are still treated this way. The church which Robert Moffat and his colleague Robert Hamilton built at Kuruman has a cow-dung floor, and it is quite beautiful: smooth, polished, cool to the feet, without a trace of odour.

In July 1820, Mary Moffat found she was pregnant. By December, she was so ill that her husband kept the gravity of her condition from her parents. The nature of her illness is unrecorded, but it persisted to the point where she 'prepared herself calmly for her deathbed and the parting with her dear Mr Moffat'. As a Victorian, she didn't find the idea of death through childbirth foreign; as a devout Christian, she didn't find it unacceptable as long as she maintained her confidence that she was going to a better world.

But she didn't part from her dear Mr Moffat, who had done all he could to save her with the help of Buchan's Domestic Medicine and the advice of other missionary wives. Perhaps she was also sustained by the intervention of Chief Mothibi of Lattakoo, who had warmed to the young couple when they stayed there and sent messages commanding her not to die. On 12 April 1821, she gave birth to a healthy, vigorous daughter. And when, a month later, Chief Mothibi welcomed them to Lattakoo, and his wives seized and kissed the baby, clasping her to breasts lacquered with fat and red ochre, the new mother became Ma-Mary, mother of Mary, her first-born, the name she carried for the rest of her life; just as her daughter, Ma-Robert, came to bear a similar honorific in the land of the Bechuana which 'was known throughout all that country and 1,800 miles beyond'.

The emptiness of Griqualand West is eerie. Almost as soon as we leave the suburbs of Kimberley, we seem to lose the human race. Yet the great sweeps of thornveld aren't wilderness; the unrolling ribbon of road is efficiently tarred, and its verges are bordered with wire fences. Now and then, but so infrequently they become objects of visual excitement on the austere landscape, we come upon road signs warning of rare hazards: corner, junction, hill. 'What is this land?' I ask Keith. 'Who owns it?'

'It's grazing land. Sheep and cattle. Where you see fences, it belongs to farmers. Where there are none, it's communal land and grazed by village livestock.'

We see no villages, or indeed livestock. 'It will be in there somewhere', says Keith, waving a hand at the bunched fists of thorn acacia and bleached grass, dry as the hair of a bottle blonde. These farms are so big the herders often live at camps they call posts, well off the road.'

The Northern Cape is bigger than Germany. The largest of South Africa's provinces, it covers over one-third of the nation's land mass, and its population is the most sparse. Much of it is semi-desert: the Great Karoo, the southern reaches of the Kalahari and, on the Atlantic coast, Namaqualand, where once a year millions of Namaqua daisies and other wild flowers clump the land to its limits, blessing the drab plains with the blooming of the brief desert spring. The spectacle is one of the Northern Cape's few but significant visitor attractions; another is the Kgalagadi Transfrontier Park, the vast Kalahari game reserve it shares with Botswana. The N8 from Kimberley to Griquatown is a link to both in a region where tarred highways are rarities, scratching their way across mighty spaces; which may be why the Mary Moffat Museum, a very modest cultural institution in a very modest town, gets respectably visited by some 2,000 people a year.

My eyes grow tired scanning the horizon for the first intimations of the little town, but finally spot a clue: Livingstone Stores, an isolated brick emporium with a corrugated iron roof, patiently waiting for customers at the corner of a dirt road. Then the Land Rover clears one of the long, shallow inclines on the N8, and in the dip ahead I see a scatter of mature trees and some geometric shapes, before the horizon resumes its severe profile. A road sign says: 'Griekwastad', Afrikaans for 'Griqua city', reminding me that most people in these parts speak first Afrikaans, then Setswana or Xhosa, with English the fourth official language. In fact, as I'm soon to learn, the name Griquatown is today considered historical.

As we ease into the empty, sunlit channel of Main Street – the only main street – we pass the Tiger's Eye Hotel, a bottle shop, a mini-market, an ornamental phoenix palm providing pavement shade, a shop selling the neighbourhood's semi-precious stones, tiger's eye and jasper, and a tourist signboard with the symbols of campsite, caravan park and restaurant. Most of the buildings are only one storey high, with flat roofs and wide verandas.

With no difficulty at all, halfway down Main Street, we find the Mary Moffat Museum, the oldest building in town. It is squat, sturdy and stone-built with a steeply pitched thatch roof, and its doors are locked. The museum closes for an hour over lunchtime, and it's not quite 2pm. Within a few minutes, a car pulls up, a short, plump, smiling woman of late middle age climbs out, and we are swept into the building by Griquatown's cultural life-force: Hetta Hager, local historian and museum curator who, she tells us with merry despair, has been trying to retire for the last two years.

'Nothing happens fast in Griekwastad. In fact, nothing happens at all. We don't even have any crime, apart from the odd domestic fight.' Marriage has marooned Hetta in the heart of Griqualand West, and she seems astonished and amused to find she's still here. 'I'm like Mary Livingstone. You know what George Seaver said about her in his book?[1] "She had no choices, only situations." That's me.'

Hetta's situations have included running the primary school as well as running the museum. She graduated from acting curator in 1986 to curator in 1991; and the building has also found itself in several situations. It was first the mission church, built in 1828 (by which time the Moffats were in Kuruman), and then, between 1904 and 1956, the local bank. The

[1] *David Livingstone: His Life and Letters*, by George Seaver (Lutterworth Press, 1957).

founding fathers of the first colonial town north of the Orange River were William Anderson and Cornelius Kramer of the London Missionary Society. Their original name for the mission station was Klaarwater. It took its optimism, in a semi-arid region, from a spring which, says Hetta, has a more interesting name: Lion's Den Fountain. 'The hut in which Mary was born was almost certainly near that spring. It's just outside the town, about a kilometre from here. I'll tell you how to get to it after you've had a look round.'

The little museum doesn't seem to be fussed about which Mary its name honours, mother, daughter or both, and has information boards on both Moffat and Livingstone families. Here, for the first time, I see a copy of the letter which ten-year-old Anna Mary wrote to Hans Christian Andersen (see Prologue), its jaunty words failing to conceal the hurt and confusion of their young author. The other exhibits are mainly examples of early colonial furniture and artefacts, including the first mission bell and one of the yokes which turned teams of oxen into engines of slow but reliable propulsion. Hetta is most proud of the museum's centrepiece – the free-standing, beautifully crafted, hardwood pulpit of the mission church. 'This was the first moveable object in South Africa to be declared a national monument.'

She tells us that visitor numbers are now in decline, despite a minimal entrance fee subsidised by a grant from the provincial government. 'We get a good number of Scots, maybe about 10 per cent of the annual average. Lots of them with church connections.'

'We haven't paid our own entrance fee yet', I remind her. 'What is it?'

'Depends on what you have', says Hetta, eventually settling for five rand (then about 50p) from each of us. And then she tells us what Lion's Den Fountain means to the neighbourhood's Griqua population – those who still cherish the instructive mythology and traditions of their Khoisan ancestors. 'It plays a major role in the initiation of girls into womanhood. When a girl has her first period she is secluded for four weeks or so with older women, who instruct her on how to handle men. And they also warn the girl to avoid the giant water snake which lives in the spring.'

The giant water snake – and it doesn't stretch the imagination to recognise its symbolism – is a trickster who knows the way to the hearts of adolescent girls. He can turn himself into anything, including brand-new shoes or bright new ear-rings. If any girl fetching water finds these desirable things on the banks of the spring and is foolish enough to pick them up, he resumes his true identity and carries her down to the bottom of the well to do his bidding. He will give her anything she wants, more shoes, more ear-rings, but she is his slave and must 'sweep his dung floor and make his mealie porridge'. She becomes a mermaid living in Lion's Den Fountain; after which she doesn't need new shoes.

'Once their term of initiation is over,' Hetta concludes, 'the girls are considered safe from the water snake, released from their retreat and again allowed to fetch water from the well.'

I remark that our own adolescent girls would greatly benefit from four weeks' seclusion and exposure to the wisdom of their elders, with specific advice about seductive snakes. And then Hetta sets us on our way to Lion's Den Fountain, directing us down a side street 'past the Execution Tree' (Griquatown's gallows are now in someone's garden) and onwards on the scrubby grass to some trees on the communal land beyond the last house.

In *Beloved Partner*, there is an old photograph of 'the garden at the house in Griquatown where Mary and Robert lived in 1820/21, and where their first child, Mary, was born'. The book was first published in 1974 but the black-and-white photo looks much older. It shows a well-built wall and neat rows of irrigation channels. Hetta has no memory of the garden, and there is no trace of the settlement which was once there, except a low turf rampart which may be the remnants of the wall.

There is little to see at Lion's Den Fountain; just a weedy pool embedded in reeds, overhung by wind-blasted thorn trees. The lions are long gone, and there isn't even a giant water snake. Just a pair of pendulous grass globes trembling on a branch, like home-made Christmas decorations: the empty nurseries of weaver birds.

The five years which the Moffats spent between Griquatown and Lattakoo were not only arduous and dangerous but also deeply dispiriting. Mora Dickson calls them 'the years of sorrow'. Not only were conditions harsh at thirsty Lattakoo, their first formal posting, but also the physical labour was grinding and its potential reward, the saving of souls, unforthcoming. These were the years 'when Robert Moffat's days were spent standing in the saw-pit, labouring at the anvil, treading clay, cleaning a water ditch, and Mary's salting meat, tending children, scouring, cleaning, cooking, supervising other women who found her instructions ridiculous'.

A second baby was born, Ann, and the household took in two Khoisan infants, a brother and sister whose mother had died. Robert had rescued them from a kinsman poised to bury them in her grave. There were regular alarms and confrontations which sent the family retreating from

Lattakoo to Griquatown, but in Ma-Mary's letters home she complained only about the mission's lack of spiritual progress. 'Five years have rolled on since the missionaries came, and not one soul converted, nor does any-one seem to lend an ear. All treat with ridicule and contempt the truths that are delivered.'

This would change slowly at Kuruman, as Robert mastered Setswana and both Moffats won the respect and affection of the Tswana. But the perils of isolation among warring tribes and raiding parties persisted. It was a period of terrible and bloody disruption in southern Africa: the years of the Mfecane, a term variously said to mean 'crushing' or 'scatter-ing' or 'growing thin through hunger'. Between 1815 and about 1840, the warlords and warriors of (most notably) Zulu, Matabele and Makololo left their tribal homelands to plunder and dispossess less aggressive tribes. These conflicts created a ripple effect which caused mass migrations of both invading and displaced peoples, many of whom fled in advance of the armies and became predatory invaders in turn.

Historians are still arguing about the conditions which caused this long convulsion, which destabilised vast regions of present-day South Africa, Mozambique, Botswana, Zimbabwe and Zambia and brought about the defensive mountain kingdoms of Lesotho and Swaziland. There seems to have been a collision of factors, and the impact of European colonisa-tion was among them – specifically the introduction of maize from the Americas by the Portuguese. This led to agricultural surpluses and a popu-lation explosion in Zululand, while the increased competition for land and water, exacerbated by white encroachment and Portuguese slaving, fired the nationalist ambitions of the Zulu king Shaka, who also happened to be a military genius.

The swelling population supplied Shaka with thousands of conscripts for his standing army of impis. He developed new tactics, like the 'buffalo-horn' formations which, sixty years later, routed a crack British regiment armed with the most advanced military hardware at Isandlwana.[2] He

---

2 After the British invaded Zululand in 1879, one of the worst defeats of British forces in Victorian times took place at Isandlwana, in what is now Kwa-Zulu Natal. Two battalions of well-armed infantry, cavalry and artillery commanded by Lord Chelmsford were crushed by 20,000 Zulus armed with assegais. The Zulu impis (regiments) were dispatched by the Zulu king Cetshwayo from his kraal with the order, 'March slowly, attack at dawn and eat up the red soldiers'. They took the British by surprise and outmanoeuvred them with the buffalo-horn formation. Over 1,700 British and local soldiers died. As with Dunkirk, the British state's PR machine turned colossal defeat into 'victory' by awarding the Victoria Cross to eleven sol-diers who took part in the rearguard action at Rorke's Drift.

replaced the throwing spear with the short, broad-bladed, stabbing asse-
gai, which was much more effective at close quarters. He turned his
warriors into the most disciplined fighting force in southern Africa and
the Zulu tribe into a nation. He did not cause the Mfecane, but his invasion and appropriation of neighbouring territories triggered its first wave.

Far to the west, in what is now the Northern Cape and Botswana,
neither peaceable Tswana nor belligerent Boer nor lawless Griqua were
immune to the knock-on effects of Zulu expansionism. The region was
twice invaded: first in the early 1820s by Sebetwane and his wandering
Makololo, who killed and pillaged on their passage north to the Zambezi, where they later become candidates for conversion by Livingstone;
then, fifteen years later, by Shaka's rebel general Mzilikazi, who had set
up a rival kingdom near the site of present-day Pretoria, but clashed with
militant Boer farmers as they pressed deeper and deeper into the land
which became the Transvaal. In 1838, after a series of battles, he withdrew beyond the Limpopo to settle in the south of present-day Zimbabwe,
cutting a swathe through the Tswana as he went.

There, Mzilikazi founded a capital which became Bulawayo, 'place
of smoky fires'. His people, whose origins were Zulu, were called the
Ndebele – in English, the Matabele. His son, Lobengula, was their second
and last king, and the most significant African figure in the history of the
region's exploitation by the British. It was Lobengula who negotiated a
treaty with Cecil Rhodes and the British South Africa Company and who
granted them limited access to his kingdom's minerals, only to discover
he had been duped. It was always the intention of the British adventurers
to claim and settle his territory and, when the deception was exposed,
Lobengula launched a heroic but futile war. Matabeleland was on its way
to becoming Rhodesia.

A century later, in the early 1980s, the warrior spirit of the Matabele
came back to haunt the newly independent state of Zimbabwe. Bulawayo
and its hinterland were the heartland of resistance to the independence
agreement and Shona dominance of Robert Mugabe's government, which
ruthlessly crushed 'the Matabele dissidents' and killed thousands of innocent members of their tribe.

Robert Moffat was the first European to appreciate that, for all their
bellicose reputation, Mzilikazi and the Matabele had many fine qualities.
In his efforts to bring them the Christian message, he formed a lifelong
friendship with the much-feared despot. In his years at Kuruman, the
towering, full-bearded missionary became a trusted interlocutor in the
complex politics of the tribes. His name was honoured as far north as the
Zambezi valley, in the distant redoubt of the Makololo – which was of

huge advantage to David Livingstone, husband of 'the daughter of Moffat', when he turned up there in 1851.

All this lay ahead. In their last months at Lattakoo, even with the prospect of a propitious new mission station near 'the fountain of Kuruman', even as the nursery gardener and the nursery gardener's daughter shared visions of fruit trees and vegetable beds, Ma-Mary was struggling. As Mora Dickson puts it, she was prepared to love the souls of the Bechuana, but she couldn't yet bring herself to like the people themselves. In one uncharitable and untypical outburst, she wrote: 'In the natives of South Africa there is nothing naturally engaging; their extreme selfishness, filthiness, obstinate stupidity and want of sensibility, have a tendency to disgust, and sometimes cause the mind to shrink from the idea of spending the whole life amongst them.'

But her first-born daughter had already indicated she thought otherwise. The little Khoisan girl rescued from entombment had become Mary's best friend, and remained so throughout her childhood.

9

The Eye of Kuruman

'A little paradise in this wilderness country'

On the road to Wildebeest Guest Farm there is a line of telephone poles which appears to have been bombarded with bales of hay. The top of each pole is spiked with huge bundles of dry grass, some as big as haystacks. I've seen these high-rise haystacks before, when I've been travelling in Namibia and Botswana, but I have only ever seen them supported by acacia trees. They are birds' nests; the world's largest nests, built by birds little bigger than sparrows. They are the community homes of sociable weavers, which, as their name suggests, like company.

There are many weaver species in southern Africa, but the sociable weaver's range is confined to the dry regions of the Northern Cape, southern Botswana and southern Namibia. Where trees are in short supply, perhaps because they have been cleared by farmers, the resourceful little birds improvise. Their nests are permanent, with multiple entrances on the underside and multiple chambers within. If left undisturbed, they can last for up to 100 years and accommodate up to 400 birds. They can also become so heavy that they bring down telephone wires and short-circuit electricity supplies, but the communal building of the sociable weaver is such a striking feature of the featureless roads in these lonely lands that it seems to be tolerated.

As we pass another spectacular structure on its man-made plinth I find myself murmuring: 'In my house there are many mansions'. The nest of the sociable weaver is well furnished with metaphors. Owls and vultures use the roof as a platform for their own nests, and chats, finches and barbets make themselves at home in the chambers. Even the pygmy falcon, a bird of prey, leaves the weavers and their nestlings unharmed in return for hospitality; another case of the lion lying down with the lamb. Among the few unwelcome guests is the Cape cobra; and the builders place sharp sticks at the entrances to deter this serpent in their little Eden.

It's sometimes hard to remember that the Moffat and Livingstone families lived among the kind of wildlife which, in today's South Africa, is largely interned in national parks and fenced game reserves. The gallant and gentlemanly William Cotton Oswell, generous companion to Livingstone, kindly friend to Mary, gives a breathtaking description of what the nineteenth-century traveller might expect to meet in the African bush:

On the plains between the Orange and Molopo rivers springboks were met with in vast herds ... they were to be counted only by tens of thousands. When we reached the Molopo seven different kinds of animals were within view – some, especially the quaggas[1] and buffaloes, in large herds ... Fifteen miles beyond the Molopo to the north in the well-wooded and watered valley of the Ba-Katla, rhinoceros and giraffe were abundant. Indeed, it was so full of game of all kinds that it put me in mind of the children's pictures of Adam naming the beasts in the garden of Eden – more animals than bushes.

Oswell was an adventurer of the purest kind, an honourable example of an Englishman abroad in a world of exotic places which, almost by accident, were on their way to becoming the British Empire. He was born in Essex in 1818 and educated at Rugby, then spent ten years in Madras with the British East India Company, teaching himself Tamil and other languages and, in the manner of a gifted amateur, studying medicine and surgery. He was later to bring his medical skills to field hospitals in the Crimean War.

But it was Africa that was 'the romance of William Oswell's life', as his eldest son wrote in a biography. He arrived in southern Africa in search of better health and had the income to indulge his audacious spirit, his curiosity about the blank spaces north of the Cape Colony, and his enthusiasm for hunting. Like others among the early big-game hunters, he came to regret the thrill of the chase and its casualties. He talks of coming upon 'at least four hundred elephants standing drowsily in the shade of the detached clumps of mimosa trees', and adds: 'I am sorry now for all the fine old beasts I have killed, but I was young then, there was excitement in the work, I had large numbers of men to feed; and if these are not considered sound excuses for slaughter, the regret is lightened by the knowledge that every animal I shot, save three elephants, was eaten by man, and so put to a good use.'

There are no elephant or giraffe or rhinoceros on Wildebeest Guest Farm, but there are indeed wildebeest: black wildebeest, uncommon descendants of the herds which once roamed the highveld and Karoo as freely as the white-bearded wildebeest of the Serengeti. A century ago,

---

[1] The quagga was a sub-species of the plains zebra, once found in great numbers in this part of southern Africa. It is now extinct, hunted out by sportsmen and farmers who colonised its territories.

the black wildebeest was brought to the edge of extinction by commercial hunting (its hide was the prize); but it has been saved by the efforts of farmers like Hester and Frans Groenewald, who have stocked their property with a breeding herd. Like the farm's 1,000-strong flock of dorper sheep, the rare antelope is adapted to dry conditions and sparse grazing and is, of course, a visitor attraction, along with blesbok, springbok and Khoisan rock engravings.

Keith has booked us rooms for the night at the guest farm, which is twelve miles north of Griquatown on the road to Namaqualand and Namibia. Even without directions or signpost the farmhouse is easy to find, as it sits at the heart of an oasis: a generous island of foliage and flowers on the miserly margin of the Kalahari. In another life Hester Groenewald was a botanist, and with the help of a borehole she has created her own botanical garden.

The Groenewalds have had their farm for over twenty years; and, even before they opened it to guests, their comfortable, colourful home must have been a welcoming place. It is demonstrably a Christian one, the sitting-room wall hung with antique and decorative crosses; and there is a clear-eyed look of love on the faces of the children and grandchildren in family photographs. Hester, who does the hostessing while Frans runs the livestock, is as warm as her surroundings. The next morning she drives us out to find the black wildebeest; not always easy on a 9,000-acre property, but she knows their favourite spots.

The wildebeest see us before we see them: thirty or so watchful beasts which keep their distance. They are smaller than the common wildebeest, wearing the dark winter coats which give them their name, and their wariness shows them to be wild creatures which have not been exposed to convoys of tourist vehicles. 'One of the advantages of living in the Northern Cape', says Hester.

Then we inspect the Khoisan engravings, circles set in haloes of spikes, the same solar images inscribed again and again on flat boulders. Were the early hunter-gatherers trying to make sense of their world, finding a constant in its most reliable feature, the sun? 'If you look closely, you can see the rays vary in number and length. It's my belief these different suns are calendars for different years – or different cycles, as they would measure the seasons.'

We drive back to the farmhouse, where Hester shows us round her garden. She has made a corner of this semi-arid region bloom, like others before her. Two centuries earlier, 100 miles to the north, the Moffats' vision of horticultural self-sufficiency was bearing fruit. Literally. The mission orchard had begun to supply grapes, figs, peaches, apricots and apples, and the land to produce wheat, tobacco and maize – 'a little paradise in this wilderness country', reported Ma-Mary. The harvesting of souls was finally under way, too, with the first convert baptised in 1829.

It's time we left for Kuruman.

It took a week to travel by ox-wagon between Kuruman and the Vaal River; perhaps two days for a man on horseback. When the Moffat family arrived back at the Cape after their long visit to the United Kingdom, news of their homecoming reached the mission in time to galvanise one of its recruits into riding south to meet them. The journey was no chore for David Livingstone, who was already showing advanced symptoms of restlessness. It was two years since he had arrived in Africa; two years during which he felt irked by the absence of Robert Moffat from Kuruman and dissatisfied by what he found there. The mission station was smaller and more isolated than he'd imagined, its hinterland underpopulated and its Tswana communicants tiny in number, although the church was well filled on Sundays. Indulging a recurring tendency to blame others for his disappointments, he was tempted to believe he had been misled by Moffat's oratory.

He also felt he was kicking his heels. Moffat's colleagues, the faithful Robert Hamilton still among them, were reliable and sincere, but they lacked the inspirational drive of their leader, and without him few initiatives were taken. There was little at Kuruman to challenge the energy and ideas of the impatient young man, and his first impressions of his new environment were bleak. On the journey from the Cape, he remarked how much of the landscape was similar to Scotland, but when he reached Bechuanaland in the middle of its dry, dusty, debilitating winter he reported gloomily: 'All around is a dreary desert for a great part of the year, enough indeed, from its nakedness and sand, to give its people most of that ophthalmia with which they are so often afflicted. There is not a tree near the station which has not been planted by the missionaries. Low stunted scraggy bushes, many of them armed with bent thorns villainously sharp and strong are the chief objects which present themselves to the eye.'

To ease his frustration, he took to exploring the surrounding territory. He made three long excursions to the north-east, once as far as 500 miles, getting to know the tribes and their chiefs, picking up some of their language, exercising that acute interest in natural history which was one of Livingstone's most attractive qualities. He soon learned that the 'dreary desert' is full of life: grasses and aloes, wild melons and cucumbers, lilies and fan-palms. Even the 'low stunted scraggy bushes' put out flowers, and he discovered trees which were not planted by missionaries. The Kalahari's three most valued species, the camelthorn, the shepherd's tree and the baobab, have today been given protected status.

The Kalahari is only semi-desert. Apart from its insect, bird and reptile populations, its permanent residents include aardvark, bat-eared fox, meerkat, jackal, aardwolf and other mammals, all sustained by the residue of water left by its explosive seasonal rains. The rains themselves, with the grazing they produce, are tracked by zebra, wildebeest, oryx and other antelope, which in turn are followed by their predators: lion, cheetah, leopard and brown hyena. Large numbers of elephant migrate in and out of the Kalahari, while the zebra migration is second in scale to that of the Serengeti.

Livingstone began to observe and record this elusive diversity. He grew to relish the freedom of sun-bright distances opened up by days in the saddle and campfire nights passed under skies bristling with stars. By the time he galloped up to the Moffats' ox-wagon caravan near the Vaal River, he was physically transformed: fit, sun-tanned and expert in his horsemanship; even rather dashing in a home-made suit as he thundered out of a glare of golden dust. It is Edna Healey's opinion that 'Mary would never see him in a more romantic light'. But, without testimony from Mary herself, that can only be speculation.

What is recorded is that Livingstone had begun to revise his lukewarm attitude to marriage. The London Missionary Society could hardly insist that its field workers marry, but it certainly encouraged them to take wives, who were expected to share their hardships and demonstrate that a man who brought his family into tribal lands was not looking for a fight. The LMS also believed that sexual stability would protect their missionaries from dangerous liaisons with local women, or even the rumour of them; a theory which Livingstone dismissed as a pious hope – 'with respect to scandal ... married men have been charged with incontinency ... I conclude that marriage, like vaccination for smallpox, is not specially preventative to scandal in Africa'.

For himself, he told friends, he could better bring the word of God into perilous lands if he were unencumbered by wife and children and the responsibilities that went with them. Perhaps this was more of an instinct than an informed belief, and perhaps Mary would have had a happier life if he'd trusted it. But he had now seen how the Kuruman missionaries were supported by their families in their isolation; how wives not only provided domestic and emotional comforts but also took part in pastoral work and were kindly received by local chiefs, who treated single men with suspicion.

He may also have felt the pull of his own libido, which as far as anyone knows had yet to find release in sexual experience. In later life, Livingstone insisted he found no physical appeal in African women and couldn't imagine any man wanting 'criminal sexual congress' with them. But in 1843 he was only 30, a vigorous young man living among near-naked young women, and whether or not he found them attractive they may have had the effect of liberating his fantasies and loosening the controls which upbringing and religion had imposed on his sexual appetite.

At any rate, when he rode with the Moffats on the last leg of their journey home, he had plenty of time to get to know their two marriageable daughters.

The Kalahari may be semi-desert, but in winter it shares one notable characteristic with that desert of deserts on the other side of the Equator, the great Sahara: cold nights and hot days, with the temperature climbing slowly from sunrise. On the route from Griquatown to Kuruman we cross the Ghaap Plateau, some 3,700 feet above sea level, and by mid-morning it's warm enough to take off our fleeces. By September winter is on the back foot in the Northern Cape, but there's still enough of Livingstone's 'nakedness and sand' in the hibernating veld to show the landscape at its most lacklustre. Even the undersized flowers on the thorn bushes, anticipating rain, look premature and pallid. For two hours the only water we see is the liquid in our own water bottles, but we cruise buoyantly along the calm surface of the N14. The Moffats' ox-wagons would have carried supplies from the Vaal River in barrels or hide waterbags.

'When you see how harsh the conditions are even today,' Keith tells me, 'you can really appreciate the achievement at the Moffat mission. And why Kuruman gets called the Oasis of the Kalahari.'

The Eye of Kuruman: Die Oog to the Afrikaner, Gasegonyana to the Tswana. The Tswana name means 'little water calabash' but if there's one thing it is not, it's little. 'The Eye is an inexhaustible fountain delivering 20 million litres of crystal clear water a day … it gushes from the seemingly barren dolomite rock even in the worst times of drought, and is the source of the Kuruman River … it is the largest natural spring in the southern hemisphere.' The people who compose tourist information love statistics. What do 20 million litres of water look like? Almost 4,400,000 gallons, which makes me none the wiser, or nearly 70,000 hogsheads. A hogshead is easier to visualise, and I imagine the Eye delivering its daily quota of barrels to each resident of Kuruman and the district of Gasegonyana.

The town itself has a population of about 12,000; and, as we draw near, the vegetation thickens and a cluster of rich red hills rears up from the veld. They look artificial, but so do many of the inselbergs which the South Africans call kopjes, and it's only when their mechanical infrastructure comes into view that some of the hills expose themselves as mine workings. 'Manganese and iron ore', explains Keith. 'This area also has the richest deposits of blue asbestos in the world, but they stopped mining it about twenty years ago. Too late for all those people who are still dying from cancers and asbestosis.'

Kuruman is the Northern Cape's most northern town. It feels almost metropolitan after Griquatown; and, for all its lush suburban gardens, the centre has the utilitarian presence of a mining community. Its proximity to the Kgalagadi Transfrontier Park and, of course, the presence of the Eye (declared a national monument in 1992) account for its tourist facilities, and there is no lack of places to stay and eat. Keith and I plan to do neither. We have plenty of daylight hours to spend at the Moffat Mission, which is on the edge of town, before heading north towards Botswana. What's more, Keith's 4WD is a life-support system. As a form of transport, its full title – Land Rover Defender Puma 110 Station Wagon – sounds almost as stirring as ox-wagon, and it has almost as many accessories. None of them would be familiar to the early travellers. Keith recites its special assets proudly: 'Long-range fuel tank, fresh-water tank, snorkel exhaust pipe for fording rivers, large aggressive off-road tyres and, of course, GPS'.

'Don't forget the fridge', I remind him. It's my favourite feature. The built-in fridge keeps our picnic lunches fresh and, for the hour of the sundowner, our white wine chilled, although when the night air bites we share a preference for red. Our guest farm dinners don't include wine, but the hospitable farmers wouldn't dream of charging for corkage.

It's late morning when we arrive at the Eye of Kuruman. Some translations of its Tswana name give a longer version of Gasegonyana: 'little water calabash of bubbling water'. I suppose I'm expecting the organic equivalent of an open sluice on a dam, a raw force of nature bursting from the naked rock. Instead, we find fenced gardens in the centre of town with, as their centrepiece, a small lake. The landscaped banks are hung with graceful drapery, willows, wisteria and giant ferns, the surrounding paths defined by tall and stately trees, palms, acacia, syringa and conifers. It seems the Eye can entice almost anything from the ground, although some people regret that 'improvements' to the spring in the mid-twentieth century have subdued its energy and created this pretty urban oasis.

We pay a few rand at the gate and note the 'café, curio shop and ablution facilities'. The largest natural spring in the southern hemisphere makes the most of its celebrity, but on this midweek morning there are few visitors. There is peace to reflect on our reflections from the footbridge at the far end of the lake, where faint pulses of water stir fallen leaves against a rim of rock – the only evidence of those 20 million litres arriving daily from dolomite solutions deep underground. 'Enough to fill 400 suburban swimming pools', says Keith, coming up with another helpful measure.

The Eye's surface is spotted with lily pads, and slinking among them are moving shadows: goldfish, carp, barbell and an endangered species of cichlid with a fabulous name, *Pseudocrenilabrus Philander*. VISVANG VERBODE, asserts a bilingual notice. FISHING PROHIBITED. Two centuries ago the fishermen were fishers of men, and in time the Eye acquired a sobriquet: 'The Fountain of Christianity'.

No doubt Jesus Christ would have found his way to Africa without the help of the Eye of Kuruman and the green fingers and persuasive preaching of an autodidact from Lowland Scotland. But permanent water makes for permanence. As soon as Ma-Mary, her husband and their two little girls were installed on the land leased to the LMS by Chief Mothibi, Moffat began work on a ditch to irrigate the site, which lay west of the Eye in the Kuruman Valley. The trench he built from the spring was nearly three miles long. In the same year, 1825, the first grave was dug in the station's virgin cemetery. Into it went the fragment of spent life which was the Moffats' first son, also called Robert, who died five days after he was born. There was little time to grieve, according to Mora Dickson:

'In spite of armed robbers constantly threatening, the work of the station had to go steadily forward. Planting, building, carrying, creating, salting, storing, sewing, cobbling, carpentering, blacksmithing, butchering, preaching, teaching, exhorting, pacifying, supporting, cleaning, feeding, praying, writing ...' The first convert was still four years away, but slowly the Tswana who drifted towards the community began to realise that these white people with their outlandish Son of God, whose mother had never been touched by man, whose own loving father had him nailed to a tree and whose followers took only one wife, were here to stay.

During those first years at Kuruman, little is heard of the young Mary until her parents take the decision to enrol her and Ann in the Salem boarding school. But much is heard from and of Ma-Mary. Necessity, and her own stout spirit, were turning the slight, comely young woman from Lancashire into a formidable matriarch, who ran her household with the rigorous efficiency which men like to call bossiness. (Livingstone was one such man.) Her standards were exacting, her hospitality generous to the station's visitors, many of whom were hunters and traders of slack faith; and her example to her daughters inspired their awe. It may also have inspired the fear that they could never match her achievements or meet her expectations.

Yet she was a kind mother who enjoyed her children's early years when she had time to do so, usually only when the family were 'itinerating' – travelling by ox-wagon either to meet Robert after one of his journeys to other tribal territories, or riding with him. This is when she writes at her most relaxed. Released from her domestic routine, she had the leisure to read to the children, tell them stories and play with them as the oxen hauled their mobile home across the veld. 'When we span out (or unyoke), a fire is immediately made, the kettle set on, and tea or coffee made. I would notice here that the missionary must be very regardless of his wife's comfort who does not see to that being done without her troubling herself. For my own part I never think of coming out of the waggon till there is a good fire, for it is comfortless work indeed turning out in a cold night in the wilderness with a child or children before there is a fire.'

Until the wrench of displacement arrived with her tenth year and boarding school in Salem, there is nothing to suggest that Mary's childhood was anything other than happy. Most children don't question their circumstances, and in a loving family they take for granted the protection of their parents. Kuruman, with its new stone buildings, well-watered livestock and maturing gardens, must have seemed a secure playground for the Moffat children, who would have little idea of the precariousness of its future and their lives.

They lived in a lawless wilderness, 600 miles from the nearest market, over 100 miles from the nearest doctor. The recurring aftershocks of the Mfecane had destabilised and impoverished the Tswana, and even the most downtrodden tribes were asserting themselves in conflicts over cattle and resources. The mission station could be either an insecure refuge for beleaguered Tswana or a target for plunder for roaming bands of Griqua and other Baastard nomads. Often, it was only the Christian example of the missionaries, who treated even their most menacing visitors with respect and hospitality, which stood between the family and disaster. More often, it was the calm and powerful personality of Robert Moffat himself.

What makes and remakes a hero? A noble man, a great Scot whose name is barely remembered outside missionary history and the East Lothian village of Ormiston, where a memorial was erected in 1885 by public subscription and today there is a housing development called Moffat Court? It takes more than a few moments of impulsive bravery. Certainly, as Mora Dickson identifies, Moffat 'possessed in abundant measure the virtue which is perhaps most immediately attractive – courage!' But Moffat's indifference to his personal safety was tested over and over again, and neither it nor the scrupulous moral standards which informed his courage were ever found wanting. 'He believed in trusting Africans, as he trusted his God, with his life, and, both for the valorous Matabele (whom he later met) and the timid Bechuana, this was an astonishing trait. Nor could they eventually resist the knowledge that it was in their interest and on their behalf that he used it.'

In time, too, his wife overcame her distaste for the Bechuana, which she had never allowed to compromise her humanity. Not long after the birth and death of her first son, it was reported that an infant could be heard crying, unseen, on a hillside near the mission station. Moffat and one of his colleagues went to investigate, with Ma-Mary apprehensively following. By the time she reached the spot, they had found a shallow pit covered with a slab of stone, which was resting on the face of a baby. The little girl, about five weeks old, was bruised and scratched from struggling against the rocks of her tomb, and almost fatally cold. Ma-Mary picked her up, took her home, warmed and fed her.

They discovered that the child had been left to die by her destitute mother and grandmother, who fled when they heard she'd been rescued. The Bechuana women of the mission station were unmoved by Ma-Mary's foundling. In a letter home, she wrote: 'They viewed it with indifference; said the mother was a rascal, but wondered much that we should love so poor an object'. So, Ma-Mary cared for the baby herself, spooning tiny quantities of milk into her mouth until she found a reliable Khoisan woman to be her wet-nurse. Ma-Mary was herself pregnant for the fourth time, and soon afterwards had a miscarriage. Two babies lost. The tenderness she felt for the abandoned child intensified. She decided to adopt the little girl, who was christened Sarah Roby, after the wife of a missionary who had been Robert's patron at Dukinfield.

Sarah Roby, plucked barely alive from a desperate grave, became a valued and much-loved member of the Moffat family. On their four-year visit to the United Kingdom in 1839, the beautiful young Tswana woman also became a celebrity on the missionary circuit.

While her father faced down the threats of those early years and her mother raised waifs, fed the starving and did her best, without medical training, to treat illness and injury, their eldest daughter seemed to have the sturdy temperament to tolerate lesser crises. Ma-Mary's fifth pregnancy was more successful than the two preceding ones, and Mary and her sister Ann were soon joined by a new and healthy sibling; another Robert to succeed the brother buried at five days old. He was still a baby when, once while the family were 'itinerating', their ox-wagon overturned. Chaos. All the supplies and equipment were spilled on the ground, the oxen had to be unyoked and pacified and the passengers checked for cuts and bruises. Only then was it noticed that two of the children were missing. Panic. An agitated search of the piles of possessions finally uncovered a lumpy mattress. Under it, waiting to be rescued, was eight-year-old Mary, clasping her baby brother in her arms to keep him safe.

When David Livingstone arrived at Kuruman in 1841, the church had been completed only three years earlier. It had room for a tightly packed congregation of 800, inspiring the fanciful sobriquet 'Cathedral of the Kalahari'; but Moffat's regular worshippers numbered no more than around 350. Of these, only forty or so were communicants, while the population of the villages within a twenty-mile radius of the mission station was only about 1,000, and not many could be counted practising Christians. Twenty years of proselytising had saved very few souls: this was the audit which disappointed the fretful new missionary, who had no idea what it had cost the Moffats to come so far and achieve as much.

If Livingstone was underwhelmed by the 'small village' which was Kuruman, he might be more impressed by the Moffat Mission today; not because it is much larger than it was then (which it isn't), but because it has endured. It has survived the two centuries of colossal demographic, social, constitutional and often violent change which eventually produced 'the rainbow nation'. It even survived the most oppressive years of apartheid, although the system tried to destroy it in the most invidious way. The Bantu Education Act and Group Areas Act forced multi-racial teachers and pupils to leave the mission; and, apart from the church, the buildings became derelict. Between 1950 and 1980, it could no longer function as an integrated place of worship and education.

Kuruman came alive again as the reformist government of F. W. De Klerk made moves to modify its segregationist policies. In 1981, the United Congregational Church of South Africa invited its sister churches,

Anglican, Methodist and Presbyterian, to found a trust and join a venture to restore the buildings and turn the Moffat Mission into an ecumenical centre. This is the calm green place which I reach on a diamond-bright day in September 2008. This is the place which would be recognised without difficulty by Mary Livingstone, her husband and parents.

10

Under the Almond Tree

'a matter-of-fact lady, a little thick, black-haired girl, sturdy and all I want'

High noon lasts for hours in the Kalahari. It's nearly 3pm by the time we arrive at the Moffat Mission, but the birds and insects are still idling in midday torpor. All is silent as we park the Land Rover in a sandy space, an informal car park at the beginnings of a lane lined with venerable camelthorn. The lane is a remnant of the Missionary Road to the interior. Its fine, biscuit-coloured soil is scuffed with footprints, hoofprints and the snaky track of a bicycle.

'I think you'll find that this place has a very special atmosphere', says Keith, who is making his second visit. People say the same thing about the Hebridean island of Iona where, in the sixth century, another Christian missionary, St Columba, began his task of introducing Jesus Christ to the heathens of Scotland. I know Iona well, and it isn't hard to find the spirit moved by its shining shell-sand beaches, sheep-cropped machair and ancient relics. But the rational pathways of my mind have insisted that the island's history has little to do with its atmosphere, other than stirring the imagination. I've found Iona's sacred resonances in a hundred other places of natural beauty and quiet mood. If anything, I'm a pantheist – which doesn't mean I can't be moved by the exalted aspirations of people who, for all I know, do leave a kind of spiritual DNA on the landscapes and antiquities of holy sites.

What is truly blessed about the Moffat Mission is that it is a living shrine, and a welcoming one. My first impression is one of homeliness and informality; the charm of thatched roofs, weathered stones, casually distributed relics and unimposing storyboards without the self-importance of the heritage industry. Somewhere in the background of the mission grounds, among its tall trees and rambling paths, are a modern library and resource centre funded by one of Kuruman's mining companies; a theological seminary, conference rooms, the offices of its administrators. But the foreground belongs to the past; and, as we walk the short stretch of the Missionary Road, we find two white fingerposts with multiple digits pointing to the landmarks of two lives: Griquatown 190 km, Kolobeng 450 kms, Lake Ngami 1,004 km, Linyanti 1,070 km, Victoria Falls 1,445 km,

Luanda 3,080 km and – the terminus of one life – Shupanga 2,627 km. Mary Livingstone was 1,632 miles from her family home when she died.

We wander at will, the only visitors. Here is the Moffat homestead, the oldest building north of the Orange River, whitewashed and trig, where Ma-Mary raised eight children; there is the shadowy, well-stocked graveyard where she buried two more. Here is the thatched room where Livingstone stayed on his last visit to Kuruman and 'wrote his analysis of Setswana'; there is the hand printing press on which Robert Moffat experimented with his Setswana Bible and managed to print 2,000 copies. Here is a veteran ox-wagon, its hoops intact but missing its canvas canopy; there is the mission station's beating heart, the sturdy, L-shaped stone church which Moffat and Robert Hamilton, with a mason and workforce of Tswana, built with their own hands. They stood in swamps to cut reeds for the thatch and hauled hardwood over 200 miles to make the great beams for the rafters. (The timber was gifted by Chief Mzilikazi of the Matabele, who at that time was living with his tribe in the Marico Valley, in what is now North West Province.) It took them over twelve years.

To my European eyes, with their archive of Gothic spires, cupolas, stone-carving, stained glass and flying buttresses, the squat exterior with its tiny belfry looks unimpressive. To the people of the Kalahari, it was a monumental building, the largest they had ever seen. It was indeed their cathedral. And here, on 9 January 1845, the midsummer air heavy with the scent of syringa and mimosa, Mary Moffat married David Livingstone.

Never underestimate the potency of lions. Seven months before the wedding, the missionary was delivered to the missionary's daughter by an improbable Cupid: the big male lion which famously seized Livingstone by the shoulder and shook him 'as a terrier dog does a rat', splintering the bones of his upper arm. If not for the lion of Mabotsa, any ember of tenderness kindled on the journey from the Vaal River might well have been smothered in the months that followed. Shortly after the Moffats' ox-wagons and their mounted escort arrived back at Kuruman, Livingstone was on his way to the rescue of a new and distant community of imperilled souls. He and fellow missionary Roger Edwards had already reconnoitred a site at Mabotsa and made contact with the Bakgatla tribe, whose township of 400 huts and around 1,500 people was promising territory. They had now been authorised by the LMS to set up a mission station nearly 200 miles to the north-east, near what is now the border with Botswana. For all that he had registered an interest in the Moffats' eldest daughter, he and Mary might have met again only rarely and briefly ... if not for the lion of Mabotsa.

I have seen the Hollywood version of the tussle with the lion in the grounds of the David Livingstone Centre in Blantyre. An octogenarian called Ray Harryhausen, who is married to Diana Livingstone Bruce, the granddaughter of Agnes, the Livingstones' elder daughter, designed and funded a spectacular bronze sculpture which was installed on a circular plinth in 2004. The complex arrangement of four larger-than-lifesize figures – snarling beast, struggling Livingstone and terrified Tswana – has become hugely popular with children, who remember from their visits, if nothing else, that the explorer was attacked by a lion; just as I remember from my first visit, aged five, a dusty old lionskin and not much else. Never underestimate the charisma of lions.

Harryhausen has had a long and successful career in the film industry. Among cineastes, he is celebrated for his innovative work in special effects in the days before the digital revolution made anything possible in cinema technology. During the post-war years, he was Hollywood's leading 'stop-motion' animator – the man whose ingenious models brought myth and fantasy to life in films like *The 7th Voyage of Sinbad*, *One Million Years BC* and *Jason and the Argonauts*, for which his creations won an Oscar. His painstaking craft animated Cyclops, Medusa, sword-wielding skeletons, dinosaurs, sea monsters and other fearsome oddities. It is this talent and this history which inform the epic scale and extravagant drama of his design, which was executed by a sculptor called Gareth Knowles.

'I wanted to bring heroes back into fashion', Harryhausen has said of his generous gift. This he has done, but in the best Hollywood tradition at some cost to the facts. Livingstone himself graphically reported the details of the attack in *Missionary Travels*, although, as he said, he had meant to keep the story 'to tell my children when in my dotage'. The Bakgatla were troubled by a local pride which was bold enough to prey on their cattle not just by night but also by day, 'so unusual an occurrence that the people believed themselves bewitched – "given", as they said, "into the power of the lions by a neighbouring tribe"'. Partly to dispel such tomfoolery, but mainly to deal with the problem, Livingstone mounted a lion hunt with the village warriors, which ended in chaos with the pride escaping both his firepower and their spears, whereupon most of the hunting party dispersed.

On his way back to the village, Livingstone came upon a big male lion, possibly the pride patriarch, sitting on a rock about thirty yards away, screened by a small bush. He fired off both barrels of his gun. The animal didn't drop; and while he was reloading it charged, 'and we both came to the ground together'. There follows an assessment of his situation which I have often found comforting, whether watching lions pull down antelope from the safety of a vehicle or walking through the bush in their tracks. 'The shock produced a stupor similar to that which seems to be felt by a mouse after the first gripe of the cat. It caused a sort of dreaminess, in which there was no sense of pain nor feeling of terror, though I was quite conscious of all that was happening ... this placidity is probably produced in all animals killed by the carnivora; and if so, is a merciful provision of the Creator for lessening the pain of death.'

He was saved by Mebalwe, an elderly convert whom he had brought from Kuruman to teach at Mabotsa. Mebalwe grabbed a gun which then misfired but distracted the lion, which turned on this new adversary and savaged his thigh. Another man tried to help and was also attacked – then, to everyone's astonished relief, the frenzied animal suddenly collapsed. It had finally succumbed to the wounds which Livingstone's bullets had inflicted with his initial shots.

The Harryhausen tableau shows Livingstone upright, sagging only slightly under the weight of the lion while it grips his shoulder. His two Tswana companions sprawl on the ground in desperate poses. White man standing; black men at his feet. Its tactlessness makes me wince.

Livingstone's upper arm was badly damaged, the bone broken and the flesh mauled. In Scotland's Blantyre museum and Zambia's Livingstone museum, there are plaster casts of his fractured left humerus. The splintered bone, and its imperfect healing, was used to help identify his remains when his body was shipped to London in 1874. He had to supervise the setting of his own injury, he was immobile and in great pain for several weeks, the wounds became infected and persistently suppurated, and he was grudgingly and inadequately nursed by the wife of Roger Edwards. Even when he recovered enough to resume work on his new house at Mabotsa, he was seriously in need of rest and care, and injured his arm again while trying to catch a falling building-block. A few months after the lion attack he withdrew to Kuruman to convalesce. Within three weeks he was engaged to Mary Moffat.

Were they in love when she accepted his proposal beneath a wild almond tree in the garden of Kuruman? Everyone who has ever written about their marriage has an opinion, and the opinions seem to be gender-divided. Tim Jeal's is unequivocal: 'The marriage was one of convenience and both recognised this'. Jeal rests his case on the tone and content of some of Livingstone's letters, 'which treated his impending marriage with a matter-of-factness that seemed to border on indifference'. It's true that the bridegroom described his betrothed in terms which today would be considered insensitive and unflattering – as he would do some two years later, advising people who were to send dress material for his wife that 'she is a good deal of an African in complexion, a stout, stumpy body ...'.

The key sentence which Jeal and others employ to conclude that Livingstone's attachment to Mary was stolidly pragmatic is the one he wrote to a missionary friend when he got engaged: 'Mine is a matter-of-fact lady, a little thick, black-haired girl, sturdy and all I want'. These offhand words have been picked over by most of Livingstone's later biographers, who dwell on Mary's lack of beauty and stocky figure as if to claim that only good-looking people are worthy of love and capable of winning it (something clearly disputed by many a wedding photograph) and as if they have forgotten that the Victorian model of female allure did not start at size zero.

The women who have written about Mary show more imagination and flexibility in their analyses of the courtship – recognising, more than anything, that Livingstone was an austere, buttoned-up, working-class Scot who wrote more fluently than he spoke but was still reluctant to commit his feelings to paper. This was something he seemed to overcome with the confidence of maturity; and, often when writing of his wife and children, his emotional language became not only extravagant but also melodramatic. To lose them, he wrote, when they left for the United Kingdom, was like 'tearing out his bowels', while his farewell to Mary in Cape Town at the start of the Zambezi Expedition was 'like tearing the heart out of one'.

But although he was happy to banter in his letters to college friends when he announced his engagement, his formality when writing to fiancée, in-laws or even his own family was entirely typical of his age, as it was in any public forum. Throughout *Missionary Travels* he refers to Mary as 'Mrs Livingstone' – a form of address between husband and wife which today strikes us as pompous and remote but which was routine for Victorians.

This is understood by Parsons, Healey and Forster. 'The marriage,' says Janet Wagner Parsons, 'if not the health and happiness of Mary, would survive the scrutiny of sceptics, while few would realise the depth of their devotion.' Edna Healey maintains that Livingstone knew he could never find a better wife, while Margaret Forster insists that it insults them both to question that their relationship 'lacked genuine mutual attraction'. She argues it was not in Livingstone's nature to take any action, including getting married, which lacked conviction, even passion; and, in her comment on his pen portrait of his future wife, she points out that, at the very least, the phrase 'all I want' is ambiguous. 'It has been taken to mean "not up to much but she'll have to do", whereas if the emphasis is put on the "all" it can just as well be read as "everything I want" (which is how I read it).' She quotes one of the letters he wrote to Mary when he returned to Mabotsa, when the prospect of his coming wedding seemed to stir more urgent emotions. 'I wish I could embrace you', he confesses in one.

Elsewhere, reinforcing the utilitarian case for his marriage, Livingstone makes a sober, sanctimonious statement to the director of the London Missionary Society, in which he concludes it is his 'duty to enter into the marriage relation ... not without much serious consideration and earnest prayer ... and if I have not deceived myself I was in some measure guided by a desire that the Divine glory might be promoted in my increased usefulness'. But a few weeks later he is writing gaily to Mary to remind her father to apply for the licence, adding, almost recklessly: 'If he forgets then we shall make it legal ourselves. What right or portion has the state church in me? None whatever. If they don't grant it willingly let them keep their licence. We shall license ourselves.' Not the sentiments of a bridegroom drearily determined to see things through in the interests of missionary service and domestic convenience; nor was his admission to college friends that he was so overwhelmed words almost failed him, but it would comfort them to know that he had become 'as great a fool as any of you'.

A fool in love, by the sound of it. And what of Mary? She was 23, and by all accounts kind, good-natured and even-tempered. After the Moffats returned from the United Kingdom she had settled into the life for which she'd been trained, formally and informally, from childhood. She taught in the mission school and energetically practised the skills essential to isolated mission life. She knew how to butcher and dry meat, preserve fruit and vegetables, bake bread, make candles, soap and clothes, improvise remedies, manage servants and barter with the Tswana. She was not an extrovert; she was self-effacing and shy, but she knew her worth, and knew it was valued by her parents and other mission families. 'To be of use to everyone was her personal mission,' writes Janet Wagner Parsons, 'and she had long since gained the love and respect of the Africans among whom she lived and worked.' At this stage in her life Mary was not the victim she later became.

Livingstone was almost awe-struck by her expert Setswana, which he struggled to master. It would be easy to assume he calculated that this and her other accomplishments would be useful to him; and perhaps he did. But that doesn't exclude the possibility that he also respected and loved her for them, or that he was physically attracted to his 'little thick, black-haired girl'. Was she attracted to him? Her replies to his letters from Mabotsa have been lost. Once again, Mary becomes a phantom in her own story; but, as she walked in the mission grounds with the intense young man, religious ardour blazing in his dark eyes, there's no reason to doubt that his attentions may have excited her. She was no stranger to the heady idea of romantic love; she had grown up with her parents' love story, and perhaps reached out for their example in a tentative court-ship which even by today's standards soon became a whirlwind romance. Mary Smith and Robert Moffat waited three years to begin their lives together; Mary Moffat and David Livingstone waited eight months.

Without Mary's testimony, despite the conflicting accounts of the bride-groom's attitude, we can only speculate on what the couple felt as they stood before the Reverend Prosper Lemue in the church at Kuruman. (They were married not by Robert Moffat, but by a neighbouring mis-sionary from the Paris Evangelical Society.) There is consensus in one area only. For all the long gaps in their life together and the hurt these caused Mary, everyone agrees that the union swiftly became one of profound mutual affection – something which couples in enduring marriages often take for granted and only fully appreciate when one partner dies, espe-cially if the loss is premature and unexpected. 'I loved her when I married her,' Livingstone wrote after Mary's death, 'and the longer I lived with her the more I loved her.'

Loved and desired her. During the years they spent together, Mary was annually pregnant. Despite the heat, dust, discomfort, danger, illness and exhaustion of their years in Africa and the instability of all the later inter-ruptions, their sex life remained vigorous to the end; there were even signs, hinted at by Dr John Kirk, that during their final reunion on the Zambezi she had again conceived.

Shortly before he died, I discussed their relationship with Andrew Ross, author of *David Livingstone: Mission and Empire* (Hambledon and London, 2002). At one point, the elderly cleric hesitated, perhaps judging that the remark he was about to make was unbecoming to a minister of the Kirk. Then he said bluntly: 'They couldn't keep their hands off each other'. Something, he added, which made Livingstone's Victorian biogra-phers deeply uncomfortable.

Like the syringa trees planted by Robert Moffat, the almond tree, or much of its trunk, is still there. The life of the tree was extinguished by lightning, but a substantial stump nearly five feet high survives. It has the rough elegance of a wood sculpture, and a weathered brass plate with an inscription: 'Under this almond tree David Livingstone proposed to Mary Moffat. They were married in this church 9th January 1845.' I can't help noticing that the engraver has given the groom's name larger letters and greater prominence than that of the bride – as history has always done, reasonably enough. But, on the occasion of their engagement, history had yet to be made by Livingstone, and Mary had yet to discover that Africa and ambition would become her bedfellows and, in time, her unassailable love rivals. It may be that there was a coded warning in his pre-nuptial letter of advice from Mabotsa: 'Let your affection be towards Him much more than towards me, and kept by His mighty power & grace I hope I shall never give you cause to regret that you have given me a part'.

There was at least one period in her life when she *did* come to regret that she had given 'a part' – if not to the man, then his mission. Those lost letters which may have been destroyed by self-appointed guardians of the Livingstone reputation, or perhaps by Livingstone himself, almost certainly put in writing the misery of her years alone in the United Kingdom, when her faith became undermined by her feelings of abandonment, and when she was known to make resentful remarks about the lot of missionary wives.

For the moment, however, all was delight at Kuruman, where the almond tree is now the centrepiece of the 'Love Garden' – so called not to celebrate human love in sickly theme-park style but to press home the scriptural message at the gate. Here, Livingstone said, he learned the truth of the words of Jesus: 'There is no man that hath left house, or brethren, or sisters, or father, or mother, or wife, or children, or lands, for my sake, and the gospel's, but he shall receive an hundredfold now in this time, houses, and brethren, and sisters, and mothers, and children, and lands ... and in the world to come eternal life'.

There were indeed houses, brethren, sisters, children and an outspoken mother-in-law to follow in rapid succession over the next few years, not to mention lands whose discovery Livingstone claimed for his own. The Moffat parents were enthusiastic about the match. Despite Livingstone's initial reservations about the achievements of Kuruman, he and Robert

Moffat were strongly taken with each other. They came from similar backgrounds, and in the nineteenth century there were many working-class Scots like them, driven by new opportunities in industry and commerce or, in their case, inspired by religious faith to educate and improve themselves well beyond the expectations of their social rank. Livingstone's respect and affection for his father-in-law, who outlived him and helped carry his coffin into Westminster Abbey, lasted his lifetime. Moffat saw his younger self in the younger man, who had all the energy and enterprise to build on his own example in the mission field. Ma-Mary, although impressed by her new son-in-law's piety, and happy that her daughter would remain near them, was soon to become more sceptical.

'Many things she admired in David Livingstone,' writes her biographer, Mora Dickson, 'but not all. She thought him wild, unpredictable – which he was. She was never sure of the purity of his motives when the urge to uproot came upon him. Although he loved and needed his wife and family, he retained the instincts of a bachelor and she did not hesitate to rebuke him when she considered him neglectful of his duty to his family or his mission.'

The rebukes came later. The newlyweds spent the first few weeks of their married life in the Oasis of the Kalahari, then began the twelve-day ox-wagon trek to Mabotsa, which they reached at the end of March before the land began to wither beneath the shrivelling winds of autumn.

The Reverend Kudzani S. B. M. Ndebele, in his mid-thirties and built like a prop forward, lives in the present and plans for the future. He isn't expecting us; but the new director of the Moffat Mission, who has held the position for only a few months and could probably do without surprise visitors, receives us courteously when we track him down in his office. Again, the totemic name of Scotland opens doors: 'I'm going to be in your country in 2010 for the theological conference in Edinburgh', he tells me. 'Also, our church, the United Congregational Church of South Africa, has been invited by your United Free Church to send a youth delegation to Scotland in 2011. But of course you will know of these events.'

I don't have the heart to tell him that the indifferent secular world I inhabit pays little attention to the international outreach of the ecumenical cause, or to the invisible threads which bind the Christian churches together to reinforce the fabric of their faith. It wasn't always thus. When I was a young journalist on the *Scotsman* newspaper in the 1970s, the news desk annually assigned two reporters, sometimes three, to cover the General Assembly of the Church of Scotland during its week-long conference in May. Digests of the Assembly debates on internal, national and world affairs, often of high intellectual and rhetorical standard, daily filled a page of the broadsheet newspaper. Today, the press takes a meagre interest in the opinions of the Kirk or the activities of any other church unless it has scandal, sensation or divisive controversy to report, like the ordaining of gay ministers, or sectarianism in public life.

'Your name', I remark, when I've explained my interest in Kuruman. 'You must come from Matabeleland. You can't be called Ndebele and not belong to the people of Mzilikazi and Lobengula.'

The director, who has degrees from the University of Zimbabwe and the University of KwaZulu-Natal, looks amused by this misguidedly arch reference to his warrior forebears. 'Yes, I'm Zimbabwean. I come from Plumtree, just over the Botswana border. Let's take a walk and I will show you the church, where people still get married, and tell you a little about the work of the Moffat Mission today.'

The grounds and gardens have been scoured of shadows by the hard light of afternoon. The watercourse dug by Robert Moffat and lined with clay has been replaced by a concrete channel; and the vegetable garden, growing cabbages and onions, might be a British allotment. Few of the trees are in full leaf; and, in the confusing way of southern Africa's seasonal cycle, which is turning towards early spring, the land looks wintry but the air feels hot. As we stand in the sun, the Reverend Ndebele also warms to his themes: the training of ministers at the mission's Kalahari Desert School of Theology, education and leadership issues within the community, child literacy and early learning programmes and – pursuing the example of Robert Moffat 'to this day' – agricultural development programmes.

We move into the church, which, like churches everywhere, is dim and cool, with walls thicker than most to repel the desert heat – massive enough 'to withstand a cannonading', as Livingstone observed when he first saw them. Whitewashed plaster, age-dark rafters and pews, a commanding stone pulpit and the famous cow-dung floor, which has an undersea look about it: the colour of sea grass seen through deep water. I slip off my sandals and test its surface: smooth and cold as polished marble, balm to my overheated feet. 'The dung is renewed and mixed with mud and the floor replastered twice a year', explains the director. 'The ladies do it, and keep the shine bright. It's hard work, but they do it for God.'

On one wall is a notice requesting visitors NOT to ring the bell (which is connected from belfry to nave with a tempting rope-pull), and on another a roll of honour: the thirty names of all the London Missionary Society staff, two of them women, who served at Kuruman between 1816 and 1966. At the top of the list is gentle, self-effacing Robert Hamilton, whose reputation has been eclipsed by Moffat's, but who arrived in the Kalahari before him, got things under way, helped build the church and remained at the mission for nearly forty years until he died of old age in 1851.

Robert Moffat's fifty-year service from 1820 is noted (in 1870, with great reluctance, he and Ma-Mary returned to the United Kingdom) along with David Livingstone's brief commitment between 1841 and 1843. But almost a century passes before an African name appears among the catalogue of English ones: Maphakela Lekalake, 1911-47, the Tswana people's first ordained minister, who was 97 when he died and, as a boy, knew Livingstone. He is remembered elsewhere on the mission station. The accommodation complex, which sleeps thirty and has meeting rooms, dining room and kitchen, is called the Maphakela Centre.

The light is losing its cutting edge as we say thanks and goodbye to Kuruman's helpful director and staff and walk back down the Missionary Road to the Land Rover. From the 1850s to the 1870s, as new generations of LMS disciples foraged for souls in the interior, the Missionary Road was pushed up country as far as Shoshong, once the seat of the founder of the Khama dynasty and the site of another LMS station. In 1902 the Bangwato tribe of Khama the Great moved their capital to Serowe when their water supply dried up. Today both towns lie well north of Gaborone, Botswana's purpose-built capital, near the highway to the Zimbabwe border and Matabeleland.

South-west of the capital, not far from the border with South Africa, is Kolobeng, the mission station which shakily secured the Livingstones' family life for five years. To reach it we pass through two places whose names tell their stories – a town called Hotazel and the border-crossing at McCarthy's Rest – and attach ourselves to the 1,000-mile lifeline of the Trans-Kalahari Highway. You can drive across the Kalahari on tar roads these days. Its vastness has shrunk and its challenge has dwindled. A long-range fuel tank and the Shell Tourist Map of Botswana will get you from east to west, from Namibia to South Africa. There are hard surfaces to take you northwards, too, from Lobatse and Gaborone to Francistown and Maun, gateway to the Okavango Delta; and to the Boteti River, which was once called the Zouga, where Mary Livingstone gave birth to her fourth child. But the stupendous sandy space which the Tswana called 'the thirstland' has not lost its mystery for me, or diminished the urge to follow the Livingstones across it to Lake Ngami and beyond.

1 *Mary Livingstone in her late thirties.*

2 *Signed photograph of David Livingstone, taken after he returned from his transcontinental journey a national hero.*

SHUPANGA HOUSE
Where Mrs. Livingstone Died.

Mrs. Livingstone's Grave

Two Contemporary Sketches. Probably
The Only Record That Remains

3 *Shupanga House and Mary's grave beneath the baobab tree, sketched by a contemporary artist.*

4 *Beginning at the end: Mary Livingstone's grave today, with Chupanga church in the background and our flowers on her tomb.*

5 *The Livingstone family in 1857, the year they were reunited in London after Livingstone's return from his transcontinental journey. Left to right the children are Oswell, Thomas, Agnes and Robert. Anna Mary is not yet born.*

6 *Kuruman Church, where David Livingstone married Mary, oldest child of Robert and Mary Moffat of Kuruman Mission, on 9 January 1845.*

7 Traffic on the
Ngami trail.

8 The communal nest of
the sociable weaver on
a convenient man-made
'tree'.

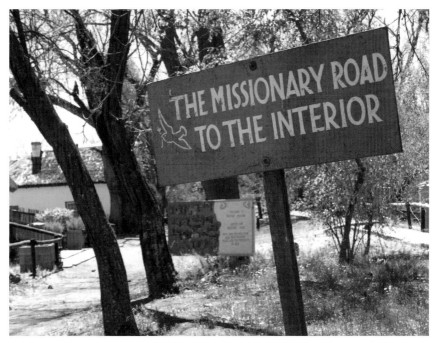

9 *The entrance to Kuruman Moffat Mission, with the Moffats' homestead in the background.*

10 *The memorial at Mabotsa, site of Livingstone's first mission and Mary's first married home.*

11 *Alfred Piet shows me around the foundations of the Livingstone homestead at Kolobeng.*

12 *Keith Rampton and I meet the Kalahari meerkats of the Makgadikgadi Pans.*

13 *Chapman's Baobab: a stupendous landmark and welcome camp site for the Livingstones in the Kalahari. The explorer carved his initials on the trunk.*

14 *Safari guide Jeff Gush at the Boteti River ford which he believes was used by the Livingstones.*

15 *Synchronised sisters. These two lionesses relaxing in the early morning sun were part of a pride of seven I photographed in Moremi Wildlife Reserve, near the route to the Chobe River.*

16 *The four surviving Livingstone children. Left to right: Oswell, Agnes, Anna Mary and Tom, photographed around 1865. By then their mother and brother Robert were dead and their father had left, or was about to leave, for Africa for the last time. They never saw him again.*

17 *Robert, their oldest child, aged about 15.*

11

Marriage, Monuments and More about Lions

'The woman is the glory of the man'

From all that's known of Mary Livingstone when she was in her twenties, she was not an imaginative woman. 'Matter-of-fact', said her husband. 'No romantic.' The surface personality described by those few contemporaries who bother to mention Mary, and by Livingstone's biographers, is steadfast and solid: a good woman but (goes the sub-text) drab and dull. I've often asked myself if this is the reason why her life, which in many ways is a tormented love story, and which has all the allure of exotic locations and life-threatening adventures, has never been turned into a novel or a film. Some things even Hollywood finds daunting. Who would play the leading role? How could she be presented as romantic heroine or glamorous adventurer?

Yet, in later life, she began to question the faith which had been hard-wired into her psyche since infancy. To me, this suggests that a searching intelligence was trapped inside the carapace of obedience and reserve with which her upbringing had equipped her. Livingstone himself was not only highly intelligent but often imaginative, with an ability to empathise with the Tswana and the Makololo who became his closest supporters and companions; it seems unlikely that he would not have found something in his wife to reflect these qualities, even if he never expressed his thoughts on mission strategies or his more radical ideas for Africa in his letters to her. Tim Jeal takes for granted a 'disparity in their respective intellectual gifts' (and almost certainly there was), but then goes on to make something of a deductive leap: 'Later he would confine his serious thinking to letters written to more famous men, and Mary would never be told about his plans for commerce and colonisation'.

How do we know? How do we know what Livingstone discussed with Mary in their private moments? How do we know how much of his germinating vision for Africa he confided in his wife? Not by letter, perhaps, but over the supper table, or in the intimacy of pillow talk. After all, 'In our intercourse in private,' as he once reflected, 'there was more than would be thought by some a decorous amount of merriment and play'. If merriment and play, why not also dreams and ambitions? Theories and ideas? As ever, Mary's version remains adrift in a sea of speculation.

The word Mabotsa means 'marriage feast'. Even the slowest imagination must have quickened at the prospect of starting married life in a place so propitiously named. By the time Mary arrived at the first of the three houses which, in the space of seven years, were the only homes she would ever call her own, the building was complete. It had stone walls to waist height, where layers of dried mud took over to roof height, and a thick thatched roof. A European–Tswana architectural hybrid. It was capacious and well built; and, in the scrupulous manner of her mother's example, the young bride was swiftly able to provide her husband with clean bed linen, mended clothes and regular meals, not to mention marital comforts of the kind which may have inspired Livingstone to describe the first months of their Mabotsa life as 'the sweet time'. With the zeal of the convert, he wrote to a friend: 'The woman is the glory of the man. I am very contented and very happy in my connection.'

It's likely the couple were less inhibited than many God-fearing Victorian virgins about exploring their sexuality. The naked body, male or female, held no mystery for either of them. Livingstone, of course, had a medical degree, and Mary had been raised among people who had their own sexual taboos, but nudity wasn't one of them. Both may have lacked experience, but they would be very familiar with the nature of the sexual act. And from then on at least one if not both showed great enthusiasm for it. We have little idea, as usual, whether Mary welcomed and responded to her husband's sexual energy, as her cultural and religious values would require her to tolerate it; but now that he was married abstinence – even restraint – was not in Livingstone's nature. Seven years later, when he was finding reasons for dispatching his family to the United Kingdom, one of his less plausible and more extraordinary excuses (offered in a letter to the Reverend Arthur Tidman of the LMS) was that separation from his wife was the only way to prevent 'the frequent confinements which, not withstanding the preaching of Dr Malthus and Miss Martineau, periodically prevail'.[1]

---

1 Thomas Malthus, who gave his name to Malthusian economics, was the English scholar and clergyman who believed that population growth should be controlled, if necessary, by sexual abstinence. Harriet Martineau, often called the first female sociologist, maintained that no analysis of society was complete without an examination of women's lives, marriage and children – a novel idea in Victorian Britain. The theories of both were in wide circulation in the mid-nineteenth century.

After she left her Salem school, Mary had trained as an infant teacher in Cape Town. Her course was cut short by the Moffat family's long visit to the United Kingdom, but when she returned she took up this role at Kuruman. She was soon running the new school at Mabotsa, which also served as church and meeting house. Although they were fascinated by their first white woman – and although their parents were instructed by their chief to send them to school – the children of the Bakgatla had other duties: herding, tending crops, caring for younger siblings, collecting firewood and water. The number of Mary's pupils fluctuated randomly between five and fifty. Her reading and sewing classes for women also suffered from the demands of the field and domestic work in which many African women labour to this day, but in any case her plans for the Mabotsa school soon became unsustainable – not because she gave them up, but because her husband was again restless, couldn't co-operate with his fellow missionary, Roger Edwards, and quarrelled badly with him. Within months, he was petitioning the LMS to support his latest project, which required a move even deeper into the interior, to a place called Chonuane.

Livingstone had met Sechele, paramount chief of the Bakwena tribe. The meeting was momentous; it was to determine the next few years of their personal lives and influence the policies of the LMS and the Cape's colonial government. Sechele is a colossal figure in the history of his time and place, active in the region's fractious intertribal politics and in the wars of attrition between Boer settlers, Tswana tribes and British expansionists. In time, he became a unifying force among the Tswana and can be legitimately described as one of the founding fathers of Bechuanaland, the British protectorate which eventually became Botswana. These days, among Europeans, he is more glibly remembered as 'Livingstone's only convert'. As Mary began to look forward to the birth of her first child at Mabotsa, her husband began to build a new house at Chonuane. Here, some forty miles to the north, Sechele had settled with his people.

Today, both mission stations are scattered stones, their empty sites marked by the rugged cairns and memorial plaques of South Africa's Historical Monuments Commission. They lie among wooded hills and rolling veld between the commercial centre of Zeerust, near Mafeking, and the Botswana border. The rural economy of this quiet, friendly region of North West Province is a mixture of cattle ranches, mixed farms, orange orchards and small-scale mineral mines. Both Zeerust and Mafeking were once villages whose Tswana names meant 'place of stones' and 'dusty place', and stood on the route of the Missionary Road. In the closing decades of the nineteenth century, this route had little to do with Christian proselytising. It had long been used for trading and transporting ivory and skins as much as for preaching. From its informal terminus at Shoshonge other wagon trails ran to Ngamiland, on the edge of the Okavango Delta, and to Matabeleland and the Zambezi. In the 1880s and 1890s it became strategically important to British interests, wedging a stake of land between German South West Africa (now Namibia) and the Transvaal Republic.

Cecil Rhodes called this sliver of territory the 'Suez Canal', a conduit from the Cape Colony to Central Africa. Its final alignment as a major trade route was confirmed when a railway line was built from the diamond mines of Kimberley via Mafeking to Francistown, now Botswana's second city, and Bulawayo. The line is one of the links in the uncompleted 'Cape to Cairo' railway which Rhodes set in motion. He imagined that a rail corridor between southern and northern extremities, passing through Britain's African possessions, would give the British unassailable control of much of the continent. Most of the line is still in operation today, although there is a large gap between Uganda and northern Sudan, while the stretch between Bulawayo and Victoria Falls is often cited as one of the world's great railway journeys. The irony of Rhodes' hegemonic vision is that it can be traced back to the tracks of those who arrived in southern Africa to liberate its people from the bondage of their paganism.

Mafeking, now the capital of North West Province, is a famous name in British military history. Here, during the Second Anglo–Boer War, a 2,000-strong British force resisted the efforts of 6,000 Boers to take the town in a siege that lasted 217 days. The British commander was Robert Baden-Powell, who recruited a corps of about a dozen boys to act as scouts and couriers: the prototype of the Scout movement. The Relief of Mafeking in May 1900 was a triumph for the British and a humiliation for the Boers in one of our least glorious foreign adventures. I have never forgotten the family history of an Afrikaans woman, a former major in the South African Army, who was my guide for eight days in Namibia. Her grandmother had been interned in one of the tented camps which were part of the British campaign's scorched-earth policy, implemented by Lord Kitchener. 'My grandmother could not say the words English or British', she told me. 'She couldn't bring herself to speak the name of the people she considered inhuman.' Salome's grandmother had seen her own and her neighbours' farmhouses burned, livestock slaughtered, wells poisoned and fields contaminated with salt. In the camp, she watched many of her friends die from neglect, insanitary conditions, lack of medical care and malnutrition.

Over 26,000 Boer women and children lost their lives in internment from hunger or disease. Thousands of black Africans, who were not the enemy but were held separately in similar camps to clear the land of those who worked it, also died. Nobody has bothered to record how many. The British were not the first nation to intern civilians, but the British gave the name to concentration camps. The scale of their casualties was much smaller and their aim different from the infamous camps of the Third Reich, but to the Afrikaner the name strikes a chill which pre-dates the Nazis.

Mabotsa is easy to find; Chonuane less so. The site of the first of Mary's married homes has an open aspect in a wide, shallow bowl of hills. The valley is well watered and lightly populated. It has the random look of much of rural Africa, where the land is communal and fields rarely have fences, and a scatter of cinderblock houses and water towers are landmarks of progress. On the valley floor the woodland is thin, depleted by decades of domestic fires or cleared for small-scale cultivation; but the hills which were once alive with game, where the lion of Mabotsa attacked Livingstone, are still rich in trees.

The mission-station site is enclosed within a tall fence with a locked gate. 'The parish pastor keeps the key', Keith has told me. 'When I phoned him he said to drop by his house.' The parish pastor is not at home, but his adult sons produce the key and point us in the right direction.

There is nobody around. The ground area of the newlyweds' home can still be traced in fragments of foundations. The house that Livingstone built – some say to impress his in-laws, although he'd started building it before he proposed to Mary – was almost pretentious for its purpose and context. It was unusually large, with bedroom, parlour, study and glazed windows. He had brought the glass up country from Kuruman. Today, its centrepiece is the Historical Monuments Commission memorial, a hefty, stepped, square-cornered edifice about ten feet high, built with local stone from the ruins. The verdigrised plaque says simply: 'THIS MARKS THE SITE OF LIVINGSTONE'S FIRST MISSIONARY STATION, 1843–1846', the English repeated in Afrikaans and Setswana. A mature acacia, seeded long ago in the shell of the house, has been left standing over the monument like a protective canopy.

Mary was almost certainly happy here. Livingstone and Edwards had built water sluices to carry water to their houses and gardens, and Mabotsa had the potential to be another Kuruman. Mary planted lettuces, turnips, carrots, onions and 'scotch kale', and glimpsed the possibility of recreating her childhood home without the interference – well-meaning but officious – of her mother. Despite her husband's estrangement from Edwards and his wife, the couple were not isolated from European company. They often had visitors, some of whom they had already met at Kuruman: William Cotton Oswell, Thomas Steele and Frank Vardon, officers of the British Army in India who had taken leave to explore and hunt in this exhilarating game-rich country, so much emptier of people and wilder in nature than India. Mary enjoyed entertaining and impressed the adventurous young men with her accomplished housekeeping. Mannerly and well educated, they respected the courage and perseverance of the couple in their self-imposed exile from everything the sportsmen would eventually reclaim in the United Kingdom. The Livingstones were to name two of their children after Oswell and Thomas Steele.

But no sooner was she settled than Mary had to come to terms with upheaval. She would enjoy the produce of her vegetable garden for one season only. Livingstone was determined to press ahead with his plan to transfer his attentions to Sechele and the Bakwena, even if it meant building a new house at Chonuane at his own expense and the expense of the Bakgatla, whom he considered 'dry bones indeed', unreceptive to the Gospel. Sechele was more than interested in welcoming him to his township, initially for pragmatic reasons. He had resettled his people four times in four years to avoid raids by the Matabele, and found he could not trust the Boers, who were rapidly becoming a new enemy. He felt he might do better looking for protection from the British, especially their missionaries. This shrewd, open-minded and exceptional man had an instinctive appetite for learning, and was quick to appreciate that they had much that was useful to teach him. He was also interested in acquiring guns.

A horse was procured to allow Livingstone to commute between Mabotsa and Chonuane, and he was considerate enough to use the animal to gallop south to his wife when she felt unwell (which she often did during her pregnancies) or was alarmed by the lions which came down from the hills to prospect for livestock around the mission station. She had little in common with Mrs Edwards, who was a sloppy housekeeper; and their relationship was also strained by their husbands' mutual antagonism, inflamed by professional jealousy. Roger Edwards felt, with some justice, that in his dealings with Kuruman and the LMS Livingstone took all the credit for Mabotsa – something he was to do in his later career as explorer, when William Cotton Oswell generously allowed him to accept an award from the National Geographic Society for registering the 'discovery' of Lake Ngami in 1849. In fact, the expedition had been funded by Oswell and was jointly undertaken by Livingstone, Oswell and the latter's companion, Mungo Murray – the first three Europeans to cross the Kalahari and reach the lake on its northern side.

With her husband increasingly preoccupied with building and preaching forty miles away, Mary was lonely. During one of his absences, her sister Ann arrived from Kuruman to keep her company, travelling as usual by ox-wagon. A. Z. Fraser, in her 1913 memoir *Livingstone and Newstead*, writes with awe that the young woman 'travelled quite alone, save for a native maid and the two Kaffir waggon boys, and it is noteworthy that the only danger thought of in those days was that from lions and other wild beasts. Danger from man there was none – rather a melancholy reflection upon our boasted civilisation of present times, when few women would care to attempt such a solitary and unprotected journey.'

It was to be Ann's only visit. On the return journey, there was a drama which discouraged any further excursions to Mabotsa. In a letter, their brother John described what happened: 'The oxen had been unyoked and were grazing near the waggon, a fire had been lighted and the kettle put on, and the tired travellers were sitting in the peaceful twilight. A sudden rush was heard ... and one of them [the oxen] fell with a lion on his back, not fifty yards from where Miss Moffat was sitting.'

Ann and her escorts spent the night in the wagon listening to the predator dismember and consume its kill.

Lion. Never underestimate the magnetism of Africa's wildlife superstar – and never overestimate its menacing reputation. In most daytime situations, the lion is anything but lion-hearted; and naturally Livingstone had something to say about that. 'Nothing that I have ever learned of the lion would lead me to attribute to it either the ferocious or noble character ascribed to it elsewhere. He chiefly preys upon defenceless creatures ...' And he jauntily describes what happens when you meet a lion on foot: 'If he is encountered in the daytime he turns slowly round after first gazing a second or two, walks as slowly away for a dozen paces looking over his shoulder, quickens his step to a trot till he thinks himself out of sight, and then bounds off like a greyhound. As a rule, there is not the smallest danger of a lion which is unmolested attacking man in the light.'

As a rule, this is true. The lion attacked Livingstone because he attacked it, although there are other occasions when you don't want to tangle with the fraudulent king of the beasts. I once did a short field guiding course in the Masai Mara and was taught how to approach game on foot by Matt

Gurney, the strapping, Kenyan-born son of a British medical missionary. Matt's personal *bête noire* was the lone buffalo bull, and he told us his heart always thumped when he walked through croton bushes, 'where the grumpy old boys like to snooze'. But he was comfortable with cats. One day, walking on the savanna, we spotted five lions about 300 yards away, lounging under their parasol of preference, the flat-topped acacia. 'Shall we try to get a bit closer?' invited Matt. We'd taken only a few steps when he signalled 'Stop' and quietly told us to retreat. Two of the lions had become active – the pride male and one of the females.

'They're mating,' said Matt, 'one of three occasions when you should never approach lion on foot. The male's hormones will be firing him up. The other two circumstances are when they're on a kill and, of course, if there are cubs around. A lioness with cubs is a fearless and fearsome animal.'

I've had other encounters with lions on foot, and they have done exactly what Livingstone said they would do, except faster; most memorably in Zambia's Luangwa Valley, where I was camping and walking with Deb Tittle. This handsome, athletic Englishwoman has become one of the industry's leading guides, and, in the seraphic hour of sunrise, backed up by Deb's rifle and an armed scout, we went looking for the neighbour- hood pride. We had heard them kill during the night: a tragic groan, the last gasp of an antelope, followed by the usual snarling squabbles over the table plan. We found most of the females and juveniles relaxing with full bellies on a bank of the Luangwa River, and watched them for a bit as they watched us; they were distant enough for us all to be undisturbed. But Deb wasn't satisfied. 'Let's go and find the male.'

The male found us. As we walked along the edge of a shallow gully there was a sudden gruff grunt, almost a woof. 'Look-look-look!' urged Deb. I swung round just in time to see the big cat leap up the opposite bank, mane bouncing, hastily followed by two of his ladies. All three charged off into the bush as if we had tied firecrackers to their tails. They had been lying unseen in the bed of the gully, perhaps fifteen yards from our path, and had heard or smelled us before we heard and saw them; hard to say which party was more surprised. 'That male is a big girl's blouse', com- mented Deb, as excitement subsided all round.

On the Masai plains of Kenya and Tanzania, Maasai youths were once obliged to spear a lion before they could start the process of circum- cision and apprenticeship which would admit them to the warrior class, *il murran*. This has now been outlawed in East Africa, but any herder or *moran* who does kill a lion (either to defend himself or his livestock, which is allowed) acquires celebrity status; so, in some areas, a certain amount of covert lion-hunting still goes on, with or without legitimate excuse. The big cats recognise and seem to carry in their race memory the image of the Maasai hunter, his tall staff and spear and knife-blade silhouette, and respect it. Many of the camps and lodges of the plains employ Maasai as night watchmen because, as I was once told by a Kikuyu guide, 'the lions know they are Maasai and run away'.

There are no occasions at all when you'd want to walk into any lion at night, when darkness arms even the faint hearts of big girls' blouses. After sunset, the lion undergoes a personality change, cutting a swathe of fear through the quivering bush with the night vision, acute reflexes and surging adrenaline of an expert hunter. Once, following a pride on the Busanga Plains of Zambia, I sat in an open game vehicle while a lioness crouched so close to the chassis I could have touched her. She was using the Land Cruiser as cover to stalk puku, a common antelope in Zambia. To her, I was just part of the vehicle, neither prey nor threat; but she knew I was there. She glanced up, and by the light of the moon we exchanged looks. From an arm's length away, I gazed into her yellow eyes with their round, very human pupils. Her expression was neither hostile nor friendly, merely neutral, but my breathing stopped.

The number of safari tourist deaths from lion is so tiny it can barely be measured statistically; but attacks do happen once or twice a decade, usually because the tourist has done something insanely stupid, like get out of a self-drive car to take photographs at close quarters. Otherwise, lion attacks are freak events which almost invariably happen at night and pass into the campfire repertoire of safari guides: the woman at the luxury lodge in South Africa who left the open-air dining area to fetch a sweater from her room and didn't come back; the gap-year student who was dragged from his open tent on a walking safari in Zimbabwe; and the fisherman at a public campsite beside the Zambezi who took an early-evening shower and lost his life.

These rare holiday disasters are on record, and everyone remembers them, sometimes too vividly. There was a night in northern Tanzania, in a wilderness area near the Serengeti, when our small camp attracted the attention of a hunting posse of lions. Our torches picked out four sets of eyes as they grumped and woofed in the darkness beyond the circle of firelight, imposing their presence on these intruders who had walked into their territory. They soon sloped off to look for more familiar mammals; but an hour later, as I was falling asleep in my flimsy dome tent, the pride male returned, gave an explosive roar to announce 'I'm back', and plumped himself down beneath a tree on the edge of camp – something I observed, trembling, through two inches of unzipped tent flap. Our escort of four Maasai warriors didn't seem to have the required impact on their historic foe, who sat there placidly for twenty minutes, watching with interest as they hefted spears, stoked the campfire, fiddled with bows and talked jumpily among themselves. Perhaps the shadows obscured their identity. Then he heard his women make a kill, and sauntered off to supper. Eventually, amazingly, I went back to sleep.

The next morning, our chief guide, who had not left his tent despite being the only man with a gun, dismissed the lion's visit with the remark: 'Best to leave him alone. He was just curious.' Yes, all cats are curious and have a special fondness for dark, enclosed spaces. The lion that enters a tent when it finds it open is not necessarily looking to attack; but, when the occupant panics, screams and lashes out, there is mayhem. The lesson: always sleep with your tent flap closed, and remind yourself you are there by choice, a voluntary thrill-seeker, rarely at risk. If you are a rural African living and working in lion country, the dangers are greater.

The man-eating lion has acquired almost mythic status, but did and does exist. Since the 1990s, a number of delinquent lions have been causing problems in southern Tanzania, the country with the largest number of the cats living outside protected areas. Misconceptions about man-eaters persist. The serial man-eater doesn't creepily acquire 'a taste for human flesh'. It turns away from its usual diet of ungulates for reasons which can be summed up as opportunism combined with learned behaviour combined with special circumstances, such as a scarcity of prey species; nor do man-eaters always suffer from disabilities or wounds which handicap their hunting skills. Research has shown that only 14 per cent of repeat man-eaters have fallen into this category, while most serial killers were in their prime.

It's true that tooth problems sometimes alter the predator's behaviour, along with scavenging on human remains left by battles or natural disasters. The first thing the lion has to do is lose its fear of humankind, and the second thing is to discover that an unarmed person is much easier to kill than bad old buffalo, which fights back, or fleet-footed zebra, which runs faster. Almost invariably, the man-eater strikes at night, or during the crepuscular hours when its preferred targets are out and about on their routine tasks: herding goats, fetching water, gathering firewood – the duties of children and women. Lions quickly learn that the weak and frightened are more vulnerable than the strong and fearless. They are drawn to the sound of a crying child as they are drawn to the bleat of a distressed buffalo calf.

Livingstone was right when he said that the lion 'chiefly preys on defenceless creatures'; but there have been some memorable exceptions.

The victims of the infamous man-eaters of Tsavo were all well-muscled men, construction workers building a bridge over the Tsavo River in southern Kenya. It was 1893, and Britain's colonial entrepreneurs had embarked on their most ambitious project: the Kenya–Uganda Railway from Mombasa to Lake Victoria. Over a period of nine months, the workforce camp was besieged by two lions which became bolder and bolder in their predations and more and more expert at evading traps and bullets. They always attacked at night, despite defensive bonfires and thorn barricades, dragging the sleeping labourers from their tents, and were given the superstitious names of 'The Darkness' and 'The Ghost'. Estimates of the number of victims hover between 100 and 135. The railway project manager, Lt-Col. John Henry Patterson, gave several figures in his 1907 book *The Man-Eaters of Tsavo*.

One of the lions had a badly damaged tooth, discovered when Patterson finally shot them, while his partner-in-crime, which only joined the hunts after the first few attacks, almost certainly learned his behaviour from its innovator. (Male lions are expelled from the pride when they are two to three years old, and two or more may remain together to form alliances called coalitions.) They were otherwise healthy, vigorous animals which turned man-eater probably because an outbreak of the imported cattle disease rinderpest had destroyed most of their prey species, although both had an unusual feature for mature males. They had no manes. There is a genetic strain of maneless lion in the Tsavo region, now Kenya's largest national park, which persists today; and one theory is that the high levels of testosterone which inhibit hair growth in bald human males may do the same in lions, making them more aggressive.

Problem teeth and absent manes don't explain the record-breaking death toll of the man-eaters of Njombe, which are much less celebrated but were much more persistent. Between 1932 and 1947, when Tanzania was the British colony of Tanganyika, three generations of the same pride, the young following the diet plan of their elders, killed and ate between 1,500 and 2,000 people. Their line ended when the last fifteen were eventually hunted down and shot by a British game warden called George Rushby; and it's believed that once again the lions had changed their behaviour when their prey species were deliberately culled to control the spread of rinderpest among cattle.

Different circumstances have produced more recent examples of serial man-eating. During the civil war and its aftermath in the 1980s and 1990s, refugees and illegal immigrants from Mozambique regularly walked across the border into South Africa – by way of Kruger National Park. These furtive crossings were made by night, and unknown numbers of people were killed by lions. The cats responsible were almost accidental man-eaters, presented with an irresistible meal on a plate, but it didn't take long for the behaviour to become habit-forming. Kruger continues to have problems with lions picking off illegal immigrants who risk the hours of darkness; while one researcher has pointed out that, for almost a century before the border was sealed, Mozambicans had been walking through Kruger in daytime with very few problems.

Between 1990 and 2005, in southern Tanzania, 563 people were killed and 308 injured by lions – a rise in attacks which coincided with a 50 per cent rise in the Tanzanian population. The demand for land has pushed subsistence farmers deeper and deeper into lion territories, reducing the prey species through poaching and loss of habitat. Although hungry lions have broken into village homes and snatched people from their beds, most of the attacks take place during harvest time, when farmers sleep in make-shift shelters in their fields to protect their crops from foraging bush pigs. The bush pig is almost the last wild mammal of any size available to the lion diet in these rural areas; and lions chasing bush pigs into farmers' fields are often surprised by the presence of larger mammals, with predict-able results. The human anguish involved rarely gets the global headlines which flag up freak attacks on white tourists, but these predations have caused conservationists to rethink their policies.

The lion is also under siege; in conservation terms it is not yet 'endangered', but it is 'vulnerable'. In sub-Saharan Africa, there are only about 40,000 animals left, with a 30 to 50 per cent decline since the 1990s. Half of them live in Tanzania; and the attacks on humans have subsided as villagers take action to protect themselves and their livestock. By killing lions. The lion's population downturn may already be irreversible.

We have lost *panthera leo* from home ranges which once included the Americas, Europe and Asia. After the last ice age 10,000 years ago, it was the most widespread large land mammal in the world after humankind. Within historic times, we have lost the lion from North Africa and most of Asia, while there are only relic populations left in west and central Africa. Conservation ideology is a bit like religious faith; either you believe that the human race is diminished every time it puts its own interests before those of every other sentient creature on the planet, or you don't. After all, says the non-believer, has it really handicapped the inexorable advance of human achievement that we no longer have the dinosaur – not to mention some 90 per cent of extinct species lost to natural causes, without any human intervention at all?

There are sound scientific reasons why biodiversity is important, but I'm a believer for reasons which are more emotional. I have been too often thrilled and charmed by lions to wish them gone. Yes, charmed. Watch lion cubs playing with their father's tail, and you watch kittens playing with a length of string. The great beast bends his majestic head towards them with a look which is merely tolerant, but some might call tender; the youngsters wrestle in a tangle of legs, while mothers, aunts and sisters, reconvening after the night's hunt, shake the dew from their sun-gold skin and greet each other with a rubbing of foreheads. Gazelle and zebra wander by, unconcerned; they know that the lion family socialising in the celestial morning light has put aside its arsenal of teeth and claws. The grazers and browsers have survived another dawn; and, on the immense, unblemished savanna, predator and prey share a few hours of peace.

For all her birth and upbringing in the bush, Mary Livingstone never lost her fear of lions; and there were more to come, even if they were not the reason why the move to Chonuane was disastrous.

12

Babes in the Bush

'His breathing was like the cooing of wood pigeons'

Not far from the Chonuane mission station is a scattered town called Ramotswa. It is an uneventful place with a wheat-flour mill, a railway station stranded on a stretch of the 'Cape to Cairo' line (so underused it looks abandoned) and an immigration and customs post. It is the tribal capital of the Balete people, who have, unusually, a woman chief – the first female paramount chief to serve in the House of Chiefs, the advisory body to Botswana's parliament.

Ramotswa sits on the border near Gaborone, and the name makes me ponder. It is tantalisingly familiar. It takes me several minutes to tease out the reason why: *The No. 1 Ladies' Detective Agency*. 'Of course. Mma Ramotswe, Precious Ramotswe. Almost but not quite RamotsWA. Maybe Ramotswa's woman chief gave Alexander McCall Smith the inspiration for the name.'

Keith is distracted by his GPS unit, and merely grunts as my musings lead me to the English-reading public's favourite fictive symbol of African decency: the 'traditionally built' heroine of Alexander McCall Smith's beguiling mysteries, set in Gaborone and its hinterland. Keith is trying to solve his own mystery. We are close to the Botswana border and the Ramotswa crossing but still in North West Province, jerking over rock-hard ruts between thickets of thorn acacia, losing the trail from time to time, thrusting through tough, spiny webs of branches as the Land Rover targets the co-ordinates on its satnav display screen. 'Is this what they call bundu-bashing?' I ask meekly, conscious that our search for the Chonuane site may be compromising some very smart paintwork.

'You could say that. *Bundu* means wilderness, or back country, and although this is more back country than wilderness, we're certainly bashing it. A popular South African activity.'

We are driving across tree and shrub savanna, flat ranch land marked only by animal tracks and droppings which, to the Livingstones, might have signalled buffalo but today signal cattle. Keith is frustrated. He has been given the Chonuane co-ordinates by the Historical Monuments Commission, and this is his second attempt to find their monument. It is so isolated and so rarely visited that it has no custodian, like the parish pastor at Mabotsa; there are no heritage signposts in these parts, and the only significant landmark is a long whaleback ridge called Sechele's Hill. Without the co-ordinates, we have little chance of finding the site in the maze of sketchy trails and sprawling woodland; and the co-ordinates have already failed Keith on his earlier visit. 'The satnav can only do so much, and the bush was thicker then. I hunted around on foot but couldn't find anything but a borehole and its water tank. Here they are.'

We pull into a clearing where the borehole pump, with its little windmill and solar panel, rises above the trees, and the concrete reservoir squats beneath them. Lack of water condemned the Chonuane mission from the start. Nearby, two ranch hands wearing beanie hats are tinkering with a fence. Without much hope, Keith jumps from the Land Rover to ask their advice. Will the name Livingstone mean much to the young rural blacks of today's South Africa? Watching, I see the man in the red knitted hat straighten up, nod confidently and lead Keith into the trees. When they return after several minutes, my guide has a satisfied grin on his face. 'Just a few metres from the spot indicated on the satnav. In among some cows. You're not scared of cows, are you?'

I resist the urge to snort. Buffalo yes, elephant often, rhino certainly, but not cows. I've been walking through fields of them since I was a child. 'Let's go.'

The Livingstones, now a family of three, arrived on the semi-arid plain beneath Sechele's Hill early in 1846 – to an unfinished house, a river shrunk to puddles, and a hot, fretful wind that scoured the topsoil from the ground where they planned to grow vegetables and wheat. Unlike fertile Kuruman and Mabotsa, conditions at Chonuane were unremittingly harsh, and before too long they found that the shortage of water was chronic, not just seasonal. There were no mechanically pumped boreholes in those days, only improvised wells scraped by thirsty animals in the sand of the river bed, or dug by Livingstone himself, guided by their example, as he drew gritty water to nourish their seedlings and meet their basic needs. The Bakwena were also struggling. Already Sechele had begun to look elsewhere for a well-watered home for his wandering people, and had planted crops at a place called Kolobeng, forty miles to the north-west. He was eager to take the missionary family with him, and needed only a nudge from Livingstone to uproot his tribe again.

For Mary, who had become Ma-Robert to the Tswana, the next eighteen months were often miserable, limiting the delight she might have taken in her first child. Robert was born in January, shortly before they left Mabotsa, delivered by his father on their first wedding anniversary. Mary's pregnancy, like all her pregnancies, had lasted ten months; and their son was not an easy baby. He was to grow into a febrile, over-sensitive boy and a volatile, unhappy teenager, but the problems of his infancy could hardly be said to anticipate the temperament which eventually snared him in a bizarre series of events and led to his early death. He was fractious; not unusual in an unweaned baby whose mother, losing weight by the week on an exiguous diet, was probably unable to provide him with enough milk.

In some ways their daily life at Chonuane, where the only interruptions to physical labour, domestic drudgery and anxious parenting were preaching and teaching, held a perverse satisfaction for Livingstone. He relished his position as the missionary who was, literally, farthest in the field, on the edge of the known frontier of southern Africa; and his letters emphasised the hostile nature of the environment and its wildlife. The hardships also resonated with that religious tradition of martyrdom which began with Christ on the cross: no gain without pain. But he had also begun to articulate the ideas which made him a maverick to the duller policy-makers of the LMS. He was convinced that their African mission lacked vision and risked stagnation; and his remedy for this – although self-evident today – shows the kind of thinking which made him for his time an exceptional European among Africans.

He strongly believed, writes Janet Wagner Parsons, that 'missions in the established south were so well provided for that the indigenous people had become coddled and spoilt ... They were never asked to take up the responsibility for their own religious life. The effectiveness of those missions was meagre, while costs ran high. The worst aspect of the situation was that resources of staff and funds were being expended that might be put into new areas.' (Here, the pull of the unknown interior, the explorer's itch, make themselves felt.) 'In new country he intended to establish a network of stations under "native agency" – Tswana evangelists – who could be trained and supervised by only one European to save expense.'

There was more to Livingstone's proposed strategy than the need for efficient budgeting. In social-policy terms today, his approach might be summed up as 'African solutions for African problems', although, as Christianity was entirely new to southern Africa, it was clear that some hand-down education was needed. He pursued a programme of training and delegation with his own followers, the Kuruman converts who included loyal Mebalwe, the man who had saved him from the lion. But he was irked by the knowledge that only the establishment of a theological college or seminary could properly take the Tswana to new levels of evangelical practice and responsibility. It says something for his far-sightedness that sixty-five years were to pass before the first Tswana minister was ordained.

Mary had taken on her usual role as village teacher – women and children only – when she discovered she was again pregnant. Robert was not only demanding but often unwell, the internal walls of the house were still unplastered, and by the middle of the year she had to surrender the school to her husband's trainee missionaries, her reserves of energy and good temper almost exhausted. To the rescue rode Ma-Mary with her three youngest children, all aged under ten, and a large escort of Tswana hunters. Robert was her first grandchild, and the long journey from Kuruman was no deterrent. It allowed her to indulge the pleasure and interest she took in ox-wagon travel through new territory – the farthest journey she had ever made to the north. 'I was perfectly enraptured', she wrote to her husband, 'on entering the first valley of the Bakgatla; and it being necessary for me to get out of the waggon on account of the rugged path, I could examine the shrubs to my great delight.'

The Bakgatla of Mabotsa, of course, had been left in the hands of Roger Edwards when Livingstone deserted them for Sechele and the Bakwena. When she reached Chonuane, Ma-Mary found less occasion for rapture. She was aware that the mission station was toiling, and her expedition was loaded with supplies for the family. She used all her powers of encouragement to lift her daughter's spirits, and with all sincerity complimented her son-in-law on his drive to break new ground, where, she maintained, she saw the first Christian shoots beginning to sprout. 'The homestead reverberated with more laughter than it had heard since their arrival from Mabotsa.'

But, when her visit was over, this intrepid and inspiring woman set off back to Kuruman with private misgivings. The Livingstones' isolation, the haggard appearance of her pregnant daughter and the health of her baby grandson were all worries, and she knew that Mary was sometimes without her husband's support when he travelled into the infant Transvaal Republic to prospect for villages where he might install Tswana evangelists. (This meant negotiating with suspicious Boers; and the excursions were largely fruitless, as the uncompromising, self-serving brand of Christianity practised by the Boers would not tolerate indigenous preachers.) Ma-Mary had good reason for her anxieties; shortly after she left, Robert became ill with bronchial pneumonia.

The attack was so severe that his parents feared for his life. His father's efforts to treat him seemed useless. When he recovered, Livingstone allowed himself a colourful description of the boy's symptoms, the first example of the offhand, even frivolous way he chose to write about the ailments of his 'brats'. Anyone who has ever suffered from or listened to the painful labouring of congested lungs must wonder how apt the metaphor when he observed that the child's feverish breathing was like 'the cooing of wood pigeons'. But the pretty metaphor no doubt disguised the relief of a man who was by no means an unfeeling father.

Time was running out for the mission station at Chonuane. The restless Livingstone mounted another expedition into the Transvaal, this time taking Mary and Robert with him; and, as they forded a river on the return journey, the baby's fever recurred. His temperature shot up, and again he seemed close to death – an episode which reduced his weak and demoralised mother to tears of despair. Again Robert recovered; but there was little to sustain them when they got home. Ma-Mary's supplies had been eaten, the vegetable garden was well nigh barren, the persistent drought had destroyed their wheat, and the supply of beads they used to buy maize was depleted. Although Livingstone had pressing business at an LMS committee meeting near Kuruman, a visit to the Oasis of the Kalahari was also an imperative if his family were not to starve.

The cattle have bells round their necks, hides the colour of glossy chestnuts, and huge, floppy ears. There are eight. Some of them have been dehorned, and most of them are comfortably couched on the bare earth, no longer chewing the cud but perhaps still concentrating on processing vegetation through their four stomachs. They look cross-bred, although Keith guesses they carry the genes of the tough red Afrikaner breed, slightly humped at the shoulder. Their condition is good despite the lack of any visible grazing. It seems little has changed at Chonuane. Maybe they get supplementary feeds.

As we approach, they stare blankly at us with expressions so incurious I'm inclined to feel insulted. Are they so bored with strangers in this semi-wilderness? Do they have no race memories of some fairly recent predators? Here, Mary Livingstone lay awake listening to the primordial roar of lion and trying to hush her babies, whose crying lured the cats to the homestead. Only a bull calf, perhaps two weeks old, gets to his feet with a wary twitch of interest. He hasn't yet grown into his ears, and they look big enough to power him skywards. I have a soft spot for cows, although it feels strange to meet them in the kind of context where I've learned to expect woodland antelope like kudu or bushbuck, or maybe even elephant. 'They're not far away,' Keith tells me, 'but behind fences. There's a very exclusive game reserve called Madikwe just east of here.'

The reclining cattle are grouped near a rough stone pyramid, about nine feet high, with a familiar verdigrised plaque, its English legend again repeated in Afrikaans and Setswana. Only the dates are different: 'THIS MARKS THE SITE OF LIVINGSTONE'S SECOND MISSIONARY STATION, 1846– 1847'. There is no trace of the foundations of the house which Livingstone built, but it probably faced the dip of the river course, which is typically empty. The trees must have regenerated many times since the family lived here, as any tribal settlement would have cleared the land for planting and firewood. Mary would have had an open view towards Sechele's Hill; but, by August 1847, the Bakwena and her husband were in retreat from Chonuane, and she was almost alone at the homestead. Livingstone had taken most of their helpers with him to Kolobeng to start building the third and last house she would ever call her own; but not before their second child, a daughter, was born at Kuruman.

There may have been food, safety, comfort and love waiting for the Living- stones at Kuruman, but there was also humiliation. For them both. They arrived in March, Mary eight months pregnant, her husband looking for a means of supporting himself and his family which didn't compromise his resolve to push his mission deeper into the interior. He was virtually des- titute. He had funded their move to Chonuane out of his own pocket and hoped to reclaim the costs from the LMS's district committee, who were meeting near the Moffats' mission. When he was reminded that he had not been authorised to leave Mabotsa and build a new mission station, he walked out of the meeting. There was nothing for it but to borrow money from his father-in-law.

Mary's appearance shocked the Tswana women of Kuruman, who were uninhibited in their assessment of her transformation from sturdy, vigor- ous young bride to gaunt and exhausted mother, who carried only the weight of her unborn child. 'Bless me! How lean she is! Has he starved her? Is there no food in the country to which he has been?' they exclaimed within her husband's hearing – remarks he recorded in a letter to his friend D. G. Watt. The status of women may have been low among the

Tswana, but the health of a pregnant woman and the birth of a child were important to them. 'The husband on these occasions', as Livingstone himself wrote in *Missionary Travels*, 'is bound to slaughter for his lady an ox, goat, or sheep, according to his means.' Mary looked as though she'd been living on locusts since Robert was born, and the chatter stung her husband.

Not enough, however, to abandon his plans to move even farther into the interior and the unknown. He felt stifled by the missionary politics and critical gossip of the settled missions, and longed to be away; but it was nearly two months before Mary went into labour after another long pregnancy, and he delivered the little girl who was briefly to become a confidante and companion after her mother's death and the collapse of the Zambezi Expedition. She was called Agnes, after Mary's mother-in-law whom, of course, she had never met. In his later life, Agnes was to be become closer to Livingstone than any of his other children, and after his death she maintained strong links with south-central Africa through her marriage to an entrepreneurial Scots colonist called Alexander Bruce. I'll return later to Agnes Livingstone Bruce, whose son was to take over Bruce's Nyasaland estates at a place with a familiar name and a persistently troubled history: Magomero.

By July, the family of four, generously provendered by the Moffats, were on their way back to Chonuane, which Livingstone soon left to start labouring at Kolobeng. The house there would take nearly a year to build, and for most of that time Mary and the children lived in a temporary hut of poles and reeds – uncomfortable, dusty, bug-infested but preferable to remaining at Chonuane, which was half-deserted. As it was, they were left behind for several weeks. To John Moffat, his wife's brother, Livingstone wrote: 'Mary feels her situation among the ruins a little dreary, and no wonder, for she writes me yesterday that the lions are resuming possession and walk around our house at night. Kolobeng means "haunt of the wild boar" but it seems to be the haunt of everything wild. Hyaenas abound exceedingly, buffaloes in immense herds, and zebras quite tame in the thickly wooded country. Elephants too have left their traces ...'

The haunt of wild boar, the haunt of everything wild. Livingstone was exhilarated, his spirits careering into euphoria at the prospect of a fresh start 'riding on the world's backbone, and snuffing like zebras the free pure delightful air of the great western desert!' He worked tirelessly on the new house, while Sechele undertook to provide the school and meeting house, maintaining that it would be 'a house for God which is the defence of my town'. The 'God House' of Sechele was the Kolobeng church, its framework of poles and reeds raised in record time on a hill above the river. But, when Livingstone returned to Chonuane to collect Mary and the children, his mood turned dark. The place reminded him of destitution and failure – and, perhaps to obliterate its associations, perhaps for reasons more vindictive, he decided to destroy both house and school to prevent their occupation by loitering Boers, who were showing an interest in the abandoned mission station.

If Mary watched her second married home go up in flames, there is no record of her reaction.

We approach Kolobeng not from Chonuane but obliquely, on a long loop from Kuruman, crossing the border at McCarthy's Rest, watching the sand turn red as we head north to join the Trans-Kalahari Highway. Keith wants to drive me through the desert; and I'm more than willing to spend a day in the southern Kalahari, which is new to me. I've been in northern Botswana several times, either driving across the border from Zambia or Zimbabwe on the route from the Victoria Falls to Chobe National Park, or flying into the Okavango Delta on light aircraft. I was first there in 1990, before you could drive on tar to the dusty, sprawling village of Maun, the safari 'capital' on the delta's south-east edge. Back then, Maun had streets of sand and all the derring-do and free spirit of a frontier town. The only vehicles were 4WDs; strapping men in khaki roared from the bush to get drunk at the Duck Inn; crocodiles lurked in the Thamalakane River; and in and out of the airport shuttled hardy little Cessnas with payloads of high-end tourists. Then as now, their passengers were bound for the luxury camps in Botswana's wilderness of mirrors: 9,000 square miles of watery labyrinth, its shifting lagoons and channels pieced together by islands of woodland and floodplain, its rafts of water lilies and pontoons of papyrus tangled with clouds in dream-like reflections.

The Okavango Delta was my introduction to the northern Kalahari, where I was bemused to find I was drifting through desert on water so pure it was safe to drink. The canoe guide pulled a fistful of sand from the shallows and waved a hand at the vegetation: aquatic figs, vigorous mopane, flowering rain trees, thickets of papyrus and bulrush, meadows of glossy grass. 'This is desert. This is all desert. If it weren't for the fault lines which trap the water it would look like the rest of the Kalahari.'

The great sand sheet which covers most of Botswana used to be all water: the Kalahari 'superlake', formed two to three million years ago when seismic shifts tilted the land upwards and blocked the southward flow of three major rivers. The Okavango, Kwando and Zambezi are believed to have once debouched into the Orange and Limpopo rivers; and, when the land rose, a vast, shallow basin of water was created which dried up only about 10,000 years ago. The convulsions altered the courses of the rivers, redirecting the Zambezi eastwards towards the Indian Ocean but containing the Kwando and Okavango in new water systems. Today, both rivers rise in Angola. The Kwando drains into the Linyanti marshes on the borders of Namibia and Botswana, while every year, pumped full of rainwater from the Angolan highlands, the Okavango River bursts its banks and spreads across the northern Kalahari, its gravitational pull towards ocean or confluence thwarted by geological fault lines.

The Okavango Delta is usually described as the largest inland delta in the world, but I find it easier to think of it as an immense floodplain, because its character is seasonal. As the Kalahari dries out after its own rainy season, the delta swells with fresh supplies of water from Angola's rains, and the grazers and browsers of the desert head towards it, followed by their predators. The delta shrinks during its dry season but never loses permanent water, and its vitality supports a prodigious ark of wildlife. Through a policy of low-volume, high-yield tourism, with hefty park fees for non-domestic visitors, and rigorous 'green' criteria imposed on safari operators, the shrewd Batswana have so far protected their glorious natural asset. Little did Mary and David Livingstone know, when they camped by the Boteti River and played with their children on the shores of Lake Ngami, that they were the forerunners of an elite tourist industry.

Today, Kolobeng is only a long day's drive south-east of Ngamiland, whose lake and rivers are part of the delta drainage system, and half an hour from the western suburbs of Gaborone. Keith and I expect to reach the mission site by early afternoon after eight hours and 500 miles of desert travel. We have spent another night in the Northern Cape, at a bush camp near the Botswana border and the eastern edge of the Kgalagadi Transfrontier Park, which is famous for its muscular black-maned lions. This is not quite as adventurous as it sounds, as the bush camp is one of the accommodation options offered by Soetvlakte Guest Farm and is within sight of the farmhouse, where we have dinner. The only big game around are one or two antelope species. But it's good to be out in the tingling night air, sleeping in huts with thatched roofs and half-walls open to the stars. Keith gets the chance to build a giant campfire while I take a picture of the outdoor loo, which is an avocado flush toilet plumbed into the sand and screened by a thornbush kraal. When I go to my hut, I find I'm sharing the eaves with a tiny, well-mannered scops owl, which soon takes off to hunt.

We're on the road as the sun rises. Will I ever tire of African sunrises, which seem to remake the world? As we enter Botswana at the lonely post of McCarthy's Rest, I practise my two words of Setswana, courtesy of Alexander McCall Smith and his illustrious lady detective. '*Dumela, Mma*', I greet the female immigration officer, and feel foolishly pleased when she gives me a huge smile, returns the salutation (a courtesy often ignored by impatient Europeans) and welcomes me to her country. Mma Ramotswe would be proud of her bureaucratic sister.

Our route takes us half the distance to Kolobeng on tar and gravel until we join the well-paved Trans-Kalahari Highway at the town of Sekoma. As soon as we cross the border, the open road, like an infinite runway in the sand, opens up even more. 'It's such a pleasure to see no fences', remarks Keith, neatly turning a negative into a positive. 'Even if we do have to slow for the livestock. Much more of the land is communal in Botswana, mainly because it's too dry for crop farming.'

Botswana is also the empire of the donkey. There are far more donkeys on the road than vehicles, which make only rare appearances, their distant windscreens beaming the sun's reflection towards us like searchlights. I am mesmerised by the donkeys, which are unusually pretty. They have round bellies, thick, chocolate-brown coats and creamy muzzles, and give every appearance of leading independent lives on the broad verges. They sit. They stroll. They graze. They suckle their foals. And, every so often, they decide to go somewhere and move into the centre of the road, walking in twos and threes with an air of stolid purpose. They have no regard whatever for other road-users. 'Where on earth are they going?' I ask Keith. 'It's the middle of nowhere.'

'Heading back to their homestead, I guess. They all have owners somewhere. Donkeys are the local transport for those who don't have trucks or bikes. Mules, too. You often see them pulling little carts, loaded up with goods or families. We call these wagons Kalahari Ferraris.'

The view ahead repeats itself in low, sweeping surges of ochraceous land, rising now and then just high enough to give an overview of scattered woodland, spreading canopies, camelthorns putting out their first bloom of yellow flowers. A desert parkland. But, soon after we join the Trans-Kalahari Highway, wider, faster and just as free of traffic, the trees disappear and the land becomes pancake flat, its sand stubbled with sparse blond grass. Mile after mile unrolls, minutes mount into hours, and from time to time my head jerks. Keith, composed and straight-armed at the wheel, seems tireless. 'I've driven through the night on this highway, and it can be dangerous. People fall asleep, springbok jump into the road. You're not supposed to dip your headlights at oncoming cars in case you hit an animal.'

From a long way away, we see the first red pimples of rock as we near Kanye, where we leave the highway for the road to Kolobeng. There is a corridor of land in the south-east of Botswana where sandstone and granite are bunched into hills. This is where most people farm and live, within reach of the life-giving Limpopo and Marico rivers. The country is the size of France, with less than 3 per cent of France's population. No wonder the roads are empty; but this one gets busier as we head towards the capital. Houses appear, with solar panels on their roofs and plots spiked with aloe vera. Thirty miles short of Gaborone, we start looking for a bridge. In a land with few rivers, bridges are not common; but this one is hard to miss, as it's flagged up by a signpost with the word 'Kolobeng' printed vertically on the slender white board.

We have reached the Kolobeng River, and beside it the remnants of the Livingstones' last family home. Mary was only 31 when she left it, believing she would one day return. She had known hardship, fear, birth and death in this pleasant little valley on the edge of the Kalahari, but also a quality of contentment she would never know again.

The site was chosen by Sechele and Livingstone because the Kolobeng was 'the river that never dried up'.

But it did.

13

Haunt of the Wild Boar

'Rhinoceros is our frequent fare'

'A mountain with several caves in it.' So said the Bakwena of the house that Livingstone built at Kolobeng. Its size, 50 feet long by nearly 20 feet wide, astonished them. More peculiarly, it was a four-cornered mountain with square caves in it. Before Europeans arrived in southern Africa, the vernacular architects took their design cues from the natural world, where there are few straight lines and no squares. Africans built in the round; even the mysterious, monumental stones of the Great Zimbabwe[1] flow into curves and circles, concentric passageways and elliptical enclosures, while the imposing citadel's only remaining tower is conical. Today, many rural Africans still live in round huts built traditionally with the raw materials to hand – mud or stone walls, pole and thatch roofs. They need regular maintenance, especially after the rains, but their ventilation is good and their organic fabric makes more sense, in a hot climate, than the cinderblock and tin-roof boxes which have replaced so many of them. The aesthetics of the natural world are also more pleasing – so much so that these rondavels, as they're called from the Afrikaans word 'rondawel', now have their luxury plumbed and wired versions in safari lodges, holiday villages and even modern housing estates.

The Moffats' homestead at Kuruman was the first four-cornered building north of the Orange River. Their daughter's house at Kolobeng was the most northerly example of European building in the southern continent. Its site was attractive. It stood on a flattened knoll overlooking the river and was modelled on the style of Kuruman, which in turn replicated a design set by the first settlers in the Cape. It had a veranda with views over the reeds and tall grasses of the river's floodplain to the wooded hills of its valley. Inside were a combination work and sitting-room called a voorhuis, a central fireplace, two bedrooms, a study for Livingstone and

---

1 The Great Zimbabwe is the ruined city which was once the capital of the Kingdom of Zimbabwe, which lasted from about AD 1100 to 1400 during the region's Late Iron Age. To the dismay of the white supremacists of Rhodesia, the discovery of these ruins and those of smaller stone settlements demonstrated that black people were capable of sophisticated building practices. It is now a national monument.

for Mary a lean-to kitchen, which her mother had always insisted upon, as 'a woman must have an integral kitchen for her own convenience and to prevent servants from pilfering'. The foundations were raised in stone to waist height and the walls completed with mud bricks. Livingstone, his left arm permanently damaged by its mauling from the Mabotsa lion, found it too difficult to build in stone. The steeply pitched roof was thatched and the walls whitewashed. In the green season, the house must have looked much like a crofter's cottage in rural Scotland – but for the veranda. The window frames had been with the couple since they set up home. They were salvaged first from Mabotsa and then Chonuane, while a grant of £30, finally awarded by the district committee for his Chonuane expenses, allowed Livingstone to acquire more glass from Kuruman.

Now the LMS had to tolerate the move to Kolobeng, which they did with the reproachful comment: 'We hope we may now regard you as permanently settled, knowing well the disadvantages attending frequent changes of this nature'. They did not know their man, who was soon brooding on the 'insensible hearts' of the Bakwena, who did not share their chief's enthusiasm for the god of the white strangers. When he failed to make progress, the missionary was to have little compunction about leaving them to their pagan practices as he had left the Bakgatla of Mabotsa.

His inner demon of restlessness was stirring within weeks of moving his family into the new house. In a letter to his close confidant D. G. Watt, he wrote: 'Here I live with the people ... as soon as I can leave them under native instruction – Forward I go ... Who will penetrate through Africa?' Concealed in the question is a supplementary question: 'Who if not me?' Far to the north-west of Kolobeng, on the other side of the desert in the land of the Batawana, he had learned there was a great font of water, a remote and shining lake which no European had yet reached. To Livingstone, it held all the allure of a holy grail – and he was already calculating how he could reach it.

But Mary felt settled, especially when her husband placed a metal plate on a wall of the house as evidence of its permanence. On 4 July 1848, the family were finally installed, and she felt confident enough to ask her mother to send her desk and other personal treasures from Kuruman and to suggest that Livingstone order a sofa 'with air cushions' – an 'awful extravagance' which her husband indulged but which was to be her only luxury, much underused. From her years at Kolobeng, which began well but became increasingly distressing and hazardous, a clearer picture of Mary surfaces, if only through the observations of her husband, who was nothing if not eager to share with his correspondents his admiration for his wife's industry and dedication. This was the period when she became his 'heroine', his 'dear rib', 'the best spoke in the wheel'. Livingstone's public loyalty to Mary and praise for her qualities seem at times excessive, as if he is trying to persuade himself, as much as a distant audience of potential critics, that his choices were also hers.

Within missionary culture, he had no need to justify himself. 'A missionary family was expected to give complete support to the man in his work', writes Janet Wagner Parsons. 'If he was called to serve God, then they could have no nobler place than beside him, or so ran the ideal of the day. What might be called the missionary family ethic held sway with every man, woman and child in the missions.' Personal disasters, family tragedies, premature deaths were considered worthwhile sacrifices to the Christian salvation of the heathen. 'Martyrdom was not only accepted; it was expected.' This was the destiny, and these were the risks to which Mary was consigned first by birth and then by marriage; and, for the early years of her life with Livingstone, she faultlessly exemplified the ideal. Was it any wonder she came close to losing her sanity when she was cast out of the system to fend for herself in a foreign country?

The Land Rover pulls off the road and rocks down a dirt track to a fence, a gate and a hut. As recently as the 1930s, the remains of the Kolobeng homestead's mudbrick walls were still standing, and excavations had disinterred fragments of walls lined with floral wallpaper. The site was later cast adrift in its rural backwater, grazed by cows and goats, occasionally visited by historians, archaeologists and Christian pilgrims but scarcely noticed by the subsistence farmers and casual travellers in the district of Kweneng. But the growing prosperity and improving infrastructure of diamond-rich Botswana made Kolobeng more accessible. The tar road from Kanye, with its link to Gaborone, and the bridge over the river were built in 1992; and the Botswana National Museum took action to protect the site, now a national monument, and encourage visitors. Today, it has an information board and a guide-custodian, who shoots out of his hut with the extravagant welcome of a man who is tired of his own company.

He is Alfred Piet, native of Gaborone, 59 years old and soon to retire from a job he enjoys when he is able to guide rather than guard. 'You are my first visitors for three days', he tells us. 'School holidays are over, but August was a busy month. See!' He produces his log from the hut and displays the numbers with their nationalities: 1 Australian, 1 Brazilian, 2 British, 2 Indians, 5 Italians, 1 Norwegian, 4 Americans, 5 Zimbabweans and 420 Batswana. When I remark on Batswana interest in the Kolobeng legacy, which is credited with introducing the country to irrigation and European methods of building as well as its first school, church, Christian convert and medical doctor, he nods. 'Yes, we are all taught about Livingstone and Kgosi Sechele at primary school. They are part of our history. But there's a nice picnic site down by the river, and that also brings a lot of people at weekends.'

Kolobeng is still a lonely place. It's easy enough to turn a deaf ear to the occasional truck crossing the Kolobeng bridge and a blind eye to the power line on its far side; and, when you turn your back on both, the landscape is timeless. Alfred leads us up a path which climbs gently to the foundations of the homestead. There is really very little to see except the views the Livingstones saw: the river's tree line, cattle standing on the floodplain (they had ten skinny cows to provide them with milk) and the rising ground of the valley, more scrub than woodland now. These are the hills and ridges which were once the haunt of wild boar and 'the haunt of everything wild'. Livingstone could shoot buffalo from his doorstep; the family roast might be giraffe or eland; the trees were browsed by kudu and stripped by elephant; bushbuck, water buck and zebra made early-morning sorties to drink at the river; and the nights were often noisy with hyena and lion. 'Rhinoceros is our frequent fare', he recalled – a diet to break the hearts of conservationists today. The landscape is timeless in every way but one: it has been cleansed of all the creatures which reminded William Cotton Oswell of 'the beasts in the garden of Eden'.

Alfred Piet has been showing visitors round the site for fifteen years. My instinct is to spend some time there on my own, but I haven't the heart to deny him company or belittle his experience. Besides, the vestiges of the community which once lived there are now so sketchy that some interpretation is useful. The volcanic rock of Kweneng district is rich in iron ore, and the large foundation stones which define the outline of the homestead are the colour of rust. Where the ground falls away from the level site towards the river, short metal posts linked with chain trace the position of the vanished veranda, but there is still shade – from the evergreen foliage of a squat shepherd tree. 'One of our protected species,' says Alfred, 'but it isn't as old as the site.'

He points to a conspicuous boulder beside a gap in the foundations. 'This was the front door, and on this rock Dr Livingstone held his surgery. It was his dental chair, too. The Bakwena would come from the village with all their sicknesses, especially the ladies in labour. He saved many lives.'

'And Mary?' I ask, although I know the answer, 'where was her school?'

'At the *kgotla*. Come.'

The *kgotla* was – and remains – a forum for tribal democracy among the Batswana, a public meeting which serves as community council and traditional law court. Every village has one, and every villager is allowed to speak without interruption. Kgosi Sechele, as Alfred calls the Bakwena chief (*kgosi* is the Setswana word for chief or king) not only settled disputes and dispensed justice through the co-operative decision-making of the *kgotla*, but was himself answerable to it – a system which has encouraged modern Botswana's claim to be one of the world's oldest democracies. It was the *kgotla*, with its emphasis on consensus, which discouraged Sechele from commanding his people to adopt Christianity at the end of a rhinoceros-hide whip, and almost cost him his chiefdom. The bizarre beliefs and conditions of his new religion came close to persuading his troubled tribe that their *kgosi* was deranged.

Perhaps, if more of them had had the advantage of Sechele's warm relationship with Livingstone, they would have been less sceptical of the missionary's challenge to their belief system. When they first met during one of his early excursions from Kuruman, the missionary was instantly impressed by the chief's bearing and intelligence. Sechele was in his mid-thirties, tall and good-looking if 'rather corpulent', with an enthusiasm for European gadgets and clothes, including formal suits made from hartebeest and leopard skins. His adaptations of European fashion often looked comical to those who met him, but few underestimated Sechele. He made an impact on all the Bechuanaland travellers who recorded their encounters with him – trader, missionary or English gentleman-hunter, including William Frederick Webb, who became Livingstone's friend and an admirer of the Bakwena chief. Webb's daughter Alice, as A. Z. Fraser, wrote the charmingly genteel if ingenuous *Livingstone and Newstead*, published in 1913. (Newstead Abbey, a country house in Nottinghamshire, was the Webb family home, which often hosted Livingstone and his children after Mary's death.) Her memoir describes Sechele as 'singularly well-bred in his ideas, and far removed from all popular conceptions of an African savage'.

Livingstone had quickly identified the potential for conversion in this untypical 'African savage', although Sechele's interest in all things European was initially self-interested. But, from his first exposure to the missionary's preaching, he was stirred by the potency of its Victorian fundamentalism and by the choice offered: salvation and paradise or damnation and hell. Immediately, he grasped its implication. 'You startle me', he told him; 'these words make all my bones to shake; but my forefathers were living at the same time yours were, and how is it that they did not send them word about these terrible things sooner? They all passed away into darkness without knowing whither they were going.'

For nearly three years Sechele astonished Livingstone with his understanding of the scriptures and the speed with which he learned to read them, not to mention his initiative in organising his own worship. At Kolobeng, unprompted, he gathered together his household for Bible study and prayers in the same way Livingstone did with Mary, Robert and Agnes. But there was still an impediment to the baptism he so sincerely desired. He had five wives. Then, quite suddenly, shortly after the Livingstones moved into their new house, Sechele announced he was now prepared to divorce four of them.

The Bakwena were scandalised, angry, almost mutinous. These young women had been loyal to their *kgosi*, served him well and given him children, and now they were being punished on the whim of a preposterous god. The chief's counsellors tried to insist that they continue to live in the village, but Sechele, fearing either the disapproval of Livingstone or the temptation of their presence, would only compromise: he sent the women back to their parents with all the possessions they had acquired while married, as well as new cloth, skins and beads and the kingly message that he found no fault with them. He was merely following the will of God.

Ironically, the younger wives were among Livingstone's best pupils, themselves on course for conversion, and he was not only appalled by the misery caused by the demand his faith made on Bakwena culture but also plagued by doubt. Was he sacrificing several souls in order to save one? The case of Mokgokong, daughter of a Bangwato chief, was particularly upsetting, as Parsons recounts. 'She had borne Sechele three children that she must now abandon to return to her people, although her parents were dead. She begged Livingstone to let her work for Mma-Robert or anyone else so that she might be allowed to stay and nurse her youngest.' Uneasily, it was agreed she should remain at Kolobeng.

Livingstone was convinced that there was also a spiritual reason for the wives' distress. 'The tears chased each other down her cheeks', he wrote of Mokgokong, deciding that they sprang from the knowledge that she would be going 'where there is no word of God'. When another wife, Makhari, who got no such reprieve, tried to give him back her Bible he wouldn't take it, refusing to accept that the despairing woman might have lost her appetite for the word of such a heartless god. She left it behind anyway.

But Sechele hadn't lost his appetite for Mokgokong. When she soon became pregnant he freely admitted responsibility and vowed to continue to 'love Christ' despite his ban from Holy Communion, which lasted only three months. Even Livingstone understood that having sex with a very recent wife was not the moral equivalent of having sex with another man's wife. 'He had become so accustomed to their customs it was like his ordinary food', was his unromantic comment.

And what of Mary, herself the mother of two young children, now carrying a third? Her voice, as usual, is silent. But the woman with the 'bright and kind smile', the infant teacher who was already loved by her pupils, had grown up with the practice of polygamy, saw how it worked (often rather well) and perhaps didn't think it so very sinful. After all, as her mother had remarked, Mary was not the most pious of her family. Duty to her husband, rather than the God he served, was more sacred to Mary.

Whatever her opinion of the *kgosi*'s decision, she almost certainly shared the anguish of the rejected wives and exiled mothers, whose emotional future, if she had but known, would not be very different from her own.

Alfred leads us up the path once trudged by Mary 'no matter how broiling the sun, to impart instructions to the heathen ...' to the site of the *kgotla*: the multi-purpose Bakwena meeting house, Christian school and church which never became permanent. Nothing suggests that anything once stood there except more posts and chains outlining its footprint; but this co-operative enterprise was the scene of Kolobeng's most enduring achievement. The baptism of Sechele took place on the first day of October 1848, when the ceremony was able to take advantage of two handsome baptismal chairs newly arrived from a congregation in Birmingham. Sechele wore a cloak which Livingstone had ordered from Scotland; and, to the relief of the nervous crowd, the *kgosi* was not required to drink men's brains from the baptismal cup – the prevailing rumour.

Sechele's conversion was thus formalised. It had far-reaching consequences for the country which is now Botswana. The deep friendship and mutual respect between the two men survived, despite strain, Livingstone's decision to take his mission north to the Zambezi and the Makololo, and encouraged the Bakwena chief to favour the British at a time when he and his people were harassed and eventually attacked by Boer expansionists. In the words of Parsons, Sechele 'prepared the ground for a nation', although the significance of Kolobeng was for long overlooked and the site largely neglected in the British protectorate which Bechuanaland first became.

Today, more generously, the Botswana National Museum acknowledges the role of this peaceful rural landmark in their country's history. Alfred Piet tells us earnestly, in the manner of one who has memorised a text: 'Sechele's alliance with the British was pursued through friendship with Livingstone and the embracing of European ways. Eventually this contributed to the declaration of Bechuanaland as a protectorate and the evolution of Botswana as a republic.'

I resist the impulse to applaud.

In the winter months of their first year in the new house, the river that never dried up soon indicated that its reputation was fraudulent. By November 1848, the dust was beginning to settle on the uproar over Sechele's baptism, but it was also settling on the bed of the dwindling Kolobeng. Livingstone had a new worry. 'Long for rains', he wrote to Watt. 'Everything languishes during the intense heat; and successive droughts having only occurred since the gospel came to the Bakwains, I fear the effect will be detrimental.' He could do nothing to prevent the Bakwena from importing a rainmaker to summon rain; and, although this sorcerer's efforts were no more successful than his own Christian prayers, the rainmaker's presence diminished the missionary's status.

Mary had little time to worry about anything other than her immediate tasks. Her Kolobeng days were hard but fulfilling, and encouraged her to believe that she and David were at last securing their family life. Its practical demands might have been what prevented her from writing more than a few postscripts to her husband's letters to their families; or, unlike her mother, she may have had no interest in recording her own reflections on their challenging circumstances; or the letters have been lost. Whatever the reason, the fragments of text which have survived from her Kolobeng years are little more than shopping lists or notes of thanks. 'There are a few references in her husband's letters to requests she made', writes Parsons, 'and these reflect a frontier woman's preoccupations with necessities: soap, a comb, socks for David ... a bonnet ...' On one of Livingstone's letters to his sisters in Hamilton, she thanked them for a tartan shawl and bonnets sent from their hat shop, and in a request for stockings remarked that missionaries' wives had no time to knit stockings – implying, not for the first time, that her role was often that of 'domestic drudge', as she once opined.

At least some of the drudgery involved a little creativity. When they ran out of soap, she made it herself from the ashes of the plant salsosa. She poured animal fat into moulds to make candles, and skimmed the cream from the cows' milk to churn butter in a jar. She sewed their hard-wearing clothes from strong calico and sailcloth ordered from Scotland, mixed and kneaded dough and baked all their bread in an oven improvised from a termite mound. But most of her household chores were dreary: washing, sweeping and scrubbing, soaking the dirtiest clothes, maintaining the cowdung floors, milling maize for porridge or, when their coffee supplies were depleted, for a disagreeable brew which substituted for the drink. Unlike Boer families or other European settlers, she had little domestic help, and adopted her mother's system of enlisting successions of Tswana women, one at a time for a month at a time, in order to improve local practices in hygiene, nutrition and child care. But their training was also time-consuming, and she could rarely delegate.

After their midday meal, Mary left Robert and Agnes (who, of course, made their own claims on her day) in the care of a 'nurse girl' and toiled up the hill to the meeting house to teach the village children, for whom she had managed to provide a motley wardrobe of shirts and frocks to supplement the inadequate Tswana version of a cache-sexe – a few strings dangling from their waists. They hated the bonds of their European clothes but during school hours endured them for the sake of Ma-Robert, who was strict but kind, and for their enjoyment of the number rhymes and alphabet songs with which she engaged their interest.

Mary, according to Parsons, was a very good teacher and, unlike her husband, had the huge advantage of fluent Setswana. 'After the lesson she stayed to teach the girls sewing, then walked into the town to talk to the women and distribute what she could spare to those who were most in need. Since the rains had failed, the people had very little and hunger always struck hardest at mothers and children. At home at dusk, she bathed Robert and Agnes without benefit of a bathtub, put them to bed and took out her work basket while David sat writing at the table.'

A similar snapshot of their lives together, but with a shift of emphasis towards 'him', was given by Livingstone in another letter to his friend Watt: 'The daily routine: up with the sun, family worship, breakfast, school, then manual work as required – ploughing, sowing, smytheing, and every other sort. Mary busy all morning with culinary and other work; a rest of two hours after dinner; then she goes to the infant school with an attendance of from 60 to 80. Manual work for him again till 5 o'clock; then lessons in the town and talk to such as are disposed to listen. The cows are milked; then a meeting, followed by a prayer meeting in Sechele's house, which brings him home about 8.30 too tired for any mental exertion.'

For all his evening exhaustion, the industrious missionary still had the energy to write copious letters, keep a journal, analyse Setswana grammar, record tribal customs, observe the minutiae of the natural world and have sex with his wife. While the drought persisted, the crops withered, the game dispersed to look for water and the Bakwena resorted to grubbing for bulbs and roots, the infallible fertility of Mary Livingstone was the only guarantee of new life. For all the short rations of her pregnancy, when she grew so weak that she had to discontinue her classes at the meeting house, her second son was born on 7 March 1849 after only three hours' labour and no complications. Despite the primitive conditions of their remote household, it was Mary's greatest asset that her husband was a gifted doctor who kept in touch with medical developments reported in *The Lancet*, even if he was never able to get hold of the chloroform which had gone into production as an effective anaesthetic. 'From the accounts I see of its operation,' he wrote to Robert Moffat, 'I expect the old ladies will be wishing they could begin again.' Livingstone's wit was nothing if not mordant.

The christening of Thomas Steele, called Tom, named after his father's friend the big-game hunter, was followed by some short-lived showers of rain and problems of a different kind. In the first months of 1849, militant Transvaal Boer farmers threatened to attack the Bakwena and evict the missionary family from Kolobeng by force. Their purpose was land-grabbing; their excuse was that Livingstone and other missionaries supplied arms to the Tswana and fomented resistance to Boer expansionism. Their resentment had festered since the early 1830s, when the United Kingdom outlawed slavery in all her colonies. Rather than submit to British authority, thousands of Dutch settlers in the Cape Colony had loaded up their ox-wagons for the Great Trek north and east of the Orange River into the territories which were to become the Boer Republics. In the infant Transvaal, their grievances had become ever more focused on LMS outposts. Kuruman was too strong to intimidate; Kolobeng was more vulnerable.

The attacks were eventually to come, but not in 1849. The menace, however, gave momentum to Livingstone's restlessness. He was also becoming disaffected with the Bakwena, who continued to resist his proselytising even when he tried to associate the benefits of Christianity with the technological and economic progress of European civilisation. Gradually, grudgingly, he began to realise that the Tswana were largely content with their own culture and values, despite the seasonal hazards of their environment and the chronic struggle to feed themselves. They were pastoralists and hunter-gatherers and very recent agriculturalists, which was challenge enough. What use had they for an industrial revolution? He retained his admiration for Sechele, although the chief's sexual lapse had been a fall from grace and a hurtful blow. But, after eight years in Africa, he had christened only one convert.

He was increasingly frustrated and bored. A bout of 'itinerating' into the Transvaal demonstrated that there was little hope of taking his mission eastwards, where the obstructive Boers were well entrenched. He was hatching another plan – an expedition which would not only scratch the itch of his wanderlust but explore the possibility that elsewhere in Africa were people more dynamic than the Tswana. (He didn't seem to appreciate that their apparent lack of enterprise was as much to do with the lethargy of malnutrition as with their passive nature.) He wanted to find tribes which would seize the opportunities of his mission as much for its economic possibilities as its spiritual rewards. He knew that such people existed – there was no lack of ambition among the Matabele, for example. And Sechele had told him about the wise Makololo chief Sebetwane, who had sustained the Bakwena *kgosi* in exile and was now living with his tribe well north of the thirstland, near the banks of a mighty river. Would the Gospel fall more fruitfully on Makololo ears?

Livingstone's growing ambition to reach more co-operative heathens contained the seeds of the vision for sub-Saharan Africa which would drive him for the rest of his life: Christianity, civilisation and commerce, inseparable allies if the indigenous people were not to be degraded by European contact, would bring new economies regulated by the administrations of colonial governments. He was a convinced colonist, but an idealistic one; he believed that prosperity would improve the lives of Africans and that the word of God would flourish with the stability it provided. For all his considerable foresight, he could not anticipate that European appropriation of much of the continent would create more problems than it solved far beyond the nineteenth century.

He sought escape from his setbacks at Kolobeng as he had evaded errors of judgement at Mabotsa and Chonuane – by moving on. This set the pattern of his future career, when he never flinched from the unimaginable obstacles and risks of African exploration but always sought to avoid the humdrum hurdle. He wrote to William Cotton Oswell, who, after a spell in the United Kingdom, had revived an interest in crossing the Kalahari to find the great lake which no European had yet reached. Soon, Oswell and his friend Mungo Murray were back at the Cape, assembling horses, oxen, wagons and supplies. They agreed with Livingstone that they would start the trek at the end of May, to take advantage of the dry, cooler winter months. Sechele, with an eye to procuring ivory from the lake country, would provide an escort of Bakwena, but pointed out gloomily that even his people, 'who are more accustomed to thirst than you are, cannot cross that desert'.

Some of their route was known to traders and hunters and fell within the fief of the Bangwato chief Sekgoma, a distrustful despot whose capital, Shoshong, lay among hills on the eastern edge of the desert. They had been told that beyond Shoshong and Serotle, which Oswell called 'the portal of the desert', was an immense wasteland of emptiness to the north-west, with few water holes and few people. Only the nomadic San, hunter-gatherers, lived with confidence in such a place; and they hoped to hire Bushman guides. If they found their way across the heavy sands, the flat, featureless thornveld and white-hot salt pans, they would reach the lake and the country of another tribe, the Batawana, who lived beside more water than the entire Tswana people could ever use.

But, before the expedition got under way, the fidgety missionary had to secure the safety of his family. Rumours of Boer hostility rumbled on and, fortuitously, gave him the excuse for a temporary withdrawal from Kolobeng. This would free him for his travels and allow Mary to visit her parents, who were only too willing to receive their daughter and grandchildren, including the new baby, into their care. Mary was less enthusiastic. In April 1849, he dispatched the excited children and their reluctant mother to Kuruman, riding with them on the first leg of the two-week journey. 'My poor lady', he reported, 'is away out crying all the road in the full belief that I shall not be seen by her again.'

If he suspected that his departure into the enigmatic wilderness marked the beginning of the end of their life at Kolobeng, it was unlikely he would share this hunch with Mary; nor could she anticipate that, on two more expeditions across the Kalahari, she and the children would travel with him and come close to losing their lives.

14

Grace Under Pressure

'she was not Dr Moffat's daughter and Livingstone's wife for nothing'

What went wrong with Mary Livingstone? When she returned to her parents while Livingstone made his preparations for the journey to Lake Ngami, it was only her second visit to Kuruman in over six years of marriage. The marriage itself was happy. She had three children who had all been born healthy and, despite a diet drastically short of vitamins, fresh fruit and vegetables, had so far overcome every infection which came their way. She had an important role in her husband's work. She had much to be grateful for. But the wan, haggard, downcast woman who arrived with her undernourished children at the Moffat mission in April 1849, dismayed and puzzled its population. For the second time, they asked themselves what had become of the buxom, buoyant bride in the few years since she had taken her wedding vows.

Physical debilitation accounted for her appearance, and perhaps her low spirits, but there was more going on to undermine her emotional health. The disappearance of Livingstone, the prospect of months of separation were sending out the first symptoms of that morbid dependency on her husband which was eventually to become dangerous. There were other warning signs, including her response to the speculation about his absence which was to torment Mary at home and abroad. The persistent questions asked by gossips black and white, in Bechuanaland and the United Kingdom, first began to surface at Kuruman. Why does he spend so much time away from his wife? Does he care nothing for her company?

Mary was uneasy, self-conscious, even embarrassed to be back at Kuruman without her husband, despite its abundant benefits for her children, who soon began to gain weight and recover their strength. Kuruman was never to be a solution for the 'problem' of Livingstone's family when he later decided to leave them for two years (which turned into four) to investigate the Zambezi and its tribes. He knew that Mary would find it humiliating to be returned to her parents, but hinted that her unhappiness was less to do with her relationship with her powerful mother, as some have claimed, and more to do with rumour, as 'more reports made and circulated by the natives would render my wife miserable'.

While Robert and Mary Moffat got to know their grandchildren, Mary Livingstone fretted – so much so that her mother observed she needed 'sustaining grace' to see her through the months before she could return to Kolobeng. This conclusion might be read as an implied criticism, suggesting tension between mother and daughter, but the remark could equally be interpreted as an oblique criticism of Livingstone – the architect of hardships more severe than Ma-Mary, even in the earliest years of her marriage, ever had to endure. She was becoming more and more concerned about her daughter's health and happiness and the welfare of Robert, Agnes and Tom. If it hadn't been for the food parcels she sent north with every traveller passing through Kolobeng, the children would have suffered even more during the drought, when the air was so dry that the bindings of Livingstone's books fell apart, and Mary's new-baked bread hardened as soon as it was cut.

Robert was now three, underweight for his age, often withdrawn. Although he was surrounded by potential playmates at Kolobeng, he sensed his difference from the near-naked children of the Bakwena, who wanted to be friendly but confused him by staring and giggling at his white skin and European clothes, which he was obliged to wear in the hottest weather. His closest companion was Agnes, an exuberant, good-natured, dark-eyed toddler who followed him everywhere, as Robert followed his father. From an early age, it was clear he adored Livingstone, who was amused by the boy's attempts to imitate his various tasks but often too abstracted to give him undivided attention. Robert was every bit as obstinate as his father (he went through a phase when he refused to use English and spoke only Setswana) and had much of his father's intense personality. Their wilful natures, as happens typically in family dynamics, were often in collision. Soon, Robert was being described as 'difficult'; and although Livingstone admired the stoicism of his son when he was punished, writes Parsons, 'he was not averse to giving him a thrashing when he deserved it, and once he accidentally broke the boy's finger. Corporal punishment, meted out by the parent he idolised, almost certainly made the boy worse. Intelligent but sensitive, he was destined to become a non-achiever and deeply troubled.'

All three children were deservedly pampered at Kuruman, where, for the first time in many months, they could have regular baths and well-balanced meals and the refreshment of new and loving faces. Ma-Mary devoted herself to improving their health and noted Robert's intelligence and Agnes's charm. Tom, just two months old, was the most robust, although he was to become a delicate child, possibly because his constitution was weakened by the acute malarial attacks he later suffered beside

Lake Ngami, and by a persistent bladder infection picked up on the same journey. He was nicknamed Tau, which is Setswana for lion, because his family fancied that his thick fair hair looked like a mane. The only person who didn't enjoy their 'holiday' at Kuruman was their mother.

Perhaps Mary did feel a little oppressed by Ma-Mary's immediate resolve to take charge; but, beyond that, there is no hard evidence that she and her mother had a difficult relationship. Livingstone once wrote that his mother-in-law was inclined to 'find fault', but that may be because she found fault with him – in no uncertain terms over the fraught issue of family responsibility, a crisis yet to come. On this occasion, Mary had no reason to feel she was being judged or found wanting in the care of her children. She could not be held responsible for the consequences of prolonged drought, and had proved her ability to rise to challenges over and over again at Mabotsa, Chonuane and Kolobeng. She lacked neither courage nor resourcefulness, nor the skills to manage a well-run home in the most inhospitable conditions. She was her mother's daughter in many ways. If there was indeed any strain between the two women, then its source was more likely to be Livingstone. At this stage in her marriage, Mary's loyalty to her husband was absolute. If she sensed her mother's disapproval of his expeditionary exploit, then it would be her instinct to support him – and, by extension, endorse the choice she made when she married him.

She was also capable of resisting Ma-Mary's forceful personality with a stubborn defence of her own independence. Livingstone had been vague about the length of his absence, but she knew he hoped to complete his return journey before the advance of the Kalahari summer, with its fierce temperatures and hindering rains. Although there might be standing water and replenished wells in the desert during summer, there would also be mud – the greatest obstacle to ox-wagon travel. Accordingly, to her parents' concern, she decided to return to Kolobeng in early August – perhaps a week or two before she could expect her husband, but in plenty of time to spring-clean the homestead and prepare to welcome him. The Moffats didn't try to stop her, but loaded her wagon with food and other supplies to last the family for months.

And so, the lone woman with her three infant children and a minimal wagon crew left the security of Kuruman for the insecurity of Kolobeng, trekked north from the eternal fountain of the Eye to the exhausted Kolobeng River, and exchanged the bountiful orchards, healthy livestock and productive wheatfields of the Oasis for the barren plots and starving cattle of the Kolobeng valley, where the only reliable vitality was to be found in the strength of the dust-thick wind. Was there something desperate in this act of valour, whose only purpose was to bring her two weeks and 300 miles closer to Livingstone?

Mary feared lions and overturning ox-wagons but not much else in her semi-wilderness. 'Mrs Livingstone's nerve' is a topic in A. Z. Fraser's *Livingstone and Newstead*, some of which is based on her father's experience of the Livingstones at Kolobeng. 'It was some six or seven inches long', she writes of a centipede which suddenly appeared on Mary's bare arm. 'Such centipedes are dangerous as well as loathsome, since they can inflict a very painful wound. To attempt its removal would have only precipitated the catastrophe, and her companions, therefore, could but watch its movements in helpless horror. But she was not Dr Moffat's daughter and Livingstone's wife for nothing, even where a centipede was concerned. Equal to the occasion, and with a quiet word of reassurance, she stood perfectly still, whilst the repulsive creature ran over her bare skin until at last it reached her dress.'

Whereupon Mary shook it off. Fraser reports that her father declared this 'the most surprising example of nerve he had ever seen in a woman. He even doubted whether any of the men present could have shown such self-control.' As I've already mentioned, Fraser's 1913 memoir is charming but naïve. Mary had grown up with an entire cast of neighbourhood creepy-crawlies and is unlikely to have been spooked by the 'centipede', which was almost certainly one of the giant millipedes known locally as shongololos. The name comes from the Zulu word *ukushonga*, which means 'to roll up'. This is what the shongololo does when it's threatened. If danger persists, it might then release from its pores hydro cyanic acid, which smells disgusting if you get it on your hands, which is no doubt why Mary was reluctant to touch the millipede. But it doesn't bite, and its defensive secretions are far from fatally toxic, although they can irritate the eyes and mouth. Fraser's 'loathsome' and 'repulsive' creature is often found endearing by those who encounter the shongololo, rolling along on its many little legs. Some people keep them as pets. When trains first appeared they were called shongololos for their similar locomotion. There's even a tourist train in southern Africa called the Shongololo Express.

Another of Fraser's anecdotes offers a more convincing example of Mary's cool head, and 'is given by Mr Oswell during the 'Ngami journey a short time before, when the waggon in which she was travelling caught fire. There were, as she knew well, more than a hundred pounds of gunpowder in it, but she did not stir, contenting herself with calling to her husband who happened to be near: "David! David! Come and put it out."'

Sometimes, the rescued became the rescuer. In *Missionary Travels*, Livingstone describes an event which clearly left him nervous, if not phobic, about snakes. 'At Mabotsa one morning a man came to me early, and going to the door in the dark I set my foot on a serpent. The moment I felt the cold snaky skin twine round my leg I jumped up higher than I ever did before, or hope to do again. The reptile was shaken off by my leap.' Thereafter, if there was any reason for Livingstone to get out of bed in the night, it was Mary who lit the candle and went first; just as she needed a different kind of nerve to take a pair of 'shoemaker's nippers' and, on her husband's instructions, wrench a diseased tooth from his jaw. The operation, which had Livingstone shouting and heaving in agony, left them both exhausted.

So, Mary was not given to panic; nor was the collapse of her emotional fibre sudden. Her psychological health frayed slowly as her dependence on Livingstone grew. When he was there, the woman who feared lions was herself lion-hearted; when he was absent, she lost her confidence, her nerve and her peace of mind. On their arduous, life-threatening expedition with William Cotton Oswell, their admiring companion put on record that he 'never saw her fail him but once – when it was proposed to leave her behind'.

October is called 'the suicide month' in the southern half of the African continent. The land has shrivelled during the winter months, and from September onwards the heat intensifies and the atmosphere grows heavy with the promise of rain which doesn't always fall. The combination of heat and humidity tests the tempers of those who live there, and the most fragile find it unendurable. Mary was without her husband for two months at Kolobeng before he returned in the second week of October, and had become more and more dispirited. No rain had fallen in her absence, and the last weeks of winter had further undermined the health of the Bakwena, who suffered seasonally from respiratory infections. The malnourished, the diseased, the very old and the very young looked to Ma-Robert for aid. She was Moffat's daughter and the wife of the *ngaka*, their sorcerer of European medicine, and must know his secrets. When they came to the homestead, she gave the weakest what food she could spare with the spoonfuls of medicine which, rightly or wrongly, they believed helped them.

Robert, Agnes and Tom also fell ill, although the benefits of their recent Kuruman diet helped them recover. As the weeks ground by and there was still no word of the expeditionary party, the suspense of waiting became an ordeal. Only her domestic chores, her sense of duty towards the Bakwena and the responsibility of her children prevented Mary from succumbing to despair. She had expected her husband to be back in August; but, at the beginning of August, after various obstacles, the party had only just reached Lake Ngami, and Livingstone was in no hurry to return. Livingstone, in fact, was euphoric. He had crossed the unforgiving desert, with its mendacious salt pans which offered mirages of the shimmering lake, to reach the generous, wooded, game-rich land of the Batawana. He was intoxicated by the almost forgotten spectacles of coursing rivers and shining water.

The lake, he estimated, was about seventy miles long; and, thanks to the self-effacing Oswell and Murray, its 'discovery' was the achievement which launched his reputation as an explorer. But he did little exploring around its perimeter; he was soon less interested in shallow Lake Ngami than in the plentiful waters of the Zouga, now called the Boteti, and the Thamalakane, which flowed from 'a country full of rivers – so many no one can tell their numbers'. (His local informants were describing the Okavango Delta.) He was in the grip of the obsession which was to dictate the course of the rest of his life: the pursuit of a navigable highway into the interior.

Such was his excitement with the amplitude of water on the other side of the desert that Livingstone seemed to forget the family who waited 600 miles to the south-east. But he didn't forget to take nature notes. *Missionary Travels* gives a rapturous account of the variety and abundance of wildlife on the banks of the Boteti, including elephants in 'prodigious numbers'. He observes the wisdom of elephant matriarchs, which knew how to sabotage the pits dug by the Batawana to trap animals as they came to drink. 'Reeds and grass are laid across the top; and are then strewn with sand ... Some of our party plumped, more than once, into these pitfalls ... Old elephants have been known to precede the herd and whisk off the coverings of the traps on each side the whole way down to the water.'

He admires the 'magnificent' trees of the riverine woodland and measures the girth of an enormous baobab (76 feet). He notes that the fishermen take ten different kinds of fish from the river with nets and spears and that their canoes are hollowed out of a single tree-trunk, so that 'if the tree has a bend, so had the canoe'. (Today's visitors to the Okavango will recognise the mokoro, the punt which takes them game-viewing in its lagoons and channels; although these days, to spare the delta's hardwoods, the mokoro is made of aluminium.) He was turning into a superb naturalist. With Oswell and Murray, he identifies three new (to the Europeans) species of antelope which live on floodplains or wetlands: the puku, the sitatunga and the lechwe. He calls the lechwe a 'water-antelope' and accurately describes its bounding gallop through shallow water from reed bed to reed bed, when if alarmed 'it lowers its head, and lays its horns down to a level with its withers'.

New aspirations for his Christian mission further stimulated his mood, which remained exalted, although in retrospect it had its sombre moments. As he later wrote to Arthur Tidman of the London Missionary Society, 'I could not help feeling sad as I looked down on the steady flowing waters of the Zouga (exactly like the Clyde just above Bothwell Bridge) and thought of the thousands who have paddled over them in total ignorance of Him who bore our sins on his own body on a tree'. He had not been given LMS permission to leave his post at Kolobeng, and it was important to impress upon the directors that his purpose was evangelical. He had in his sights, however, not the Batawana but Chief Sebetwane and the Makololo who, it was confirmed, were living beside even more tremendous streams only 200 miles to the north. And at this point Livingstone's behaviour became very strange indeed, as his euphoria climbed into something which looks like hypomania.

The season was turning towards the hottest time to travel and his family expected him at Kolobeng, but he told Oswell and Murray that he wanted to continue alone to find Sebetwane's capital. Oswell pleaded to be allowed to go with him; but the plan was thwarted by the Batawana chief. Lechulathebe had welcomed them and was eager to trade but, when he learned that Livingstone wanted to reach the warrior Makololo, feared the consequences. If the expedition chose to sell guns to the northern tribe, his own people would be in danger, so Lechulathebe refused to let them cross the Boteti at the fords he controlled. Undaunted, Livingstone spent days on the riverbank trying and failing to construct a raft with wood which was rotten and wouldn't bear his weight. 'I worked many hours in the water, for I was not then aware of the number of alligators in the Zouga, and never think of my labours without feeling thankful that I escaped their jaws.'

Bizarrely, he then proposed to swim across the river, without explaining how he would then equip himself for a 200-mile trek to the north. Oswell was astonished by his behaviour, which he called 'Scottish', and not a little alarmed. He persuaded him to postpone his visit to the Makololo until the following year with the promise of a boat which he would bring from Cape Town. Livingstone also had second thoughts about swimming the Boteti because he was shy of exposing his white nakedness to the bemused locals. The madness slowly subsided.

The expedition began the long haul back to Kolobeng. It was slow, hampered by dying oxen and the activities of Chief Sekgoma of the Bang-wato. Jealous of his monopoly on the ivory coming out of the interior, the chief was suspicious of the travellers and tried to sabotage their outward and return journeys by filling in all the water holes in his fief. As they skirted his capital at Shoshong, a frantic plea for news reached them from Mary. Back at the homestead her spirit was almost spent.

In her book *The Livingstones at Kolobeng*, Janet Wagner Parsons makes every effort to be fair to the nature of the Livingstone marriage, its Victor-ian context, and the exceptional demands made on Mary by her husband's immutable sense of purpose, which he believed was God-given. (There is plenty of evidence, in fact, that he was also driven by personal ambi-tion.) She tries not to pass judgement on the reckless way he neglected his family when seized by a new idea and gripped by the prospect of travel, but his late return from Lake Ngami provokes reproach: 'He might have foreseen the circumstances and duration of her lonely vigil and distress. He had always known that epidemics overtook the country every winter – diarrhoea, bronchitis or pneumonia – and that every year one or more of them struck a devastating blow to malnourished people, his own frail children among them.'

Livingstone hadn't seen his wife and children for six months, and his homecoming letter to the anxious Moffats was a flurry of excuses to explain his long absence: Oswell had arrived late with the oxen and wag-ons, they had miscalculated the distances involved, the chiefs had been obstructive. No mention of his hyperactivity at the Boteti and his wild scheme to push on northwards to the Makololo, which would have caused much more delay. That rush of blood to the head, however, had merely receded, to be replaced by cooler calculations, although by most people's standards the risks of his new plan were extreme. The fourth chapter of *Missionary Travels* begins with the bland words: 'I returned to Kolobeng and remained there till April, 1850. I then left, in company with Mrs Livingstone, our three children, and the chief Sechele, with the intention of crossing the Zouga at its lower end, and proceeding up the northern bank till we gained the Tamunak'le. My purpose was next to ascend that river and visit Sebituane in the north.'

The family's settled life was effectively over.

We have one last relic to visit at Kolobeng before we leave the haunt of the wild boar to its present duties as heritage site: the graveyard, if you can call a burial ground without monument or headstone a graveyard. Alfred Piet leads us down the hill towards the river and a thicket of wild mimosa, where there is a clearing staked with more posts linked with chain. In the rough grass are three shallow mounds. Two of them cover the remains of two men who died near Kolobeng in 1851 – the year the family was struggling back from its most challenging journey to the interior, the year Sechele and the Bakwena left Kolobeng for ever, and the year Livingstone made up his mind to uproot Mary and the children from their African home and send them to Scotland. The unmarked graves have been identified, although there is some mystery about the deaths. 'They are Alfred Dolman, an English adventurer, and his servant John Coleman', explains our guide. 'People think they were murdered by another traveller, but by the time the bodies were found the scavengers had got to them.'[1]

The largest mound, more firmly defined by uncut stones, covers the smallest remains: the scraps which were briefly Elizabeth Pyne Livingstone, who was born within days of Mary's return from her first trek across the Kalahari and died six weeks later. Her grave is also unmarked; but one visitor, perhaps a child, has left a posy of artificial marigolds inside its border of rocks.

It's almost exactly a year since I left four fresh blossoms on the distant grave of Elizabeth's mother. The marigolds will last longer.

We have spent four days and covered nearly 1,300 miles on the journey to Griquatown, Kuruman, Mabotsa, Chonuane and Kolobeng, and still we have only brushed the hem of the great sand sheet of the Kalahari. For the moment, we've run out of time. Keith has commitments, work

---

1 Alfred Dolman was a young English artist from a prosperous home who had left school to travel to the Cape and explore the interior. He was interested not in trading or hunting but in drawing the land and its wildlife. At some point, he met Livingstone; and it is believed he was trying to join the expedition to Linyanti when he was killed.

and family, in Johannesburg; I have commitments, work and family, in Edinburgh. 'Next year?' I suggest. 'Let's aim for May or June, when the Livingstones travelled.'

'You bet', agrees Keith. 'That will give me plenty of time to do some research on the route and how long it will take us. It's pretty straightforward as far as Maun, but the road to the lake is a bit obscure, and once you get into Chobe National Park you run into an awful lot of soft sand.'

It will also give me time to explore ways of supporting my return to Botswana to follow Mary Livingstone across the desert to Lake Ngami; then northwards to the 'country full of rivers', along the edge of the Okavango Delta and across the Mababe Depression to the Chobe River, where four countries rub shoulders as it flows into the Zambezi.

15

Ragtag and Bobtail

'We are still in deep anxiety about the Livingstones'

June 2009

Not for nothing is the currency of Botswana called the pula. In Setswana, *pula* means rain, which has been valued for longer than the diamonds now prised out of the Kalahari by the Botswana government and De Beers. While I have spent the winter in Scotland there have been good rains during the Botswana summer, and they should be over. But a maverick weather system has migrated from the Atlantic and lodged above the desert, dumping torrents of water on its confused animals and plants and reversing the seasons. 'It's official', Keith Rampton tells me. 'It hasn't rained like this in June since 1994.'

It is insensitive, even ignorant to complain about rain in much of Africa – and as Keith and I approach Botswana's south-east border I do my best to smile approval at the clouds hanging over the Manyelanong Hills like dingy, dripping washing. We are on the road again, and the Land Rover is even more comprehensively equipped with expedition essentials for a journey which may find us running out of daylight and camping in Chobe National Park. But it begins in urban Botswana. We are heading for Gaborone through customs and immigration at the familiar post of Ramotswa. This time, I notice more of the town and take my usual delight in the inventiveness of African trading names. If you scavenge scrap from old motor cars and farm equipment, why wouldn't you call your recovery business Vulture Scrap Metal? Or if you make your living as an undertaker, why wouldn't you name your parlour One Call Funerals? Sooner or later we all receive that One Call.

Ramotswa's near-namesake, Mma Ramotswe, is on my mind, displacing Ma-Robert for at least a day. I've planned a series of travel articles which will help me stay in Botswana for longer than my budget would otherwise allow. For one feature, I want to write about Gaborone's new international celebrity, and have made contact with a guide who takes clients round the landmarks of *The No. 1 Ladies' Detective Agency*. The film series based on the McCall Smith books has just completed a season on BBC television, the set is still standing on the outskirts of the city, and Botswana's unspectacular, little-known capital has been sprinkled with the kind of stardust which makes drive-through tourists break their journeys to the stellar regions of the country's wilderness. I've arranged to join the Ramotswe tour the following morning, before I slip back into the nineteenth century and pick up the trail of Mary Livingstone.

During the Edinburgh winter, I've also spent time trying to find support for Gaia Allison's heritage trail to Mary's grave, but I've had only polite interest from the Scottish churches, while the Royal Geographical Society is happy to 'raise the profile' of Livingstone's wife but can't offer financial help. I need to find a friendly philanthropist with an interest in the Livingstones, but my enquiries are interrupted by disappointing news from Mozambique. Gaia is leaving Beira. Her contract with the provincial government has not been renewed, and, although she has tried to involve the Archdiocese of Beira and the British Embassy in Maputo in the project, she is no longer on the ground to drive it forward. 'Not sure I'll be able to do much from Tajikistan', she tells me when we meet over the Scottish border in Cumbria, where she is visiting her family before taking up her next job in international development. 'But we'll keep in touch. Maybe when your book is published we can try again.'

The book is now dependent on this second expedition with Explorer Safaris, which is more ambitious than the first. Earlier in the year, Keith has done part of the route with two clients, an American pastor and his wife by the name of Livingston. Different spelling, no relation. 'We found Lake Ngami, according to the satnav co-ordinates, but we couldn't find any water. The locals say the lake has been virtually dry for years.'

This is not unexpected. Even Livingstone noticed that Ngami's surface area had diminished on his second visit and made some early comments on the 'desiccation' of Africa. The lake has been changing its size ever since, shrinking and swelling but mainly shrinking at the whim of the complex river system and drainage of the Okavango Delta, where the often mysterious movement of water is believed to have more to do with fractional shifts in tectonic plates than the volume of rainwater in any given season. 'In 1849,' writes Oliver Ransford, who described its vagaries after a visit in 1971, 'the lake was a noble sheet of water. Thirteen years later Baines found it no more than a pan. In 1925 it again covered an extensive area, but in 1950 it was quite dry. During 1951 it had increased to five miles of water but when the author visited it twenty years later it was represented by a star-shaped pond, only fifty yards across.'

According to Ransford, another factor affects the size of the lake: the quantity of sudd, massed vegetable matter, on one of the Okavango channels which feeds it. Another channel runs into a ridge of the Kalahari sand which deflects its water southwards as the Thamalakane River, and then eastwards as the Boteti River – one of the few Okavango drainage systems which flows deep into the heart of the desert and even reaches the salt pans where Livingstone, Oswell and Murray saw mirages of Lake Ngami. They were perplexed by the intricacies of this drainage system, as the higher they climbed the Boteti, the broader it became. 'The explanation lies in the fact that, as it flows, the Botletle loses much of its water by evaporating, and literally dies in the desert', says Ransford, who uses the Setswana spelling of the river's name.

The Boteti has been dry since the early 1990s. Its vitality seems to come and go in forty-year cycles; but, just before I leave for Botswana, I get exciting news from Mena a Kwena, one of the camps where I've arranged to stay on our route to Lake Ngami. It sits on the lip of a sandy gorge – the bereft channel which, in 1851, was brimming with sweet water when Mary Livingstone gave birth to her fifth child. Now the Boteti has started to flow again. Delta floodwaters have been pushing slowly but persistently into the dry river bed, and the camp tells me this will transform the lives of local people who, unlike the wildlife and their own nomadic ancestors, don't have the option of upping sticks and looking for water elsewhere. Like most reputable safari operators, Mena a Kwena is closely involved with its neighbourhood village, and has been helping to organise a water-aid programme along with pumping water holes to attract game to the camp's environs. But muddy pools can't compete with living waterways. Mena a Kwena means 'teeth of the crocodile', but has seen no crocodile for a very long time. There is hope now that these ancients will return, along with other aquatic characters and all the fabulous bird life of an African river.

Can a lake be a lake or a river be a river without water? The news from the Boteti makes me hopeful that Ngami is also a beneficiary of record water levels in the Okavango Delta, but meanwhile Keith and I have our own weather system to negotiate. The depression over south-central Africa shows no sign of budging. We drive into Gaborone in a deluge. The Botswana capital is better equipped than many of its continental counterparts to cope with heavy rain; the city is less than fifty years old, and most of its roads and street lighting are comparable to any in the West. Gabs, as the locals call it, was purpose-built as the seat of government when Bechuanaland became the Republic of Botswana in 1964. Older Batswana, black and white (and almost certainly Mma Ramotswe), have mixed feelings about its urban personality, which is not organic. Most of it was built in three years. It's also the economic centre, and one of the fastest-growing cities in the world. Some 200,000 people, about 10 per cent of Botswana's tiny population, live there, tucked into the country's south-east corner less than ten miles from the South African border.

This is the city which 'does not fit badly' or is 'not unbecoming' – the meaning of the name, which it takes from Gaborone village and its eponymous chief. (The site of the new capital was chosen because it was close to water and the railway to Pretoria, and because Chief Gaborone of the Batlokwa was a neutral figure among the central tribes.) Is Gabs 'not unbecoming'? It's almost dark when we arrive, but I'm struck by its broad boulevards, pedestrian walkways and open spaces. It was built along the principles which then informed much of Britain's post-war urban planning. It is a 'garden city'. Tomorrow, in daylight, I'll have time to see how much of the chaotic vibrancy of African cities has been sacrificed to its design.

At the end of April 1850, a small, untidy caravan of assorted men, women, children and beasts plodded northwards from Kolobeng. Its complement of Europeans and Tswana passed to the west of Kgale Hill, 'the sleeping giant' which a century later would supervise the building of Gaborone, and set a course for Shoshong, breaking camp before dawn, travelling steadily at three miles an hour until darkness fell, outspanning at noon to rest the oxen and spare themselves the worst of the midday heat. Livingstone called his second expedition to the interior 'ragtag & bobtail'. He used his own elderly, patched-up wagons and provided his own supplies, relying on an agreement reached with the LMS that at least some of his costs would be met. He had not waited for Oswell, who was on his way from Cape Town with the promised boat to cross the Boteti. Livingstone left no explanation for his puzzled benefactor, who arrived at the Kolobeng homestead near the end of May to find it empty and shuttered. Sechele and his family were also missing, along with the Kuruman convert and trainee evangelist Mebalwe.

The missionary's treatment of this big-hearted, good-natured Englishman, who loved the adventure of exploration for its own sake and had no dreams of glory, was at best discourteous and at worst duplicitous. The biographers of both have come to the conclusion that Livingstone wanted to shed Oswell in order to claim sole credit for reaching 'the country full of rivers' and the Makololo of Sebetwane. He had also found an option to the boat, a strategy which he believed would overcome the obstacle of the Boteti and the intransigence of the Batawana chief Lechulathebe, custodian of the ford. The option was Mary Livingstone.

Even without the far-flung reputation of Robert Moffat, whose name was known and honoured by both Batawana and Makololo, a white family travelling among the tribes was an act of good faith. No man whose intentions were hostile or exploitative would bring along his wife and children; and the daughter of 'Moshete', as Mary's father was called, represented considerable added value. Livingstone's diplomatic instincts when negotiating with Africans were almost always right, and he judged that his family's presence would smooth their passage across the river and onwards to the north. Confident that Mary's name would open respectful doors, he even decided to tackle the unhelpful Bangwato chief Sekgoma in his Shoshong capital, and managed to make a friend of him. The water holes which Sekgoma had again filled in were soon unblocked; and, after Livingstone treated him for an ulcer, the chief provided him with guides.

In the months since they were reunited at Kolobeng, Mary seems to have grown resigned to the prospect of this extended family outing. She knew her husband's gaze was now fixed on the north and was deeply reluctant to be without him again. The children also needed their father. Agnes and Tom were probably too young to be much aware of his absence, and certainly too young to resent it. Robert was now four, a child whom his grandmother Moffat had found bright for his age; but Livingstone remarked in a letter that he had problems expressing himself. Perhaps only to Livingstone. 'That year at Kolobeng and Kuruman,' writes Parsons, 'and the six months of his father's absence in particular, had laid their mark on the boy. He alone among the children had been old enough to comprehend his mother's distress ...'

Another consideration was the situation at Kolobeng, where security remained an issue – particularly as Sechele, his wife and children and twenty Bakwena had decided to join the expedition to explore not the land but its opportunities for trade. As Livingstone was now more familiar with the route to Ngami, he decided, presumably, that there were no great risks in bringing his family along, even though he knew there were times when they were going to get very thirsty indeed. Nor was it any deterrent, apparently, that Mary was five months pregnant when they set off, and might well give birth during the round trip – which, if they reached Sebetwane's capital, would cover nearly 1,500 miles.

At Kuruman, Ma-Mary was less sanguine. She thought the adventure lunacy. Her daughter, she knew, was often unwell during her pregnancies; she feared the possibility of miscarriage and distrusted Livingstone's ambition. The more her son-in-law insisted he must reach the farthest frontiers with the Gospel, the more she suspected that his motives were temporal: the intoxication of exploration and the celebrity which came with illuminating the mysteries of the uncharted interior. 'Her own instinct', writes Mora Dickson, 'was to settle, put down roots and engage in the long, slow battle of conversion. For this purpose she would gladly have relinquished any of her children, to live in any circumstances however dangerous; but in Mary's case she saw little evidence of it.'

Ma-Mary was wise enough not to object openly to the 'ragtag & bobtail' expedition which exposed a pregnant woman and three vulnerable infants to the extremes of desert travel; but, six weeks after they left, she wrote to a friend: 'We are still in deep anxiety about the Livingstones; we have not heard a word about them since they left – and if dear Mary is right in her calculations she is to be confined next month. It was an ill-managed affair for her to go with him and if experience does not teach them that, then I shall say they are dull scholars.'

The 'dull scholars' learned nothing, despite the calamitous outcome of Mary's confinement. And, when Livingstone proposed to mount a second family expedition the following year, Ma-Mary was a great deal more outspoken.

The Kalahari gushes. From Namibia comes news that my Mma Ramotswe contact is bogged down on safari and won't be back in Gaborone in time to show me his *No. 1 Ladies' Detective Agency* tour. But, by happy accident, we've already made a start. En route to our guest house in one of the oldest suburbs, we come upon Zebra Way; not quite Zebra Drive, the home address of Mma Ramotswe, and a little too affluent for the modest sleuth. Capacious bungalows on sprinkled lawns, security systems, and the well-defended Tiny Bubbles Pre-School and Day Care centre (Your Kids, our Pride). But surely the name is the inspiration. 'Let's see if we can find one or two more spots tomorrow', I suggest. 'I want to get some impression of Gaborone, and maybe the tourist information office can give us a steer.'

It can and it does, contributing a city map. Overnight, the deluge has eased into drizzle. Gaborone's city centre looks damp and smells nice: wet vegetation from the gardens of the Government Enclave. Outside the Parliament Buildings, a bronze statue of Sir Seretse Khama balances on a boulder of Kalahari rock, while Pula Arch, monument to independence, rises at the other end of the Main Mall, the central avenue of commercial buildings. There are the usual international hotels, including the Gaborone Sun where Precious Ramotswe sometimes enjoys coffee, and an orderly African market which may be less sober when the sun comes out. Nearby are the National Museum and Art Gallery, the Princess Marina Hospital, and to the east of Maputo Drive the National Stadium and University of Botswana. Every tree which has survived the city's development, and every tree since planted, is cherished for its shade – not much in demand on this freakish June day. To escape another downpour, we duck into the Botswana Book Shop in the pedestrian precinct. Its stock of Mma Ramotswe novels is running low, and I buy the last copy of *The Tears of the Giraffe* – an early mystery, but my favourite and worth rereading.

Outside the central business district, Gaborone, like the new towns of 1960s Britain, is designed for the motor car: ring roads, bypasses, dual carriageways and slick retail parks with on-site leisure facilities. Unlike the new towns of post-war Britain, the arteries feel temporary, although their paving is solid enough. They seem to carry an air of expectation, as if every speeding car is only playing at urban life, and the instant city might vanish into the huge, wild, empty land on its doorstep just as quickly as it appeared. The Gaborone Dam, which commandeers the Notwane River for the city's water supply, has a reservoir which is used for recreation. It is home to the Gaborone Yacht Club and the Kalahari Fishing Club and is popular with birdwatchers, but swimming is discouraged. 'Take a dip and the crocs might get you,' I inform Keith, 'which is what happened to the husband of one of Mma Ramotswe's clients.'

As a consumer of McCall Smith's entire Botswana oeuvre, I find that the No. 1 lady detective has almost succeeded in performing an act of transubstantiation. She is becoming real. McCall Smith himself blurs the line between fact and fiction by including one 'Dr Moffat' in his stories. Dr Moffat exists. Howard Moffat is the great-great-grandson of Robert and Mary, and one of many members of the dynasty who never left Africa. For several years he was superintendent of the Princess Marina Hospital, the largest treatment centre for HIV infection and AIDS in the world. (Botswana was the first African country to dispense free anti-retroviral drugs.) There isn't time to look him up, but when I'm back in Scotland we make contact to productive effect. He puts me in touch with an Edinburgh Moffat who answers some of my outstanding questions about Mary's grave – more of which to come.

Keith and I take to the Land Rover to drive around the outer capital, which is thinly spread on the surface of its recent bushland. The industrial zones and residential suburbs consume space in a manner which, in cramped Europe, would be considered wasteful. Gaborone's flat uniformity would be dull but for its dominant natural feature: Kgale Hill, 4,000 feet of raw, rugged, piled-up Africa on the city's south-west boundary. And it's here, in the rain, at the foot of Kgale Hill, in the custody of a chain-link fence and a handsome Alsatian dog, that we find an illusion of the small human world of Precious Ramotswe.

Kgale View is a neat complex of low-income housing, and 'Kgalewood' is the nickname of the mothballed film set of *The No. 1 Ladies' Detective Agency* on its outskirts. Through the fence we see fading pastel colours, blue, pink and green, on flaking plaster, Mma Ramotswe's place of business with its proud signage, the Last Chance Hair Salon and sundry small shops. All is hushed in the deserted lot but for a tentative bark from the guard dog, which seems confused about its role. When we approach the padlocked gate he approaches us from its other side, wagging his tail, but the look in his eye is stern. The guard in him wants to scare us off; the dog welcomes the company.

'*Dumela, Mma, Dumela, Rra.*' The greeting comes from behind us and makes me jump. Mr JLB Matekoni, perhaps, proprietor of Tlokweng Road Speedy Motors and shy suitor of Precious Ramotswe? No, a muscular, smiling young man who represents Security but also seems glad to see us on this dismal morning. He is happy to answer questions. Yes, people come on tours to visit the film lot, but he doesn't know if and when it will be used again.[1] No, the real Tlokweng Road Speedy Motors is on Tlokweng Road and has a different name, but the set has a lock-up which doubles as the mechanics' workshop. Yes, this was the first major production to be filmed in Botswana, and everyone in Gaborone was very excited.

And then Security, who is armed with a set of keys, proves he is no jobsworth. When I explain my mission and ask if we can take a closer look at the set, he pauses only to say: 'Let me first tie up Rocky and the other dogs. There are two more inside.' Which is how I come to have a photograph of myself standing on the veranda of The No. 1 Ladies' Detective Agency. Starstruck? Well, I've got an article to write.

Only when we're on the road again, clearing Gaborone on another dual carriageway, do I start to reproach myself for neglecting Botswana's national heroes in order to pursue Botswana's fantasy heroine. 'We should have made time to see the Three Dikgosi Monument', I lament, 'and pay our respects to Sechele's heir.'

---

1 The film lot at 'Kgalewood' remains mothballed. In 2007 the producers signed a ten-year lease on the site, but the television series got disappointing ratings, and no second series was commissioned. In 2011 the production company announced that scripts for two feature-length films were in development.

The Three Chiefs Monument, inaugurated in 2005 and a landmark in the new business district, honours the three paramount chiefs who secured the future of Botswana by saving Bechuanaland from the acquisitive predators of the British South African Company and the land-grabbing aggressors of the Boer Republics. But for the chiefs' pan-Batswana alliance and a journey made to London in 1895, the country would today be part of either Zimbabwe or South Africa. They were Khama III of the Bangwato, Bathoen I of the Bankwaketse and Sebele I of the Bakwena – son of the great and much-loved Sechele.

After Livingstone deserted the Bakwena for the Makololo, and the Bakwena themselves abandoned Kolobeng, Sechele devoted himself to years of painstaking negotiation to bring together the leading Tswana tribes and conserve the independence of their territories. Three years after he died, his heir Sebele travelled to the United Kingdom with his fellow chiefs to petition Queen Victoria to limit the activities of the British South Africa Company in Bechuanaland, which at first the Crown was reluctant to do. The three chiefs appealed directly to a British public which, decades earlier, had been alerted by the eloquent testimonies of both Livingstone and Sechele to the endangered status of the Tswana. Sebele, Khama and Bathoen succeeded with a compromise. Sebele's father had earlier set his boundary with the Transvaal at the Limpopo and Notwane rivers; and the country beyond the rivers became a British protectorate for much of the following century.

Sechele's relationship with the British began with his friendship with a missionary whose greatest strength was his empathy with the heathens he had come to convert. But the Bakwena chief's own qualities and vision were just as important, as Parsons identifies:

> In a career that spanned half a century Sechele had taken a few hungry and nomadic people, fragmented and harassed ... and built a populous, prosperous and cohesive *morafe* (tribal nation), the greatest among the northern Batswana. The kingdom of Kgosi Sechele, in turn, provided an example to the Bangwato and Bankwaketse, whose kingdoms formed in its likeness, and the Tswana chiefs learned strength through co-operation to create the genesis of the modern nation of Botswana.

This is the significance of the Three Chiefs Monument. Like many ambitious public projects, it arrived to a fanfare of controversy. The cost of three larger-than-lifesize bronze statues on a hefty plinth (12 million pula, well over £1 million) was an issue; and the North Korean construction company got the date wrong in the inscription. But Botswana's progress from British protectorate to independent republic has had little of the trauma of its neighbours, Zimbabwe and South Africa, both still tormented by their colonial past. The three chiefs surely deserve their tribute.

In 1850, Sechele was in the prime of life but anything but ascendant. He was taking risks to guarantee a future for the dispersed and beleaguered Bakwena, and the greatest risk he took was his commitment to Christianity, which almost cost him his authority. The Livingstone family expedition across the Kalahari gave him relief from the disapproval of his counsellors. He had his own wagon and brought with him his children and his remaining wife, and he enjoyed hunting for the pot as the motley procession made its way from Shoshong to the Boteti. They travelled throughout May as the surface water began to evaporate and the last thin scatter of summer growth disappeared. Only the solitary shepherd tree kept its evergreen colour on the bleached wasteland, and it was a rarity. But the desert had its compensations. At sunrise and sunset, the Kalahari glows as if lit by fire from within.

For pregnant Mary, who, unlike her mother, did not enjoy ox-wagon travel, the journey must have been always uncomfortable and often stressful – keeping the children amused, distracting them from their thirst or the unpleasant taste of muddy water, and feeding them rations which, she knew, were anything but ideal. For over three months the family lived on stewed meat, corn, milk and coarse bread when Mary was able to bake it. If they had waited for Oswell they would have been able to enjoy the bottled fruit and tinned cake which were among the luxuries carried on his generous wagons. Livingstone later claimed that he had made no firm arrangement to travel with his old companion and benefactor, but this was contradicted by Oswell's arrival at Kolobeng with the boat. Tolerant as ever, the English sportsman merely recorded that Livingstone had 'rather unwisely taken his wife and children with him', and made his own way to the Boteti, hunting from a spot where he hoped to meet the party on their return.

Only the *Sarwa*, or San, whom Europeans called Bushmen, were adapted to surviving in the harshest conditions of the Kalahari – and they were not always there by choice. The desert gave these nomadic hunter-gatherers some protection from Griqua and Boers, many of whom treated them as primitives fit only for forced labour, and thought nothing of abducting their wives and children. Livingstone, whose compassion for the most oppressed Africans was limitless, wrote tenderly of the San who owned only what they could carry. In *Missionary Travels*, he describes an encounter near the Boteti: 'A little farther on we came upon an old man quite naked and hopelessly diseased. He informed us that he had been deserted a few days before us by his daughters, that he suffered much from thirst, for though lying under the large trees which line the banks of the river he could not crawl down for water. Having supplied him with a covering and some food, we offered to carry him to the next village. "O," said he, "if they saw me they would flee from me." Socialism has but sorry fruits among these unsophisticated specimens of humanity.'

Socialism was not hugely evident among the European expeditionaries either, for all their kindness. They, too, had to abandon the old man, whose daughters' behaviour was almost certainly not callous but pragmatic. Their father was dying, their own struggle for survival was desperate and they could not afford the burden of his final days. But it would be a mistake to imagine that these 'unsophisticated specimens' lacked sensibility. The theft of their children 'was the greatest tragedy that could befall a people who loved babies above all else and had so few', according to Parsons.

There were other encounters on the road to Lake Ngami, and they were harbingers of disaster. The expedition came upon two separate parties of traders who had been cut down by malaria. Several had died, others were critical; and only Livingstone's early experiments with quinine, which by 1850 was known to fight the fever, helped their recovery. Undaunted, he continued with his family to the lake, whose level had shrunk by three feet since his last visit. He had noticed that malaria was common where there was water – 'the source is no doubt marshy miasmata', he told Robert Moffat – but at that time neither he nor anyone else had made the connection with mosquitoes. The biting insects were to be endured as an irritant, albeit a savage one. After one night's exposure to them, the children were so badly attacked he 'could not touch a square half-inch' of their bodies which was unbitten.

Unknown to him, the female anopheles mosquito – the only member of the mosquito family to carry the malaria parasite – was the tiny saboteur which would again prevent him from travelling north to the Makololo. Mary's presence had indeed had the desired effect on Lechulathebe, the young chief of the Batawana, who received them hospitably. His cooperation was sealed with the gift of Livingstone's gun; and he not only agreed to let him ford the river but also offered him guides. Livingstone planned to leave Mary and the children in his protection. She was confident she would get it, along with the support of Sechele and his family, but was uneasy about losing the expert skills of her doctor husband. Who can blame her? She was now nearly seven months pregnant, her infant children were defenceless against disease, and she had seen men comatose and dying beside the Boteti River. One of them was a young artist called Alfred Rider, who left behind a sketch which later turned into a souvenir of a rare day of frivolity on the family expedition – their 'seaside holiday' beside Lake Ngami.

Livingstone had lost interest in Ngami, where the discomfort caused by mosquitoes inspired 'more fear than anything else in the Lake country', making it unsuitable for European settlement. But he knew that the immense, shining mirror would be a thrilling novelty for children who had never seen any expanse of water, let alone the sea, and he wanted to give Mary 'a peep'. She was badly in need of rest after months of trekking and had been shaken by an accident which she had always dreaded, perhaps because something similar had happened in her childhood. Their ox-wagon lurched into one of the camouflaged game traps and overturned, spilling all its passengers on the ground. Nobody was hurt, and her husband claimed that Mary reacted phlegmatically with the words 'Is that all?' But she must have been troubled for her unborn child.

When they reached the lake, they outspanned beside the water, where the children 'took to playing in it as ducklings do' – and a bizarre impression of the scene reached readers of *Missionary Travels* when it was published eight years later. Rider's sketch of Ngami had been amplified by another artist to include the entire family in their bulky, buttoned-up Victorian clothes. Robert and Agnes stand by the shallows, watching fishermen cast their nets; Tom is barely visible in his mother's arms as Mary sits by a campfire; and Livingstone looms above her with an instructive arm outflung.

The idyll was short. Fever struck the camp. Livingstone's trek north to meet Sebetwane hung in the balance. He had decided to travel on foot with only two men, as he knew that the tsetse fly which infested the banks of the Thamalakane would soon account for horses and oxen. Then Agnes and Tom went down with malaria, Mary's distress grew more and more intense, and for once Livingstone put the interests of his family before his own. They retreated to a spot on the Thamalakane where, fifty years later when the lake dried up, the Bakawana resettled in a new capital. At the place which would become Maun, the expedition turned east. It had become a rout.

At a ford on the lower Boteti, Oswell, who had spent the past two months hunting, was waiting for them with potatoes and fruit from Kuruman (although the apples had rotted) and other supplies which Livingstone had asked him to bring from the Cape, giving him £40 for their purchase, which Oswell insisted on returning. When he saw the children, he was shocked. Agnes, who called herself 'Nannee', the little girl who had charmed him at Kolobeng, was a ghost of her lively self, and the toddler Tom was so weak he had to be carried everywhere by his mother. Livingstone was glad of his support as they recrossed the desert, but was unrepentant. He believed that God had protected his party where others had fallen; and, although the 'ragtag & bobtail' expedition had achieved nothing of its aim, there had been no loss of life and therefore no harm done.

The loss of life and the harm done were waiting for them at Kolobeng.

16

The Portal to the Desert

'I must again wend my weary way to the far interior'

Round about noon, we cross the Tropic of Capricorn. Its invisible presence is honoured by a road sign, which I dutifully photograph. The boundless highway is bereft of corners, and swoops to a flat horizon, level as an ocean rim. As I stand in a lay-by on the Tropic of Capricorn, a man marches towards me, side-stepping puddles. He is smartly dressed in suit and raincoat, carries a suitcase and grins a greeting as he tramps past. I look round, dazed by the emptiness; tree and shrub savanna as far as the eye can see, no human imprint of any kind other than the road and its signage. People and donkeys seem equally at home in this pseudo-wilderness.

'Hitching or heading for a bus stop', explains Keith. The A1 to the north is a major transport artery, linking Gaborone with Francistown, Botswana's second city, and connecting with the highway from the Zimbabwean border to Bulawayo, the city founded by Robert Moffat's lifelong friend, the Matabele chief Mzilikazi. The A1 also hugs the line of the 'Cape to Cairo' railway, and much of it traces the route of the old Missionary Road to Shoshong. At the cattle town of Mahalapye, a secondary road loops round the angular Shoshong Hills to Serowe, which became the Bangwato capital in 1903. A few miles north, no longer marked on modern maps, was Serotle, the place that Oswell called 'the portal to the desert', and nearby is our own portal to the desert: an unusual gateway with some very impressive residents. Keith has booked overnight accommodation at Khama Rhino Sanctuary.

We have left Gaborone at noon. The rain has stopped, but the sulking clouds regroup as we travel. By the time we reach Mahalapye, 270 miles north of the capital, the sky has turned so dark that it activates the sensors on the street lights. Two hours later, we flow through Serowe on a torrent. This is an important town, seat of the Khama dynasty, birthplace of Sir Seretse Khama and his son Ian Khama, the president – but it might be under water for all I see of it. Only the gleam and scale of the new Sekgoma Hospital make any impression. I think of Livingstone's manoeuvres with that saboteur of water holes, the unfriendly Bangwato chief Sekgoma, who was dead by the time the tribe moved its capital from Shoshong to Serowe. But Sekgoma's heir was Khama the Great, one of the national heroes of the Three Chiefs Monument; and, although his Christian beliefs brought him into open conflict with his father, whom he deposed, the name Sekgoma remains an honoured one.

I have been chewing an apple to keep myself awake during the long drive and relentless rainstorm, while lamenting a receding vision of chargrilled filet mignon. Few campsites in southern Africa lack the most important asset to alfresco dining, and Khama Rhino Sanctuary is no exception. We are booked into self-catering A-frame chalets at Mokongwa Camp, with bush loo, hot shower and, of course, braai facilities. Keith has stocked the Land Rover fridge with steaks, I've supplied the Cape pinotage, and we have been looking forward to an evening of firelight, starlight and prime Botswana beef, confident that its smell will attract neither black nor white rhino, both strictly vegan.

The sanctuary is only fifteen miles from Serowe and has been open to visitors since 1993. It was set up by a community trust, with President Khama as patron, to reintroduce white rhinoceros to the Kalahari, and now has a breeding population of thirty-four, as well as two black rhino. Two centuries ago, both species could be measured in tens of thousands in their home ranges, but today only remnant populations live in the wild, outside the protection of game reserves and national parks, whose security is often fallible. The story of their persecution is well known. They are poached on an industrial scale for the pseudo-scientific properties of their horns, or for their ornamental value to Yemeni ceremonial daggers, which have handles fashioned from rhino horn. Throughout the nineteenth century and much of the twentieth, they were also shot for sport by the likes of William Cotton Oswell, Roualeyn Gordon-Cumming (a famously successful Scottish hunter) and William Frederick Webb of Newstead. All three got to know the Livingstones at Kolobeng; and the prescient author of *Missionary Travels* expressed doubt about their activities, calling Gordon-Cumming's predations 'warfare with wild animals'.

'The statement of Mr Cumming as to the number of animals he killed is by no means improbable when we consider the amount of large game which was then in the country. Two other gentlemen in the same region destroyed no fewer than seventy-eight rhinoceroses in a single season. The guns introduced among the tribes cause these fine animals to melt away like snow in spring.'

The two other gentlemen were almost certainly W. F. Webb and his future brother-in-law, Captain William Codrington. In *Livingstone and Newstead*, Webb's daughter, A. Z. Fraser, mounts a defence of her father and his companion by proposing that the extermination of animals like black rhino and lion was desirable. 'It must be borne in mind that at this date it was a real public service to rid these regions of dangerous beasts, whose presence in such numbers formed the chief impediment to improvement. Traders did little or nothing in this direction, and even the regular elephant hunters were so much more intent upon ivory, that they rarely went out of their way to waste bullets upon lions and black rhinoceros. The latter were often by far the most dangerous animals, and by no means easy to shoot. They were also so numerous that my father saw no less than twelve specimens in one day. My uncle says, in his journal, that they killed so many that at last he hardly troubled to write them down, regarding them "much as one would rabbits in England". I believe, however, that they secured seventy-eight in a single year.'

The armour-plated rhinoceros with its great antique head and ruthlessly pillaged horn continues to 'melt away like snow in spring', if more swiftly and violently. The Khama sanctuary population gets round-the-clock military protection from the Botswana Defence Force base at Serowe, and is also defended by a seventeen-mile electric fence funded by Debswana, the diamond-mining partnership of De Beers and the government of Botswana. It is former hunting land, seventeen square miles of woodland, sandveld and pan, and supports over thirty animal species. Some have been translocated, others have settled naturally, and over 230 bird species have also been recorded. The herbivores include giraffe, zebra, eland, kudu and red hartebeest, and the largest predators are brown hyena and leopard. We've promised ourselves a game drive in the morning, but first we need food; not barbecued steak under a Mokongwa tree but chicken and chips in the sanctuary restaurant.

The rain has drowned custom, and the swimming pool has burst its earthenware banks. We are the sole customers of the chilly brick-and-timber dining room, which, like the chalets, is designed to repel heat and sunshine and is ventilated accordingly. Like us, the staff are huddled in fleeces; but they generate enough warmth to make us feel welcome. They are much more bemused by the weather than I am. After all, I'm genetically programmed to expect and endure rain at any time of the year. 'It's crazy! Namaqua daisies out in June! They should not be blooming until August. And the frogs who have put themselves away for winter are all popping up and trying to mate. I tell you, Mma, the desert is going bananas. Where are you heading?'

'The Boteti River, the Makgadikgadi Pans and eventually Maun.'

The restaurant manager is happy on our behalf. 'The television says it's drying out up there. You should get some sun.'

When the Livingstones passed this way in June 1849, they sometimes travelled at night to avoid the sun; and, while the children slept, Mary was relieved of her exhausting efforts to distract them from their thirst. Once, they went two days without water. But what was mere hardship during their first crossing of the thirstland became an ordeal during their second.

The family limped into Kolobeng with the emaciated survivors of their oxen and their rickety wagon at the end of July. Midwinter. Livingstone tried to trivialise their halting progress through the sand with humour, describing their uneven tracks as 'the slithering of a snake', but it was a grim homecoming. The house was thick with windblown grit which Mary, now well past term and profoundly travel-weary, felt obliged to tackle. Once again, the family were almost destitute. They had no crops to harvest, and their milk cows were producing only half a pail daily. Their other supplies, including much-needed soap, were almost depleted, and once again they had to write to Kuruman for assistance. They had been home for barely a week when Mary went into labour.

The birth of Elizabeth Pyne, 'a very lively young lady', was to give her parents only a brief hiatus from their anxieties. A few days later, Mary became ill. She took to her bed with fits of shivering and something she called severe earache, and, untypically, stayed there. It was some time before Livingstone noticed that the right half of her face was frozen, causing 'considerable deformity, especially in smiling'. Her right leg was also paralysed, and she could do little to care for her new baby, the blue-eyed daughter who, from her father's light-hearted remarks to the Moffats, was clearly underweight at birth. She was, he said, a tiny thing about the size of Ma-Mary's little finger.

There has been much speculation about the nature of Mary's illness. It's often assumed that she suffered a stroke from which she recovered well, although she had recurring pain and occasional paralysis on the right of her face for the rest of her life. Livingstone described her symptoms and tried to treat the extreme pain in her temple by 'blistering' and 'cupping' (a traditional method of relieving pressure) but didn't offer a diagnosis. Over 100 years later, another medical man attempted to explain the 'neurological disease' afflicting a woman weakened by malnourishment, exhaustion and childbirth. In *Livingstone the Doctor*, a study in medical history published in 1957, Dr Michael Gelfand speculates that it might have been Bell's palsy, or perhaps poliomyelitis. Janet Wagner Parsons doesn't exclude toxaemia in pregnancy, which can lead to eclampsia and stroke, but makes the case for 'cerebral malaria endemic in the Lake Ngami region through which Mary travelled. The P. falciparum parasite enters the liver and remains dormant until a period of low resistance or stress (e.g., exhaustion, poor diet, birth and the puerperium).' Oedema then develops in the brain, causing pain and paralysis.

Whatever the cause, the lingering effects of Mary's facial paralysis, which tended to return when she was under strain, might explain the lifeless expression of her later photographs, and the look which some of her more critical companions on the Zambezi Expedition found 'queer'.

More sickness followed. It was the season for respiratory ailments. The Bakwena, as usual, were affected; and soon the children had feverish colds which turned into pneumonia. Livingstone took heart from the memory of Robert's recovery from 'inflammation of the lungs', and Elizabeth's elder siblings did rally. But the underweight baby, not yet a month old, grew weaker and weaker, and her despairing father could do little to help her fight the infection or ease her cries. She died six weeks after she was born, declining hour by hour while Livingstone tried every useless remedy at his disposal, from liniment rubs to quinine. She was, he said, 'taken from us to join the company of the redeemed of whom she never heard'. In a painful letter to his parents, he struggles to reconcile acute sorrow with florid piety. 'It is wonderful how soon the affections twine round a little stranger. We felt her loss keenly. We could not apply remedies to one so young except the simplest. She uttered a piercing cry, previous to expiring, and then went away to see the King in his beauty and the land – the glorious land and its inhabitants.'

It goes without saying that Mary must have shared his grief, but did she find any consolation in her baby's transfer to 'the company of the redeemed'? It's known that she wrote to her mother soon afterwards, but again that letter has vanished. It would not be too surprising if its anguish was inflamed by a sense of grievance, a disloyal hint that perhaps the Lake Ngami expedition carried some responsibility for the calamities which overwhelmed the family on their return. It seems more than carelessness that so many of Mary's letters written during the various crises in her life have been lost to history.

Livingstone claimed, no doubt sincerely, that he would remember his daughter's last cry even in eternity. But her death and her mother's illness did not prevent him from planning the second family excursion across the Kalahari. Much to the indignation of his later biographers, he refused to admit – or allow himself to consider – that months of deprivation and desert travel had contributed to their catastrophic homecoming. Instead, he attempted rationalisation. He convinced himself that Elizabeth's death was the result of infectious disease at Kolobeng, and wrote in his journal: 'It was the first death in our family, but just as likely to have happened had we remained at home, and we have now one of our number in heaven.' But Parsons doesn't let him off the hook:

> The smallness of the child at birth reflected privation; her mother's cerebral haemorrhage attested to the presence of malarial infection contracted in the regions of the lake. It was a baby more vulnerable than most that faced contagion from her debilitated brothers and sister ... Livingstone, in due course, would reap the criticism he expected. The death of the infant and paralysis of the mother would influence his decisions on the future of his family. Yet in the long term, when historians and society had propagated the myth of saintliness in the missionary explorer, the child and the tragedy would be forgotten.

Not entirely. Not today. Not by the Botswana National Museum or the likes of Alfred Piet and his successors at Kolobeng. The wooden marker disappeared long ago, but the rough stones which border the grave of Elizabeth Pyne are probably remnants of the cairn the Livingstones raised to protect her remains. Their neat arrangement is carefully maintained.

When news reached Kuruman that the Livingstones' fourth child had been born and the other children were ill, Ma-Mary trekked north. She knew from experience and instinct she was needed, although she did not know just how desperately the couple were struggling in every aspect of their lives. They were effectively stranded in conditions which worsened daily. The grain and supplies left by Oswell had been used up, their oxen were too weak to attempt an evacuation, the death of Elizabeth and the paralysis of her mother had blighted the spirits of the older children, and the morale of the household was at its nadir. When Livingstone himself developed pleurisy, his own iron constitution and indomitable will faltered. A violent hailstorm had broken windows which he didn't have the energy to replace. Only a donation of maize, wheat and sorghum from the Edwards, their old neighbours at Mabotsa, kept them going until Ma-Mary arrived in the middle of October. When she learned of the baby's death and saw their desolate circumstances, she loaded the family into her ox-wagon and took them back to Kuruman.

To be rescued by his mother-in-law must have stung Livingstone's pride, but he made no protest. Despite his lethargy, his mind was on the future. The retreat from Kolobeng effectively marked the abandonment of his mission there, although he said they were leaving only 'to rusticate a little'. The family rusticated for four months, recovering their strength as the summer rains revitalised the land and replenished its stock. The breeding season of the antelope family and other herbivores is timed to produce young as new growth bursts from the earth, but the human reproductive cycle has no such internal logic. If Mary Livingstone wasn't already pregnant when they returned home in February 1851, then she became so soon afterwards.

She had made her mother a half-promise. If she were pregnant, Mary maintained, it was improbable that she and the children would be tasked with another trek across the thirstland. Ma-Mary was convinced that the expedition to Lake Ngami had contributed to the baby's death and her daughter's illness, and was dismayed when she learned that Livingstone was planning an even longer expedition to an even more remote area, with no knowledge of its potential hazards. But events were being taken out of her hands. Her son-in-law had confided in Robert Moffat, who admired Livingstone's zeal and took the attitude that the family's destiny was in God's charge, while two other interested parties had emphasised Mary's importance to the enterprise. Sebetwane let it be known that he was equally eager to welcome 'the daughter of Moffat' as he was to receive her husband, if not more so; and Arthur Tidman, the new secretary of the LMS, gave his support on the understanding that Livingstone's wife had given hers.

Had she? From all that is known of Mary, it's impossible to imagine that she tried to argue her husband out of his consuming ambition to penetrate the uncharted interior. But there is evidence from one of Livingstone's letters that she did come up with an alternative plan. On 18 August 1850, shortly after their return from Lake Ngami, he wrote to his friend Watt: 'My wife, poor soul I pity her, proposed to let me go for that time (namely a year) while she remains at Kolobeng'. This would have been a huge sacrifice for Mary, but she was never called upon to make it, for three reasons: 'the daughter of Moffat' was Livingstone's greatest diplomatic asset, and he wanted her with him; Kolobeng was still under threat from the Boers; and – the most commanding reason from Mary's point of view – she was again pregnant and did not want to return to Kuruman to give birth, or, indeed, give birth anywhere without her husband's help. She knew he was going to go, regardless of her pregnancy, so her only choice was to go with him – which was no choice at all.

'She was as helpless to influence his movements as she was to control her childbearing', says Parsons.

For once, a fragment of Mary's own voice is heard in the outraged letter that her mother sent to Livingstone at Kolobeng, although it never reached him until they were on the trail. He recorded it in full in his journal, almost as if its stinging text was a form of self-flagellation. Mary's own letter to her mother, in which she indicates she is again pregnant but they are all preparing to leave for the north, has inevitably been lost. But Ma-Mary quotes her daughter's comment on the forthcoming adventure, and the words are not those of a woman excited by its prospect or committed to its purpose. They are at best apprehensive, at worst pessimistic. 'I must again wend my weary way to the far interior,' Mary wrote, 'perhaps to be confined in the field.'

Ma-Mary shared her foreboding. Her shock could not be contained; and, although her letter begins calmly, it soon gathers furious momentum.

'My dear Livingstone', wrote the Moffat matriarch. 'Before you left the Kuruman I did all I dared do to broach the subject of your intended journey, and thus bring on a candid discussion, more especially with regard to Mary's accompanying you with those dear children. But seeing how averse both you and Father were to speak about it, and the hope that you would never be guilty of such temerity (after the dangers they escaped last year), I too timidly shrank from what I ought to have had the courage to do. Mary had all along told me that should she be pregnant you would not take her, but let her come here after you were fairly off. Though I suspected at the end that she began to falter in this resolution, still I hoped it would never take place, i.e. her going with you, and looked and longed for things transpiring to prevent it. But to my dismay I now get a letter, in which she writes, "I must again wend my weary way to the far interior, perhaps to be confined in the field". O Livingstone, what do you mean? Was it not enough that you lost one lovely babe, and scarcely saved the others, while the mother came home threatened with paralysis. And will you again expose her and them in those sickly regions on an exploring expedition? All the world will condemn the cruelty of the thing to say nothing of the indecorousness of it. A pregnant woman with three little children trailing about in the company of the other sex, through the wilds of Africa, among savage men and beasts! Had you found a place to which you wished to go and commence missionary operations, the case would be altered. Not one word would I say, were it to the mountains of the moon. But to go with an exploring party, the thing is preposterous. I remain yours in great perturbation, M. Moffat.'

The angry and reproachful eloquence of this plea reveals much of what

Ma-Mary knew and didn't know. She had long suspected that her son-in-law's sense of mission, although sincere, was fired as much by his lust for exploration as his piety, but she seems to have been kept in the dark about the aims of the 'exploring party'. Livingstone had not only made up his mind to take the Gospel to the Makololo but also had genuine hopes of resettling his wife and children among them. He had indeed found a place to which he 'wished to go and commence missionary operations' – along with a much grander design.

As his influence on the Bakwena waned, despite the efforts of the steadfast Sechele, he persuaded himself that Sebetwane's warm invitations made the Makololo more promising candidates for conversion – and this was the case he presented to the LMS. But the real attraction of Sebetwane's people was the place where they lived, the 'country full of rivers' – and this also features in his correspondence with the society. Arthur Tidman, appointed its secretary in 1850, was proving a receptive ear; so much so that Tidman's maverick missionary shared his vision with him: 'We must have a passage to the sea on either the Eastern or Western coasts', wrote Livingstone after the family returned from Lake Ngami. 'I have hitherto been afraid to broach the project on which my perhaps dreamy imagination dwells. But ... without promising anything I mean to follow a useful motto in many circumstances and try again.'

That was how he won Tidman's endorsement for his third attempt to reach the Makololo – with the proviso that the project was fully backed by his wife. Interestingly, Parsons speculates that Mary, having accepted the inevitable, may have found her own purpose in the venture and even awarded herself a diplomatic role which, if successful, would have raised her high in the estimation of her parents. It involved her father's close friend Mzilikazi, chief of the Matabele.

Like the Matabele, the Makololo were migrants displaced by the rolling disruptions of the Mfecane. They were a tribe of the Sotho group who had lived in what is now the Free State of South Africa, and were forced east into Bechuanaland by Zulu incursions, then driven north by Griquas after a battle near Kuruman. They continued moving north until they reached the Chobe and Zambezi rivers, and by the 1840s had become the dominant tribe in the Barotse valley and the Batoka plateau, both now in Zambia. But they were harassed by the raiding parties of their old enemies, the Matabele, who were entrenched in the Bulawayo area of present-day Zimbabwe, and they had retreated into their swampy redoubt at Linyanti. Its defensive position between the Chobe and Zambezi gave them protection from the Matabele but exposed them to other lethal aggressors: malarial mosquitoes. They did not know the cause of the sickness which was steadily pruning their numbers, but they knew that Linyanti was unhealthy. If they stayed there indefinitely, they risked extermination.

Sebetwane was aware of Robert Moffat's influence with Mzilikazi and had become aware that the only escape from his unwholesome capitals was to negotiate a truce with his old enemy – perhaps through the good offices of Moffat's daughter. Parsons is one historian who has concluded that Mary was intimidated by her powerful parents and preferred 'the vagabond life over domination by her mother at Kuruman', and offers the theory that she was looking for a way to impress them. 'She had always fallen short in the level of commitment that her parents felt in witnessing to the heathen, but her father had another, related dream that may have attracted her enthusiasm: peace between the peoples of Mzilikazi and Sebetwane. She could be instrumental in laying the groundwork for evangelising two renowned heathen dynasties.'

Would she have risked the lives of her children to be the broker of peace between the warring chiefs? If Mary did harbour fantasies of fulfilling her father's dream, then they were marginal to her assigned role in the expedition, which was that of her husband's 'mainstay', as he flatteringly described her; but how she squared her devotion to him with the risks to her children is difficult to understand. Maybe it takes genteel, reverential, often ingenuous A. Z. Fraser, friend and confidante of Agnes Livingstone Bruce, to grasp the simple reality of Mary's priority and spell it out: 'good and tender mother as she was, it is very evident that she was one of those women to whom children come as a secondary consideration. Her heart was ever with her husband ...'

The family left Kolobeng on 24 April 1851, almost exactly a year after the start of the 'ragtag & bobtail' excursion. This time, they were better equipped. They were accompanied not by Sechele, who had other responsibilities, but by an equally invaluable friend: William Cotton Oswell, whose respect and affection for Livingstone now extended to his wife and children. Oswell was always prepared to tolerate the missionary's ungracious behaviour for their sake, and he did everything in his power to ease their passage on the Ngami trail which, since he, Livingstone and Murray had blazed the way two years earlier, was becoming waymarked by the dead campfires and discarded detritus of adventurers, ivory traders and sundry other fortune-seekers.

Ma-Mary's letter of protest, perhaps carried by one of these unofficial postmen, didn't reach Livingstone until the expedition was well on its way. Would it have put a brake on the rolling wagons if it had reached him in time? The dry comment he attached to her indignant words when he recorded them in his journal suggests not: 'They show in what light our efforts are regarded by those who, as much as we do, desire that the Gospel may be preached to all nations'.

He was fully conscious that he was leaving himself open to criticism for so jeopardising the lives of his family. But it was clear that he believed the goal was worth the risk.

17

Into the Thirstland

'the tearful eye told the agony within'

Most of the wildlife has gone undercover. We spend an hour squelching around the game tracks of Khama Rhino Sanctuary but log only two giraffes, a morose family of zebra and a waterbuck bull whose comfortable presence in the dripping bush seems almost satirical. As their name implies, waterbuck like water; nor do rhinoceros mind the rain; and, like elephant, they enjoy mud baths. They are also much more sociable than their reputation suggests, especially the white rhino. I once saw four whites taking their ease in a muddy pool like captains of industry in their club jacuzzi. But the brimming Serwe Pan is empty of heavyweights black or white. By 8am, we have left the rhino sanctuary for the desert which is no desert, no wasteland, but a storehouse of salt and diamonds and the natural element of many sentient creatures. To the Tswana, it was always the thirstland.

Our route follows much of the original Ngami trail, now smoothly tarred. It's interrupted from time to time by donkeys dozing in the middle of the road and by disease-control gates, where we are required to demonstrate that we have no unofficial livestock or infected meat in our vehicle. (I think of Keith's perfectly wholesome barbecue steaks in the Land Rover's fridge, and later he tells me he once had six fresh fillets of beef confiscated.) Botswana rigorously protects its beef industry, most controversially with hundreds of miles of long-distance fencing which score the Kalahari as far north as the Okavango Delta. They are there to prevent the spread of livestock diseases and meet the high veterinary standards of the European Union, the market for most of the country's beef exports. The network of fences and quarantine camps partitions the land into disease-control areas which restrict livestock movements – but also restrict the movements of non-domestic animals. The desert is etched with the migration routes of some of the largest populations of wildlife in Africa – zebra, giraffe, buffalo, wildebeest and other antelope species – and, when the routes are blocked, their seasonal search for water and grazing can end in death by dehydration; or, if they try to cross the fences, by hopeless entanglement, which has the same outcome, helped along by predators and poachers.

Until the discovery of diamonds in the early 1970s, beef production was the engine of the country's economy. It has since been overtaken by diamond mining and tourism; and beef exports now contribute less than 3 per cent to the GDP. But cattle remain a social and cultural touchstone in Botswana – cattle are the traditional currency of every livestock farmer, large or small – and the barrier fencing has come to represent a bloodless battleground between beef producers and wildlife managers. Despite one of the most comprehensive game laws in Africa, Botswana's wildlife numbers, with the exception of elephant and one or two other species, are in steady decline. Among the usual suspects is the veterinary cordon fence.

The Okavango Delta, with some of the largest concentrations of game, has been spared the encroachment of livestock farming by the helpful if uncomfortable presence of the tsetse fly. It most selectively infects domestic animals but few wild ones, most of which have developed immunity to the parasite which causes sleeping sickness. Horses and cattle are vulnerable; zebra and buffalo are not. But buffalo can spread foot-and-mouth disease, and to the conservationist the most notorious barrier is the Buffalo Fence, which traverses the Delta from south to north; especially its northern section, erected in 1996. Studies report that this fence is one of the most destructive to migratory species, cutting across a major route between dry and wet areas: it is one of several reasons why Botswana's wildebeest population has dropped by 90 per cent in two decades. With the GDP contribution from tourism, predominantly wildlife tourism, now outperforming beef exports by almost 7 per cent, there is pressure on the government to rethink its fencing strategy.

There have been other massive changes in the Kalahari since the Livingstones trekked from water hole to water hole between Kolobeng and Lake Ngami; and wildlife has played its part. Although diamonds were first discovered by De Beers prospectors, it delights me to learn that termites were the pioneering miners of the richest repository of the precious stones in the world. Jwaneng's deposits were discovered by termites looking for water. Digging deep, the tiny insects brought to the surface grains of diamond, and the Jwaneng mine followed on in 1982. Today there are five diamond mines in the country, the majority operated by Debswana, the partnership between De Beers and the government of Botswana. The country has become the leading global producer of gem diamonds – which is why, unlike the Livingstones' journey, our progress across the Kalahari is not entirely self-determined.

The town of Orapa, almost midway between Serowe and Maun, is on our route; and the Orapa mine is the oldest and largest in the country. I'm curious about the town, partly because Livingstone mentions the 'Orapa well' in *Missionary Travels*, and partly for its recent history, which didn't begin until 1972. 'The Kimberley *de nos jours*', I muse. 'We could stop for coffee there and have a look at it.'

'No chance, I'm afraid', Keith tells me. 'Not just the mine but the entire town is a secure area, surrounded by fencing and checkpoints. You can't get into it without a resident's permit or some kind of accreditation. The road detours round it.'

A gated community of over 15,000 people, who apparently feel not confined but safe and privileged. Botswana's diamonds are guarded as zealously as Botswana's beef. All we see of Orapa, and the smaller mine at Letlhakane, are the distant tabletop hills of their workings; but long before we reach them I've given myself over to the mysteries of the land-scape, which, under the sunless sky has faded into monochromes and become even more homogeneous. The wet sand is grey, the thorn trees and bushes are black with water, and mile after mile the road delivers the same ruler-straight horizons, but I have found a new entertainment: home-made bus stops.

Kalahari bus routes are happy to offer request stops, but on such a highway how do you know when you've reached the dirt turn-off to your village or homestead or cattle post? You create your own bus stop. First I notice a large red plastic jug hanging from the branch of a wayside camel-thorn; then an oil drum painted yellow, standing on the verge; then a shiny piece of tin or aluminium wedged into the branch of another tree; then an old tyre skewered by a fence post. These lonely, improvised bus stops, each marking the start of ghostly tracks to invisible homes, only disappear when the fences disappear. 'The end of fencing means the end of productive land', explains Keith.

The thorn trees dwindle. Now and then mokolwane palms, like frayed exclamation marks, punctuate the sheet of sand. Near Mopipi we see our first pan, its salt crust covered with rainwater. Two donkeys, fetlock-deep in water, face each other like book ends; and a distant figure, a woman in bright clothes, walks towards this shallow lake which is no illusion, although we're now truly in the thirstland. To the east of the great pans of Makgadikgadi we thread our way through lesser pans, where Liv-ingstone, Oswell and Murray were deceived by spectral plates of water. On later treks the mirages were ignored. They knew by then that they were still some 300 miles from Lake Ngami, but could look forward to the verdant conduit of the Zouga, the Boteti River. But on Livingstone's second journey with his wife and children, when the goal was neither lake nor single river but 'the country of rivers' and the Linyanti capital of the Makololo, the expedition changed direction. Almost fatally.

Why did Livingstone abandon the established route west of the Boteti to Lake Ngami, where he aimed to strike north-east along the well-watered margin of the immense floodplain now called the Okavango Delta and reach Linyanti with the guides offered by the Bangawato chief Lechu-latebe? Why did Oswell submit to an impromptu plan which would take them due north from the Boteti into unfamiliar land where it was known that there was very little water? The early stages of the journey had passed with few obstacles. Drought, not deluge, followed them along the Ngami trail into the month of June, and clouds of honey bees, deprived of their food source, escorted the ponderous wagons. The hungry bees detected the sugar inside; and on one of their lightning raids Mary and the children, trying to beat them off, were repeatedly stung. But although they could never afford to be relaxed about water and sometimes went thirsty, they now knew the sites of underground springs, and Oswell often rode ahead with their Bakwena helpers to dig them out. (There was nothing this big-hearted sportsman wouldn't do to improve conditions for Mary and the children; and he was to offer much more before they left their homeland.)

Eight years later, in *Missionary Travels*, Livingstone outlined his plan for 'crossing the Zouga at its lower end, and proceeding up the northern bank till we gained the Tamunak'le (Thamalakane). My purpose was next to ascend that river and visit Sebituane in the north.' This was his intention on both the family treks, although, as I've already described, the plan was aborted on the first of them when 'our little boy and girl were seized with fever'. It was aborted on the second for very different reasons. By the time they arrived at the lower Boteti he had discovered something which made him want to reach Linyanti as quickly as possible, by the most direct route.

His urgency has been explained in different ways. Tim Jeal, his most severe biographer, contends that ambition designed the new, unrehearsed itinerary. When he learned that 'three other Europeans were attempting to reach the area he was aiming at … Livingstone was determined that at all costs these men should not beat him to his goal'. Janet Wagner Parsons takes a more charitable view. Two of the three men were known to Livingstone as traders and adventurers of little scruple (the third was an English naturalist), and their sights were set on the ivory of the Makololo. She maintains that the missionary feared that their mercenary interests would taint the susceptible tribe, and that he believed he must reach Linyanti before Sebetwane and his people were corrupted by their first experience of white people.

Whatever his motives, they were not opposed by Oswell, who, although he contributed so much to the family's travels, always deferred to Livingstone as expedition leader. The wagons turned north, although 'no one knew the path', and at first made swift progress across hard, flat country plated with vast salt pans, 'one of which, Ntwetwe, is fifteen miles broad and one hundred long', and found a chain of springs which sustained the families of the *Sarwa* who lived there. 'One of the Bushmen, named Shobo, consented to be our guide over the waste between these springs and the country of Sebituane', writes Livingstone. 'It is impossible to convey an idea of the dreary scene on which we entered ... The only vegetation was a low scrub in deep sand; not a bird or insect enlivened the landscape.' They had reached a region which is still difficult to cross today: the Mababe Depression, now mostly within the boundaries of Chobe National Park, Botswana's third-largest protected wilderness, but then desolate and trackless. And their guide had vanished.

Whatever Livingstone's motives for the race north, they were now thrown like dice against the lives of his infant children and pregnant wife – or, as he would see it, placed trustingly in the hands of God. He might also have credited the senses and instincts of oxen and rhino. Lost and dehydrated in an unforgiving wasteland which remains a challenge to adventurous self-drive safari tourists with all the aids of GPS and 4WD, the party eked out its water supplies for four days until the last keg was almost dry. The children cried ceaselessly, tormented by thirst, and Livingstone confessed to his journal that the 'idea of their perishing before our eyes was terrible'.

Then they spotted rhino spoor. They unyoked the oxen and sent men to follow the beasts and the spoor in the hope that the oxen would smell water. Livingstone and Oswell stayed with the family, conscious that the dice had been cast for the last time. Hours passed as they waited in the shade of their wagons, and night fell without the return of the trackers. 'This was a bitterly anxious night; and, next morning, the less there was of water, the more thirsty the little rogues became ... it would have been a relief to have been reproached with being the entire cause of the catastrophe, but not one syllable of upbraiding was uttered by their mother, though the tearful eye told the agony within.'

On the fifth day, their last few drops of water were given to the children. Still they waited for the return of the trackers; and finally the men appeared with a bottle of murky, stinking liquid infused with fragments of rhino dung. Nobody hesitated to drink. The oxen had led them crookedly to the edge of the Mababe Depression and a shrinking tributary of the Thamalakane. They were able to fill their kegs with more stagnant water which, according to Livingstone, 'never gave them any inconvenience'. His accounts of crises can't always be taken at face value. He is rarely other than blithe when describing hazards, and tended to minimise the sufferings of himself and his family when the danger was past. His remarks about the 'little rogues' dying before their parents' eyes were unusually heartfelt and a measure of how worried he must have been.

As ever, we hear nothing of Mary's thoughts on the ordeal, except when her husband mentions that despite 'the agony within' she didn't reproach him.

Today's desert water holes are filling stations. There are no gaudy complexes of 'services' on the road from Serowe to Maun, just a set of hand-cranked pumps at the little town of Rakops. Keith tops up the Land Rover's long-distance tank. It is only half-empty, but the opportunity is not to be missed. 'You can drive for 100 miles to the next filling station and then find there's no diesel and the delivery tanker isn't due for two days.' At Rakops, we exchange the tar road for gravel, which takes us to the western boundary of Makgadikgadi Pans National Park. Around noon, a line of light appears along the seam of sky and land, as if a laser beam has sliced through the cloud cover. It is the frontier of the low which has kept us company all the way from Johannesburg. We advance towards our first sight of the sun in three days as the sun advances towards us, and meet within view of a long smudge of woodland: the tree line of the Boteti River valley.

The collision of sunlight and trees, full canopies of generous leaves, makes me quite giddy with pleasure. Imagine making the journey from a European winter to a European summer in the space of half an hour, while bypassing spring. Since we left the rhino sanctuary near Serowe this morning, we have driven nearly 300 miles; and we reach Meno a Kwena, another thirty minutes along a woodland track, in time for a late lunch. There are no traffic tailbacks in the Kalahari. I have arranged to stay at the camp, whose name means 'teeth of the crocodile', for two nights. Here, there are people who can tell me more about the capricious Boteti River and its Livingstone history, and here I can gather material for one of my newspaper commissions.

When the Livingstones arrived for the second time at the Boteti, which was then the Zouga, they had been on the Ngami trail for a month. But now they are ahead of us. They are approaching the Chobe River, while we have yet to backtrack into the Makgadikgadi Pans, then press on to Lake Ngami – which, we are eagerly told at Meno a Kwena, is resurrecting itself as exceptional waters rise in the Okavango Delta.

'The world is watching, according to the *Ngami Times*!' grins Jeff Gush, thrusting a copy of the local paper into my hands. 'There's the headline – "Okavango flood excites international interest". You couldn't have timed your visit more perfectly. The Delta waters are set to exceed all levels since records began in 1936, Lake Ngami is filling up again and the Boteti waters are pushing down towards us as I speak.'

Although I've come across the overweight and the underwhelming on my trips to the bush, most male safari guides, whether black or white, manage to look the part: capable of infecting their women clients with what gets called 'khaki fever'. (I'm too much of a veteran to be susceptible to this contagion, but I've been given an insider's take on the industry by my daughter, who has worked in camps and lodges in Zambia and South Africa.) Muscular, leather-brown, sun-creased Jeff is no exception. He introduces himself as a Motswana – the singular of Batswana – and has been running his own mobile safari operation out of Maun for twenty years. During our visit, he is hosting and guiding the guests at Mena a Kwena while its owner-manager is away. And, like quite a few people in these parts, he is a Livingstone enthusiast.

'Get settled in', he instructs. 'Chill a bit, watch the elephant over the river, and tomorrow I'll take you to what I think was the main Batawana ford, the one Lechulathebe initially refused to let Livingstone use. He and Oswell and the family would have crossed there on their journey back from Linyanti.'

'I don't suppose', I ask, 'that you know where they camped while Mary was giving birth?'

He laughs. 'Shouldn't think the spot's marked on any of the old maps. Livingstone was very discreet about that event. But you can take your pick of campsites around here.'

After the flurry of handshakes and welcome drinks I am only just beginning to take in the quirky character of Meno a Kwena and its site on the edge of Makgadikgadi Pans National Park. Jeff leads me along a path to a little stockade of thorns and branches, a three-sided kraal, and opens its roughly-made door. The fourth wall is nothing but air and views. In the middle is my tent, perched on a podium of sand above a deep, broad cleft in the desert. On the opposite bank, making their way through the forest with their delicate, slow-motion stride and air of solemn purpose, are a family of five elephants. 'There you have it,' says Jeff, 'the Boteti River. In a day or two there will be water down there. The fish eagles are back already.'

And he leaves me to open my senses to the sounds, smells and sights of the bush, and the incomparable feeling of peace which comes with them.

Not for everyone; the sensations of the bush are not always pacifying. By mid-June, about 170 miles to the north, the Livingstones and Oswell had reached the deep and powerful Chobe River, which never dries up, which owes its vigour to the same Angolan rainfall which feeds the Delta. Water, water everywhere, but they couldn't relax on the Chobe's banks to enjoy the shade of its trees. A new instrument of torture waited to plague them: tsetse fly, swarms of the biting insects, big as bluebottles and urged into frenzy by the smell of oxen, horse, people and the prospect of fresh blood.

The bite of a mosquito is a pinprick which can pass unnoticed, but the mandibles of tsetse make you yelp with pain. (The Tswana gave the fly its name; 'tsetse' in their language simply means 'fly'.) Soon the children were in tears again, the adults harassed and frustrated and the wagons forced to travel at night when the flies suspended their assaults. During the day the caravan retreated from the trees where the little guerrillas ambushed them, and sheltered in the reeds of the riverbank. But this slowed their progress, and the livestock were ailing. By the time they were found by Makololo scouts, whom Sebetwane had sent to escort them across the river, they had lost twelve oxen to sleeping sickness, and fifteen were so ill that they were abandoned.

The scouts assured them that their king would replace their beasts. They were still about twenty miles from the Makololo capital, but the undergrowth hampered any further movement of the wagons, and they found a place to outspan which was free of tsetse. Here, a plan was hatched which caused Mary to falter for the first time. She had silently endured the ordeal of the Mababe Depression, but beside the Chobe came the moment which so struck Oswell. He later remembered that in all their travels together he saw her fail her husband only once – 'when it was proposed to leave her behind'.

How exactly Mary failed her husband Oswell didn't explain; nor was he indelicate enough to mention that she was now nearly seven months pregnant and had every reason to be distraught. But she must have wept or pleaded or protested in some way when Livingstone announced that he and Oswell would continue by canoe to Linyanti with the Makololo, while she and the children remained camped on the south bank of the Chobe with the wagons, their Bakwena drivers and servants and the surviving oxen – not for days, not for weeks but, with a few interruptions, for over two months.

The successful meeting with Sebetwane, the paramount chief whose militant character and high status rivalled those of Mzilikazi, had a dismal conclusion. 'He was about forty-five years of age,' writes Livingstone in *Missionary Travels*, 'of a tall and wiry form, an olive or coffee-and-milk complexion, and slightly bald. His manner was cool and collected, and he was more frank in his answers than any other chief I have met. He was the greatest warrior ever heard of beyond the colony, and always led his men into battle himself.'

But the warrior king who had long protected his people from the Matabele was fighting a losing battle against an unknown foe in the Linyanti swamps. He welcomed Livingstone and Oswell warmly, but made it clear that the two men were intermediaries. He wasted no time asking after the daughter of Moffat, as he hoped that Mary's father, the powerful old friend of Mzilikazi, would broker a truce with the Matabele. He insisted on meeting her. Soon, Mary and the children were receiving the chief and his entourage and their gifts of honey and grain at the wagon camp. Shortly afterwards Sebetwane 'fell sick of inflammation of the lungs', and within days his condition was critical. 'I visited him in company with my little boy Robert on the Sunday afternoon in which he died', writes Livingstone, describing how the chief lifted his head and told a servant to take Robert to one of his wives for some milk.

'These were the last words of Sebituane ... I was never so much grieved by the loss of a black man before.'

But the end of the chief did not mean the end of Livingstone's plans for the Makololo. It was still his purpose to establish a mission among them, although he quickly realised that it could never be at fever-ridden Linyanti. Sebetwane's successor was a woman, his daughter Mma-Motsiasane, who lived twelve days' travel to the north and gave Livingstone and Oswell permission to move freely about her territories. And so began Livingstone's search for a healthier site for the Makololo capital and his own new mission station, neither of which was ever to become a reality. What he did find was the Zambezi. Again leaving Mary and the children on the south bank of the Chobe, the two men rode over 100 miles to the north-east, saw the great river for the first time and heard described its 'smoke that thunders': Mosi-oa-Tunya, the cataract which Livingstone would reach on his transcontinental journey nearly four years later, and name the Victoria Falls.

During these weeks of exploration, nothing is heard of Mary. But much was happening in her husband's mind, and its exalted state set Livingstone on the path which would make history and change for ever his own and his family's lives, pointing them in different directions. He had discovered no suitable site for a mission, but he believed he had found his highway to the sea: a wide channel of deep, flowing water, 'a breadth of from three hundred to six hundred yards', its presence unmarked on the Portuguese maps of the time. Although the Makololo called their stretch of the river Shesheke, he was fairly certain it was the upper reaches of the Zambezi, which he was well aware debouched into the Indian Ocean. Now vision and ambition coalesced in a new resolve. He would chart the entire valley, beginning with a journey north-west to find the river's source. The need for a navigable, commercial route into the heart of Africa was made even more pressing by another discovery: the slave trade had reached the upper Zambezi.

He needed two years of travel, he estimated, to find an upland home for the Makololo mission and to survey the river. This he could not undertake with wife and children; the lessons of the Mababe Depression had taught him that. From the moment Livingstone arrived on the banks of the Zambezi, Mary, Robert, Agnes, Thomas and their unborn sibling became excess baggage.

In the middle of August, after the required period of mourning for her father, Mma-Motsiasane gave the white men and the daughter and grandchildren of Moffat permission to leave her land. There would be no more reckless path-finding on the return trek. They followed the Thamalakane to Lake Ngami, where they picked up the usual route along the Boteti, and by mid-September they had reached one of their favourite campsites, a tree-shaded bend on a river of many tree-shaded bends. Here, William

Cotton Oswell, who remained a kindly friend to the Livingstone children for the rest of his life, helped to entertain Agnes by collecting pods and seeds for a make-believe tea service, before inviting Robert and Tom to tea. They had plenty of time for games. On the morning of 15 September 1851, Livingstone announced that they would stay at the camp for another eight days, and was awkwardly reluctant to say why.

The reason couldn't be concealed for long. During the night, Mary's prediction that she would be 'confined in the field' had been fulfilled. Without fuss, she had given birth to a son – so noiselessly that nobody knew of his arrival until Livingstone, with some embarrassment, gave them the news. Typically, he downplayed the reappearance of his wife's paralysis which followed the delivery. The baby was named Oswell after their friend, and nicknamed Zouga after the river; and, in a later letter, Livingstone assured his father-in-law that Mary 'never had an easier time of it'. She slowly improved, but not before Livingstone had to deal with another medical emergency. Tom's malaria had become recurrent, and, although they moved away from the river, he had three severe attacks within two weeks. The journey back to Kolobeng in temperatures of over 40 degrees, with sick toddler, new baby and enfeebled mother jolting in a stifling wagon, soon rendered stale the refreshment they had found under the camelthorns of the Boteti.

At some point on the journey, Livingstone and Mary reached agreement about the future, and made the sketchiest of plans: she and the children would go to Britain, while he would return to Linyanti to follow the Zambezi to its source. If, as George Seaver says of Mary Livingstone, she had no choices, only situations, then this was the hardest situation of her entire life.

Birdsong. I haven't heard much birdsong since Keith and I left Gaborone, although the Kalahari has its own abundant birdlife, much of it supersized. Vultures, eagles and other raptors are plentiful, and among long-legged, long-necked terrestrial birds there are korhaans and bustards, not to mention the bird with the longest legs of all: the ostrich. There are secretary birds with their quill-pen crests, now pedantically reclassified as 'long-legged land eagles', and there is one of the heaviest flying birds in the world. The Kori bustard, taller than a turkey, is a common resident; but, in his desert travels, Keith has found it elusive. 'I've never seen a Kori bustard', he confesses. 'Can you believe it? Maybe I'll get lucky on this trip.'

None of these birds has much notion of melody, and their calls can't be called song; nor can the deep grunts which I hear in the night, the voice of the giant eagle owl which lives in a tree near my tent. But with first light come the first woodland soloists of the dawn chorus, and soon I'm sitting on the edge of the cliff in my little kraal, while the rising sun flushes the treetops across the river. I have taken a bucket shower under a beautifully burnished copper 'bucket', I have a mug of campfire tea in one hand and binoculars in the other, and it's my most valued moment of the bush day. The camp's greatest asset is the privacy of its kraal accommodation – eight rustic 'suites' of tent, shower and rondavel loo. My only passers-by are a ground squirrel, a crimson-breasted shrike, a babble of pied babblers and a small brown parrot with a yellow forehead, later identified as Meyer's. Soon, I will walk along the sand path to breakfast cooked over an open fire, bracing myself for the required sociability of camp life; sharpening my wits for the intense focus of bush walks and game drives. Safaris can be hard work. But these quiet moments alone at the start of the day make me fit for anything. They also give me time to think about Mary Livingstone.

There are wide, sweeping bends in the Boteti channel in both directions; any one of these shady curves would have made a pleasant labour ward were it not for the flies and mosquitoes. Scavengers, too, might have been drawn to the smell of the afterbirth, although Livingstone surely burned or buried the placenta and cord as soon as possible. Was Mary, with the muscles of her right side lifeless for several days, able to feed her new son? Did she use her breast, or had she carried with her a bottle and teat? The father, doctor though he was, recorded none of the details which today might be captured on video for family viewing.

At least there was plenty of water to wash linen and improvised nappies. I move to the edge of the kraal and look again into the sandy bed of the Boteti, which carries the usual waymarks of the bush: dead trees, old bones, elephant droppings, busy tracks. Pools of standing water catch the early sunlight; not the first floodwaters of the Delta, but the residue of the rain we travelled through on our way north. Jeff has told us that 100 millimetres fell at Mena a Kwena. 'We haven't had rain in June since 1994.' (I get the feeling I've already heard this.) 'I'm afraid it means there isn't much game around. The zebra migration was on its way to the Delta but the Kalahari is growing fresh grass and the herds have turned round and gone back into the desert. And the cats have gone with them.'

He has promised us our first sight of the revivified Boteti when we go to Moreomaoto, the village upriver which has the closest links with the camp. Meno a Kwena sits on tribal land, and a bed levy from each guest is paid to the community, which provides most of the camp staff. 'We do a lot with the primary school there', says Jeff. 'We hold educational workshops and bring the kids to the camp in groups to learn about the environment. The hope is always to spread the message about the importance of wildlife and tourism to local incomes.'

Silently, I think: a new faith, a new evangelism, a new economy. Not Christianity and commerce, but conservation and commerce.

Moreomaoto is about twenty minutes' drive from the camp, close to the crossing where Jeff believes the Livingstones forded the river. 'The name means "tree with legs", which is what the Tswana call the baobab.' We arrive mid-morning, when the temperature is still pleasant; we admire the smart school buildings and immaculate sand playground with its flamboyant tree, and pass a mobile-phone mast. Like most of Africa, Botswana is in thrall to the cell phone, whose networks have marched across the continent into the most remote communities, generally empowering and enriching them. I get better reception on my mobile in some parts of the bush than I do in the Highlands of Scotland, but there is at least one serious negative: cell phones assist the movements of ivory and rhino-horn poachers, whose sorties use them to warn each other of the approach of rangers' patrols.

This phone mast has been in place for five years and has been colonised by red-billed buffalo weavers, whose big untidy nests are communal, like those of the sociable weaver, but not as durable. And then, as we drive down a gentle incline towards the river, we see water – not deep, not flowing, but water stretching from bank to bank, soaking up the blue sky. Standing in the middle of this shallow flood are some bemused-looking cows, perhaps perplexed by the altered nature of their landscape but happy to enjoy the novel sensation of paddling.

The Delta floodwaters, seeping furtively into the Boteti channel, have almost reached the crossing where local vehicles negotiate the track linking the banks, but we can still walk dry-footed. We stand in the middle of the ford while Jeff sketches ox-wagons in the air, demonstrating how they would have rocked down the low approach to the river and up the other side. It's a lovely spot, with broad-leaved sycamore fig and mangosteen among the acacia and bush willow. Namaqua doves, the smallest and daintiest of the dove family, forage on the ground, and a flock of red-billed quelea perform disciplined manoeuvres above our heads, their tight formation like one entity.

I'm reluctant to move from the Boteti River. But Mary Livingstone has left Kolobeng for the last time, and the family are on their way to the Cape by way of Kuruman, while Keith and I have a rendezvous at a place called Planet Baobab.

18

The Great Nothing

'The mark of Cain is on your foreheads'

Far to the south in their Kalahari oasis, Robert and Mary Moffat waited for news of the family's return and Mary's confinement – in or out of 'the field'. Livingstone, of course, had neither seen nor spoken to his mother-in-law since receiving her long-distance tongue-lashing, and appears to have been nervous about breaking their journey at Kuruman on the trek to Cape Town, where he intended putting his family on the first available ship. Typically, he disguised his apprehension with a joke: 'From the way Mrs M has written to us for some time past,' he wrote to his father-in-law, 'I expect to be obliged to pull down as soon as we reach Kuruman and get my bottom warmed with the "taws".'

Nobody knows for sure why the hospitable Moffat mission was discounted as a home for Mary and the children during Livingstone's travels, but there has been plenty of surmise, most of it devolving on the relationship between mother and daughter. Livingstone's letters hint that the junior Mary was reluctant to be pulled back into the orbit of the senior one, but without the testimony of either we have only his word for it. He was known to bear grudges, if not for ever then for long spells of brooding. Still stung by his mother-in-law's disapproval, he may well have been the one who wanted to distance his family from her strong will and critical view of him.

He also implies that sly missionary gossip and blunt Tswana comment would upset Mary; it was a common opinion among some (and one that was later murmured by the spiteful in England) that he didn't want to live with her. More openly, he outlines the reasons which he no doubt used to persuade her of the virtue of his plan: the children's education, the Scottish grandparents they had never met and, quite plausibly, the fact that Mary would find it easier to tolerate his absence at a distance, far from any worrying rumours which might travel to Kuruman, and well removed from any temptation to try to reach him. (Equally, of course, Livingstone would be far removed from any family crisis and the obligation to do anything about it.) Mary's acquiescence probably had much to do with her children. The family adventures had been debilitating for them all, and often harrowing. Away from the bush, they would not suffer as they had suffered, they would have access to the most advanced medical attention in their childhood illnesses, they would have the security even Kuruman couldn't guarantee and the education even Cape Town couldn't provide. But there is little in Livingstone's letters to reflect her thinking.

It's possible she believed that some day they would all resume their life in Africa. But first they had to take their leave of Kolobeng, unaware that they would never reclaim their home there. They found the river almost dry and the village deserted. Abandoned by Livingstone, Sechele had abandoned Kolobeng and led his people upstream to a place called Dimawe, where water was not much more reliable but which offered some protection, among a scatter of kopjes, from the threatening Boers. (Mebalwe, the Kuruman convert and Bible-studies teacher, went with them; and, although Sechele is often called Livingstone's only convert, 'and a lapsed one at that', the Bakwena chief never abandoned his new religion, and continued to welcome Christian missionaries into the lives of his tribe.) It was a forlorn homecoming and forlorn departure, but now that the decision was taken there was little time for sentimentality. While they packed what they could carry in their single wagon, Oswell left for Kuruman with a request for Moffat to send fresh oxen, then continued to the Cape. By the middle of December, Mary and the four children had turned their backs on Kolobeng for ever.

The highway between Nata and Maun cuts like a blade through the route improvised by Livingstone when he decided to strike due north from the Boteti to reach Linyanti in advance of the party of traders. (A race he won, thanks to his near-disastrous shortcut, despite the fact that the rival expedition had a head start on the Ngami trail.) The A3 slices through the desert at the northern limits of the Makgadikgadi Pans, the 'hard, flat country' where the family and Oswell found salt pans, springs and their ineffectual San guide before veering north-west and blundering into the Mababe Depression. Although it means detouring from the Ngami trail onto the A3 and backtracking down its fast surface for nearly eighty miles, I want to see something of the Makgadikgadi Pans before we move on to Maun and the lake. With Keith's help and an invitation from Uncharted Africa Safaris, I can do this in three days.

Uncharted Africa is a name which takes liberties with established cartography but conjures up dreams of adventure at the far frontiers of wilderness tourism. The pre-eminent safari company in the northern Kalahari, it is a defining example of how the industry has evolved (to the regret of many of its old-timers) over the last two decades. The company owns four properties and runs high-end horse-riding and mobile camping safaris, but it has its origins in the bush lifestyle of a legendary slayer of crocodiles and hunting guide who opened a small camp near the sterile wasteland of the pans. Jack Bousfield, goes the story, arrived in Botswana from his Tanzanian homeland in the 1960s and asked: 'What's at Makgadikgadi Pans?' Nothing, came the reply. Nobody's been there for 100 years except Bushmen. 'Good,' said Jack, 'that's where I'll go.'

By the 1980s, Jack's Camp had achieved an elite reputation among no-frills safari enthusiasts – those who preferred expert guiding, encounters with Bushman culture and stories round the campfire to luxury tents, fine wine lists and game shared with other tourists. Grizzled bushwhacker Bousfield, head swathed in a Swahili kikoi, was the main attraction, along with his masterly innovation: quad-bike safaris out onto the pans, where the unique selling point (to use a marketing cliché) is nothing at all. No game, no birds, no plants, no insects, just the shimmering space and silence of an infinite white landscape, like a frozen sea in the desert; and at night one of the finest star-gazing spectacles in the southern hemisphere.

In those days, there were no tar roads in the northern Kalahari, no sat-nav for self-drive visitors; and Jack's Camp was truly isolated, difficult to reach by anything other than light aircraft charters, which ferried in supplies and most of the guests. Jack himself was a bush pilot of the vanishing school of seat-of-the-pants flying and, famously, survived six crashes. In 1992, his seventh killed him.

Jack's son Ralph took over, and with his partner transformed the camp and developed Uncharted Africa, conscious that the increasingly competitive safari industry could no longer rely on the charisma of odd-ball bush veterans with a minimalist approach to comfort and cuisine. But Ralph Bousfield has kept certain constants in place. The camp is a base for zoological research, its commitment to its unique environment chimes with Botswana's high-yield, low-impact policies on tourism, and the glamour of the Bousfield legacy lives on. When I heard him speak at a safari marketing event in Edinburgh, I thought Ralph looked like a poet-adventurer with his flowing, shoulder-length dark hair and his lyrical eulogies to landscape and wildlife. How can you not warm to a man who ignores the opportunity to persuade potential clients to take one of his very expensive safaris and chooses, instead, to present the latest research on the clan distribution of the rare brown Kalahari hyena?

Talking to Ralph after this idiosyncratic piece of marketing, I mentioned my upcoming trip to Botswana and interest in the Livingstones. 'You must come and see us', he said promptly. 'We're not far from Chapman's Baobab, which is a Livingstone landmark, and we've got a little museum at Jack's with some old maps.'

I hesitated. I'd never been to Jack's Camp, but I had reservations about all I knew it had become: 'an oasis of style and comfort' with a backlist of top media and industry awards and prices to match. Out of my league, which is the old-timers' division. I have no objection to comfort and good food in the wilderness, but I don't need tents fit for a Zanzibari slave merchant, Persian rugs or silver service at dinner. Ralph Bousfield's offer of hospitality, on the other hand, was hard to refuse.

As it turns out, the ten opulent tents at Jack's are all booked on the dates determined by our itinerary, so Keith and I are on our way to its more modest sister camp and neighbour: Camp Kalahari, 'a return to the traditional style of the old explorers'. This is safari-speak for not roughing it like they did. The 'traditional-style' tents will have proper beds and their own attached flush loos and hot showers, and someone will bring me my tea in the morning, put a hot water bottle in my bed at night and build the campfire. My needs are simple, but I don't like to be cold. I am the modern counterpart of Ma-Mary of Kuruman, who would 'never think of coming out of the waggon till there is a good fire'.

On the naked verges of the A3, a few miles from the town of Gweta, is a waymark which can't be missed: a giant aardvark modelled in termite cement, bigger than the elephants which cross the highway on their long marches, stripping out any tree smaller than a baobab. The ant-eater's snout points into the desert, and down a side-road we find the very tree – a whole grove of them, in which sits Planet Baobab, for which the terms 'budget accommodation' and 'wayside watering hole' do not say it all. Scattered among the baobabs are self-catering rondavel huts, a campsite, restaurant, well-stocked bar of whimsical design (the chandelier is made of beer bottles) and an extravagant swimming pool. They all add up to another venture for Uncharted Africa, and Planet Baobab is the pick-up point for Camp Kalahari. Here, we leave Keith's Land Rover and climb into an open safari vehicle for the three-hour transfer, which turns into four hours. The most direct route is still waterlogged, and there is the usual astonishment about June rain: '180 centimetres' is the excited statistic given by our driver. 'Vehicles have been getting stuck.'

Overland journeys in the Kalahari are counted in hours and days. Ox-wagon treks were counted in weeks and months. But the desert still presents many of the same problems. For the first time it occurs to me that the great salt pans of Makgadikgadi may also be waterlogged; in which case I won't be able to sleep out under the stars to marvel, like the Livingstones, at the vast space and profound silence of Ntwetwe Pan, listening to the blood singing in my ears.

The family arrived in Cape Town like bush vagrants. They were drained by six months and over 1,500 miles of travel, and dazed by the city. The only urban life the children had known were Tswana towns of mud and thatch; it was twelve years since Livingstone had arrived at the Cape, and ten years since Mary had last seen Cape Town. In their absence, the city had grown and prospered and kept pace with the times, while they were out of time and conspicuously out of place. To the fashionable colonials of commerce and shipping, and even to the evangelicals, the bureaucrats and preachers of the LMS, they looked destitute (which they were) and behaved oddly. Their clothes were patched and faded, the children wore ragged hand-me-downs, their ramshackle wagon tottered through the busy streets, and their speech stumbled to recover its English fluency.

Their greatest challenge was stairs. The children had to learn to use them for the first time, and the adults to relearn. Livingstone records that he found them so awkward he took to descending staircases backwards. Their greatest embarrassment was their appearance, their utter shabbiness in a city which did not expect to see poor white families. Yet this family's patriarch was already a local hero, the man who had reached Lake Ngami and the uncharted interior; and it was assumed he would take his place in Cape Town society along with his profoundly ill-equipped wife.

Once again, the noble Oswell was their salvation and rescued them from humiliation. He had already paid for the hire of oxen to replace the enfeebled beasts ruined on their last expedition, and without the fresh team they would not have been able to 'come out' of the wilderness. Now Oswell helped his friend to find lodgings, with a garden for the children, between Table Mountain and Lion's Head, at a cost of only £2 10s a month. He also gave him £200 to buy them all new clothes. He had thoughtfully anticipated the problems of their re-entry into colonial civilisation, and waited in Cape Town until they were comfortable. When he finally boarded a ship for England, he pressed Livingstone to draw on the account he had opened for their use, and made a rousing joke of his generosity. He had already funded it, he said, with ivory from 'Livingstone's Estate'.

Yesterday's ivory-hunters are today's ivory-poachers, the most reviled of wildlife criminals, but I am quite in love with William Cotton Oswell.

How was he to know, in an age when the study of animal consciousness didn't exist, that the violent death of one elephant traumatises the entire family? That orphaned infants, milk-dependent until they are at least two, die slowly of dehydration, often mutilated by predators too small to make a quick kill? I suspect that Alice Webb, A. Z. Fraser of *Livingstone and Newstead*, was a little in love with him, too, or at least with the idea of him. Not only was he tall, athletic and handsome, but also, as she writes, 'Of all that early group of fine African pioneers, no one came closest to the best popular type of hero than William Cotton Oswell, truest of friends, bravest of hunters, and most chivalrous of Christian gentlemen, a fact that should never be forgotten either now or in the far-off future'.

Nobody has ever rattled any skeletons in Oswell's cupboard. There is no mystery about the man, except the puzzle of a character so indifferent to acclaim that he refused the entreaties of the Royal Geographic Society to publish his own journals of his African expeditions. 'No, I won't write a line' was his mild explanation. 'I know full well that Livingstone is working hard at his book; he wants this medal, let him have it; it means more to him than it could ever mean to me.' He was so determined that he should not 'take the wind out of my good friend's sails' that, when he had a bad attack of fever (no doubt recurring malaria), he ordered his notebooks to be brought to his bedside, removed the most significant pages and had them burned in his presence to prevent publication should he die.

Livingstone, originally suspicious of Oswell's competition in what he imagined was a race for glory, came to value him above all other men. Years later, after Mary's death and his return from the Zambezi, he made this clear in a letter to Alice's father, William Frederick Webb. 'I love him with true affection,' he wrote, 'and I believe he does the same to me, and yet we never show it.'

So very Scottish. So very English.

The underground springs in the harsh, flat, semi-arid grasslands which the Livingstone family and Oswell crossed, are the begetters of islands of trees where, if you want to build a camp, you can find enough shade to supplement its canvas and thatch and hide its infrastructure, including the borehole and pump. Hyena Island comes into view long before we make out the shapes of tents among the dense acacia and mokolwane and fan palms. We arrive at Camp Kalahari in time for afternoon tea with home baking. We've been on the road, rough roads and smooth ones, for nearly seven hours, and I don't want to climb into another vehicle any time soon. But an irresistible force called Super Sande has other ideas.

'Just a short drive. No more than twenty minutes. There's something I want to show you.'

Super by name, super in scale, almost seven feet tall. Among his short, slight, lighter-skinned Khoisan colleagues, Super Sande is a black titan of the Kalanga, one of the first Bantu tribes to migrate into what is now Botswana and its neighbour Zimbabwe, where they are close kin to the Shona. He comes from Francistown, at the heart of Kalanga country, and as a youth he helped Jack Bousfield to set up his first camp. He is now the longest-serving guide in the company. 'If there's a problem,' says Super, towering over scones and carrot cake as he passes cups and saucers, 'they come to me.'

When I ask if we've been identified as problematic, he gives a powerful laugh. 'No, no. Ralph was going to show you around himself, but he's had to go to Francistown. I'll be your guide while you're here.'

Guide or despot? It doesn't take me long to learn that Super is in charge and, although I'm bone-rattled, windblown, dusty and dreaming of siestas, he will not be gainsaid. He knows best: the best restorative for the travel-weary is not shower or snooze but total immersion in the sea of land around Hyena Island, with a creative pick-me-up as the sun goes down. 'Twenty minutes' drive', he repeats, as we finish our tea. 'I'll go ahead and meet you there.'

We are just in time. Dusk is peeling off the sunset glow; the tough blond grassland is turning grey. We see the fire and the paraffin lamps before we see Super. He is standing like a mokolwane palm on the beach of a watery pan, presiding over a bar: three camp chairs, a table covered with a white cloth and – I counted them – twenty-four bottles of different spirits. He is slicing lemons and taking ice and mixers from a coolbox hoarding beers and wine. 'Welcome!' he booms. 'Welcome to the Great Nothing!'

This is my introduction to the Makgadikgadi Pans: cocktails and cana-pés on the empty basin of the Kalahari superlake, where they are still finding fossils of the earliest mammals, and the tools of stone-age Bush-men are counted modern artefacts. As the sun does its kamikaze dive off the edge of our own flat world, Super unrolls a map and anchors it to the ground with four beer bottles. By the light of the lamps and campfire, he shows us our place on it. 'We're right here. This is the north-west edge of Ntwetwe Pan, which is as big as Switzerland. It is my sorrow you won't see much more of it.'

As I feared, all quad-bike safaris and bedroll sleep-outs on Ntwetwe have been suspended. Its salt crust and the silt beneath have turned to glutinous mud. 'Don't tell me', I request; 'there hasn't been rain like this in June since 1994.' Predictably, Super goes one better. 'Countrywide there hasn't been rain like this in June since 1967.'

The good news is that we can still go to Chapman's Baobab over the dry savanna. And in the morning we will meet the meerkats.

Even in the dry season there is plenty of wildlife in the Kalahari, although some of it, like the brown hyena, is elusive, and much of it comes out only at night. On the drive back from our sundowners at Ntwetwe Pan, spring hares bounce away from our headlights on their long kangaroo legs, and we see an aardwolf, which looks like a miniature striped hyena but eats nothing but insects. Like the aardvark, it's a termite specialist and spends the nights scooping harvester termites from their burrows with its sticky tongue.

The local celebrities, however, are meerkats, and they do come out during the day, although not until the sun climbs over the horizon. 'No need for an early start', advises Super. 'Breakfast at 7:30. It's winter; they won't be up early either.'

My tea arrives at 7am, which counts as an indolent lie-in – and I'm eager to be up. It isn't often you set off on a game drive knowing exactly what you're going to find, but already I know I will see my first meerkats at close quarters. Research zoologists working at Jack's Camp have spent so much time with a local clan that its members are now relaxed in human company. They are completely wild, but they have been 'habituated', much as bigger game gets used to safari vehicles; and the meerkat morning is a stellar event at all three Makgadikgadi Pans camps. Visits are controlled: small groups at a time on a rota system. Our own group could hardly be smaller if it were a private safari. Keith and I are the only guests at Camp Kalahari, which has just reopened after a refit.

The early light is pure enough to cleanse the world of all its sins. We sit on the ground close to the meerkats' communal den, and within minutes the first sharp snout appears at the entrance to one of its burrows. The clan matriarch, head swivelling, eyes bright in their sooty patches, looks us over and pops outside. Suddenly, the grass is sprouting meerkats large and small. There are eleven of them, talking to each other non-stop in an elaborate vocabulary of squeaks, and they are in no hurry to move off. One or two youngsters seem nervous of our very close presence, but a few squeaks from their mother put them at ease. Super Sande interprets. 'She's saying don't worry, no problem, it's just Them Again.'

The clan has two priorities: look round and warm up. Meerkats always scan the ground and sky for predators before setting off to forage, and this they do by standing tall on their hind legs on the highest ground they can find. What better viewpoint on a flat landscape than a human shoulder or a human head? 'Keep very still', commands Super, who has taken charge of our cameras – but I am already frozen with delight. The pack matriarch has climbed up my arm and onto my shoulder, where she sits with ramrod back, scrutinising every point of the compass. I can feel the warmth of her body on my cheek and the grip of her long toes through three layers. Then she moves to Keith for a closer look at the sky.

'They do this without any encouragement from us,' explains Super, snapping furiously, 'but they don't choose to do it with everyone. We make no promises when we bring visitors here.' I feel childishly proud. To receive the trust of a wild creature is a huge, throat-catching moment, even if you know that the trust is prompted by opportunism.

We watch the meerkats groom each other and use their communal midden, taking turns to stand guard. Eventually, reassured by their recce, limbs loosened by the climbing sun, they scatter into the savanna and disappear.

Although a gifted and observant naturalist, Livingstone makes no mention of meerkats in his accounts of his Kalahari life. He may never have seen any. Left to themselves, these desert mongooses, also called suricates, are shy and quick to dive underground if alarmed. They are also well camouflaged in their perilous environment, where death can come from any direction. Until patient research uncovered their co-operative social system and lively lifestyle, and they became the darlings of wildlife film-makers, few people took an interest in them.

Chapman's Baobab had no name when the Livingstones and Oswell trekked across Ntwetwe Pan on their unwise route to the Chobe River. That came later, when the titanic tree had become something of a mail-drop for desert travellers. The man who gave it his name, James Chapman, was an elephant-hunter and travelling companion of Thomas Baines, the artist and storekeeper unfairly dismissed by Livingstone on the Zambezi Expedition which killed Mary. (Baines gave his name to a group of magnificent baobabs near Nxai Pan, trees which have changed little since he painted them in 1862.) But the tree described in *Missionary Travels* is recognisably the lone fist of cupped fingers which, after an hour or so of lurching along the edge of the liquid pan, we see on the horizon.

Livingstone's description comes from his second journey to Linyanti in 1853, when Mary and the children were wandering around England. 'We passed over the immense saltpan Ntwetwe, and about two miles beyond its northern bank we unyoked under a fine specimen of baobab, here called, in the language of the Bechuana, Mowana. It consisted of six branches united into one trunk, and at three feet from the ground it was eighty-five feet in circumference.'

This colossus is standing in a shallow pool of water, but its roots make stepping stones to the monumental trunk where, it's claimed, Livingstone carved a cross and his initials. As he reported, the trunk is indeed a fusion of six branches, each as thick as the bole of the mightiest oak, grey and hard as granite, and worn into veins and knuckles of bark. I peer at the spot, about five feet above the ground, which might represent a crucifix with faint lettering, but it's impossible to be certain. There are plenty of other initials etched into the bark, most very old, one or two recent. 'Vandals!' proclaims Super; not a denunciation Livingstone would have enjoyed. 'This tree is between three and four thousand years old.'

Beneath its canopy, stone-age Bushmen camped. I run my hand over the bark, warm and wrinkled like the hide of an elephant, and fancy I feel a pulse. The Livingstones and Oswell were very recent tourists.

We leave Camp Kalahari before sunrise. Three hours in an open vehicle in the early morning of the Kalahari winter leave the face numb, but on the drive back to the highway Keith achieves an ambition. The birds are also up and about, ant-eating chats on the ground, clapper larks in the air, and we meet two sand grouse performing the courtliest of courtship dances, circling each other with wings spread like capes. When the vehicle picks up speed, I cover my lower face with my scarf and half-close my eyes, and don't spot what Keith spots, although they couldn't be more conspicuous. 'Kori bustards!' We stop to admire the stately pair, tall as half-grown ostriches, with handsome, crested heads. 'Ostrich lite' is their local nickname. They walk together in measured strides, as if synchronised. The Kori bustard is so heavy it's reluctant to fly, and will only take off when directly threatened.

At Planet Baobab, with some relief, we exchange the camp Land Cruiser for the heated Land Rover, and set off up the road to Maun. I'm looking forward to seeing again the bush outpost I first knew twenty years ago, which now has a new civic role as the administrative centre of Ngamiland. Maun takes its name from a San word, *maung*, which means 'place of small reeds'. The Livingstones never knew it; it didn't exist until the Batawana moved from Lake Ngami as its water dried up along with the threat of Matabele aggression, which receded when the warrior tribe and their king Lobengula were crushed by the British colonists of Rhodesia.

Since 1915, it has been the tribal capital of the Batawana, whose rural life co-existed, over much of the last century, with a growing number of white hunters and hunting guides from the colonial neighbours of Bechuanaland. Their playground and workplace was the Okavango Delta, 'the Swamps', where crocodile-hunting was not just a sport but an industry. They were tough, salty, hard-living, rule-breaking, risk-taking men, and they made their own legends. In time, a few became aware that the great herds and the big cats of marsh and savanna, the trophy animals so prized by their affluent clients, were a finite resource. And they turned gamekeepers.

So did the Batawana. The Batawana were themselves a hunting tribe but had the foresight to anticipate that the future of the safaris which brought income and employment to their tribal lands depended on the future of the wildlife. Moremi Game Reserve, nearly 2,000 square miles of the east-central Delta, was the first tribal game reserve in Africa. Its creation in 1963 was wholly sponsored by the Batawana, and it is named after Chief Letsholathebe Moremi – Letsholathebe III, the great-grandson of that same young chief who refused to let Livingstone ford the Boteti River, then became his friend when he returned with Mary. The founders of Moremi Game Reserve launched the beginning of Delta conservation and set an example to the new Botswana Wildlife Department, which went on to establish the national parks that today protect 17 per cent of the country's land mass.

In the 1990s, the wild men of Maun were young bush pilots and Land Rover jockeys, while the veteran bushwhackers propping up the bars of the Duck Inn and Riley's Hotel had only their death-defying anecdotes to savour with their beer. The town's status as Botswana's safari capital had not only been consolidated but also reformed in an industry which had largely exchanged hunting rifles for long-lens cameras. But its reputation was still robust, and it still felt thrillingly remote. Its roads were sand or gravel, there were no saloon cars in the tiny airport car park, and there was little commercial life beyond the markets of Batawana farmers and the servicing of camps, lodges and safaris. Maun was my introduction to sub-Saharan Africa, to a town where mud and thatch rondavels rubbed shoulders with cinderblock 'four-corners', egrets and ibis roosted in the gardens, and livestock strolled in the streets. Here, I met white people who could turn the pages of their bush history over several generations, and who were still living lives which to me seemed extraordinary.

I was shown round this flat, incoherent sprawl on either side of the

Thamalakane River by a self-taught entomologist whose name was given to the new species of spider, *paraecobius Wilmotae*, which she had discovered. Wilmot was Ursula Boyes' maiden name; and the Wilmots are bush 'royalty'. Bobbie Wilmot, Ursula's uncle, was the most celebrated crocodile-hunter of his day. In the 1950s and 1960s, he and his father ran the crocodile concession for the whole of 'the Swamps' and hugely depleted their population. Then the reptile world bit back. Bobbie was killed by a cobra which struck his thigh when he was walking on a Delta island, while Botswana's crocodiles have been protected since the 1970s, and their numbers have recovered. His son Lloyd had a different relationship with wildlife. Lloyd's Camp, famously eccentric, was the making of an area called Savuti (now well known for its large, elephant-hunting lion prides); and the latest generation of Wilmots is still in the business of bloodless safaris.[1]

There was one hot topic in Maun on my 1990 visit: the sealing of the road from Francistown and Nata to Maun, now the A3. Conservationists feared the hard surface would bring too many people to 'the gateway to the Delta'; conservatives knew that it would change their frontier way of life for ever. This it did in a hurry. We drive through the suburbs in a traffic tailback. Today, Maun has a rush hour, twenty-four-hour supermarkets, Kentucky Fried Chicken, banks, offices and 'conference venues'. Even Riley's, once its only hotel, is now a Cresta with executive suites and meeting rooms. As government departments moved up the tar road in the early 1990s to administer north-west Botswana, more and more people did arrive at the gateway to the Delta, and the Batawana capital is now a town of 50,000 people.

Yet it is still a village; not just because its suburbs are still mud and thatch rondavels and its streets are dreamily sauntered by cows, goats and donkeys, but because administratively that is its designation. Village status is valued by rural communities. It absolves farmers of the need to corral their livestock, which is licensed to roam at will. Nor has Maun lost touch with the wilderness on its doorstep. Before we set off for Lake Ngami, I take a stroll in the grounds of Maun Lodge, a modern hotel on

---

1 In her memoir *Starlings Laughing*, published in 1990, June Vendall Clark gives a vigorous account of life in Ngamiland and the Okavango Delta in the late 1950s and early 1960s, when she spent eight years living on an island in the Thamalakane River. She and her husband hunted crocodile with Bobbie Wilmot, then dedicated themselves to assisting the Batawana to create Moremi Wildlife Reserve. They were greatly supported by Chief Letsholathebe's mother, the Queen Regent, 'who preferred to be called Mrs Moremi', while the young king was studying social science in the United Kingdom.

the banks of the Thamalakane, and fall into conversation with a young gardener. 'The river looks good and full at the moment', I remark. 'Do any crocodiles come this far into town?'

'For sure, Mma. And hippos, too.'

Later, in the town centre, I see a donkey using a zebra crossing – the next best thing to a zebra itself.

News of the lake is encouraging. We have seen for ourselves, on the last stretch of road into Maun, the swelling volume of the Boteti and the new grass on its verges. The Delta is filling its drainage channels, the surplus water pressing south into the withered basin of Ngami, and we have been promised more than the 'star-shaped pond, no more than 50 yards across', which Oliver Ransford saw in the 1970s. But to anyone but locals finding Ngami's recovered water is a trial of perseverance which, in our case, ends with a lucky break.

Much of the basin, which was seventy miles long in Livingstone's estimate, is now embedded in communal ranchland, with no height to give an overview, near the villages of Sehithwa and Toteng, the old Batawana capital. Toteng is only forty or so miles from Maun on a good tar road, the A35; and the stretch which runs between it and Sehithwa actually crosses the western extremity of the old lake bed. Near here, the GPS coordinates on Keith's last visit propelled him into the middle of scrub and grazing cattle. This time we take human advice.

The advice is picturesque, involving turn-offs signed by home-made bus stops and junctions marked by makeshift football posts and barriers of 'prickly burrs which you want to avoid'. An hour or so after leaving the main road, we are still bundu-bashing through acacia woodland, tangled in a skein of cattle trails and sketchy tracks, and Keith is still keeping faith with his satnav. 'Lake Ngami', he insists, 'is right here.'

We jump out onto baked earth, negotiate some thorn bushes and reach a faint incline which looks as though it might lead to the rim of something. The height we gain yields a vista of impenetrable, waist-high, desiccated stalks topped with spiky seed cases. 'Think these are the burrs we were told to avoid', I murmur feebly, conscious I'm stating the obvious.

Back in the Land Rover, each trying to suppress exasperation, we meet a pedestrian: a slow-moving ancient who turns round hopefully, eyes hitching a ride. The only word we have in common is 'Ngami', but he makes us understand that, quite fortuitously, the lake is near his village and he can show us the way. He clambers in, dim-eyed and gap-toothed, nodding smiles, and waves Keith onwards. Minutes pass and scepticism mounts. Then our hitchhiker calls a halt at an intersection of tracks which look like all the other tracks. 'Ngami, Ngami!' he announces, climbing out. Setting off along one track, he waves us down another, calling 'Ngami, Ngami' over his shoulder.

Without much optimism we follow his instruction. Soon, the woodland opens onto beds of reeds. Suddenly there it is – a sheet of blinding beauty in the afternoon sun: a full body of water at least half a mile across, blue as paradise and even more welcome. The far bank is a mirror image of the one we've reached: flat littoral, acacia woodland and reeds, empty of life but for the water birds. Jumping down, grabbing binoculars, I see a fish eagle perched on a branch and the big white shapes of two pelicans; above our heads a fly-past of spur-winged geese salutes our success. Lake Ngami has been reoccupied.

We celebrate. Keith uncorks wine. There are ghosts at the water's edge, but we can't be mournful. Beside the lake we raise our glasses to Mary and David Livingstone, and to the children who 'took to playing in it as ducklings do'.

Livingstone's family have left Africa. They sailed for Southampton on 23 April 1852, three weeks after arriving in Cape Town. Their ship was the *Trafalgar*, en route from India with a complement of Indian officers and their wives. The Livingstone children, suddenly exposed to the alien infections of crowded streets, had been ill with measles. They all embarked with bad colds which, according to Livingstone, had been caused by getting their hair cut. They left behind a husband and father who was also in need of medical attention – surgery for a swollen uvula which had pained him for some time – and who, from his letters, was also suffering emotionally. He was wretched about the decision he had taken. The preparations for his new expedition to Linyanti were moving sluggishly, and he had nothing to do but brood and succumb to depression.

His faith never faltered, but he redirected his misery, doubt and loneliness into hostile feelings for mission society and mission work. His letters became more and more grim; one borders on hysteria. 'My children are absolutely vagabonds', he wrote to Arthur Tidman of the LMS, describing how they asked when they would return to Kolobeng, when to Kuruman. 'Never! The mark of Cain is on your foreheads, your father is a missionary.'

His moods of despair obscured any rational or honest assessment of his own actions. He denied responsibility for them. For the loss of his children and their loss of a home, writes Parsons, 'he blamed conditions in Africa and the demands of Christian society on its clergy. It would not have served his purpose to acknowledge that no other missionaries in Africa had felt the need to send their families away.'

To Mary, he wrote in terms which were almost, but not quite, unprecedented, invoking the memories of the earliest days of their love affair. 'You may read the letters over and over again which I wrote at Mabotsa, the sweet time you know. As I told you before, I tell you again, they are true, true; there is not a bit of hypocrisy in them. I never show all my feelings; but I can say truly, my dearest, that I loved you when I married you, and the longer I lived with you, I loved you the better ...'

Did she read and reread this and the Mabotsa letters over the next four years? She got few other words from her husband as he rode and walked almost 6,000 miles from the day he left the Cape until the day he arrived at Quelimane, on the Indian Ocean – and none as confessional, as passionate.

Mary, meanwhile, was lost more completely than her husband in the foreign land which became her own wilderness: Victorian Britain.

19

Lost and Found

'I would beg of you to be lenient with me'

There is little to find of Mary Livingstone in Britain past or present; little publicly recorded to mark the passing of her itinerant years in Scotland and England until her husband returned a national hero in 1856. When she and the children disembarked from the *Trafalgar*, she was just another rustic colonial who attracted no attention and was not yet the wife of a public figure. She was not even of interest to the Royal Geographic Society, which had honoured Livingstone's first expedition to Lake Ngami and might have made something of the fact that she was the first white woman to reach the Chobe River, but didn't.

Over the next four years, she must have written dozens of letters to her husband, her mother in Kuruman and the several friends of her parents with whom she stayed from time to time. Few have survived. Some, no doubt, were discarded by accident or tidy housekeeping, but none of her letters to Livingstone during this period has ever been published; and, as far as anyone knows, none exists. This is a mystery.

It's known from Livingstone's correspondence that at least some of Mary's mail was lost on its optimistic journey to the explorer as he tramped through the forests from Linyanti to the Atlantic, then tramped back in the opposite direction to the Indian Ocean. But all of it? Livingstone's letters to his wife and children, although few and far between, did reach their destinations. He is still at Linyanti in October 1853 when he tells the children: 'Don't speak Scotch. It is not as pretty as English.' (He was inclined to show symptoms of what, today, we would call 'the Scottish cringe' – undue deference to all things English in an age when Scotland's sense of identity and cultural values were at risk from creeping Anglicisation.) A year later, in October 1854, he writes: 'It occurs to me, my dear Mary, that if I send you notes from different parts of my way through this colony (Angola) some of them will surely reach you and if they carry any of the affection I bear you in their composition they will not fail to comfort you.'

Why has none of her replies survived? Why did Livingstone, a committed chronicler of all his own activities, not keep and preserve them, even in the difficult circumstances of wilderness travel? If his own sentiments are to be trusted, any note which arrived from his wife in the colonial outposts and tribal villages of central Africa, where the importance of the written word was not ignored, must have been dear to him. The suspicion is that he destroyed them, embarrassed by their disturbing content, troubled by Mary's despair and, most of all, distressed by signs that she was losing her faith. This was the woman of whom he wrote, two days after her death: 'She was a good wife, a good mother, and a good but often fearful and dejected Christian'.

The letters' fate can only be speculative, although I was told by a descendant of the Scottish chemist James Young, a close friend from Livingstone's student days, that the Young family believed Mary's letters were burned. Perhaps it was not Livingstone who suppressed them; perhaps relatives or trustees, going through his papers after his death, exercised an officious discretion; perhaps his grown-up children were just as eager to protect their mother's memory, unsullied by bitterness, as their father's reputation, which was well on the way to being sanctified by Henry Morton Stanley. What is on record, however, is the correspondence between Mary Livingstone and Arthur Tidman of the London Missionary Society: fifteen letters written during the years when the LMS was her only source of income. And, despite the formal language, their sub-text is desperate: this woman is not coping.

From the earliest example it's plain that Mary is finding it difficult to manage money. It is a request for an advance on the quarterly stipend of £30 which the LMS granted the family of their maverick missionary, whose powers of persuasion had secured their permission to scout for a mission site for the Makololo and find a route to the sea. Livingstone, although out of touch with the cost of living in Britain, seems to have had misgivings about the worth of the stipend. 'If they crimp my wife and family in England they will hear thunder', he wrote to Robert Moffat. But he did nothing to petition any other possible source of support.

Mary's first letter to Tidman is dated October 1852, and the address is 6 Almada Street: the rooms in Hamilton where she and the children moved from Ulva Cottage, her in-laws' house in Burnbank Road. The tone is practical, if a little anxious, as she makes a case for the inadequacy of the first £30, listing her expenses since disembarking:

Dear Sir,
As you kindly gave me permission to write to you I now sit down to let you know how I am situated and to tell you of my difficulties. My health has been very poor since my arrival in Scotland but I am now a

little better. We are in lodgings at £15 per quarter, independent of food and other expenses. Now that will never do for me. There is a cottage being built which the owner will let me have for £7 a year, but it is not furnished ... the furnishing will be £20 at least if it is ever so plain and simple ... I shall at present give you an account of the £30 I received from you. First I paid £5 for custom house dues. The journey from London to Manchester and Scotland including luggage, £12. And £5 for house rent and £2 for other expenses. Now there are only £5 left ... The reasons I am so explicit in this, that you may see how the money has gone. Now I shall require to get winter clothing for the rest of the family. Therefore I think it will be necessary to let me have £26 of the next quarter's allowance for the house.

Mary never moved to the unfurnished cottage at £7 per year. The following month, she wrote to Tidman from a new address at 46 Almada Street, telling him that after some trouble she had 'succeeded in getting one room at £5 a year'. At such a rent, it can only have been a wretched asylum for the five of them. There is a wistful passage: 'Have you heard anything of Mr L this mail? I hope he is far in his travels in Sebituane's country.' She mentions the cold – 'exceedingly severe but the children seem to bear it well, better than we did when we first came to this country, the only one suffers from it is myself'. (Her facial ache and paralysis returned in cold or damp weather.) But she says nothing of Livingstone's parents and sisters, living a stone's throw away in Burnbank Road. Like the other silences in Mary's life, the nature of their quarrel has never been explained.

Was there even an open quarrel? There was certainly estrangement. Nothing in Mary's character suggests she was combative; but she was lonely and dislocated and often in pain and possibly moody, while her children must have been frustrated and confused by the cramped indoor life and restrictions of the Scottish winter. Oswell, born beside the Zouga, was still a toddler, but Tom, Agnes and unruly Robert must have found it hard to bear the lack of freedom during the shortest days, when light lasts only a few hours. Perhaps Mary also disappointed the senior Livingstones, who were expecting qualities more impressive of the daughter of the distinguished Moffat and the wife of their remarkable son. It's easy to imagine why Livingstone's African and Scottish families found it hard to tolerate each other, closeted in a cottage with accommodation for four, not nine.

Livingstone joked that his parents had become lairds when they moved from their Blantyre tenement, first to a house in Almada Street and then to Ulva Cottage in nearby Burnbank Road – and it was never intended that Mary and the children should become permanent guests. But their short-lived stay seems to have wounded Mary and disturbed her in-laws. The household of Neil and Agnes Livingstone was ordered strictly by its patriarch, who was not only God-fearing but also teetotal. Their two unmarried daughters were equally committed Presbyterians. Janet and Agnes, moving into middle age, might have made friendly aunts for the children and later did support them, but they would take instruction from their father, they had their own duties, including their millinery shop, and they were often preoccupied with their health. (Livingstone's sisters were probably hypochondriacs; his letters show that he was often solicited for long-distance diagnoses and treatments for their various ailments.) By any standards, the cottage must have been an oppressive and tedious refuge for the colonial family, whose life among the Tswana had its tribulations but was rarely less than lively.

In January, without telling her in-laws where she was going, Mary suddenly left Hamilton. This was certainly bad behaviour – at best discourteous and at worst heartless – but may have been the first indication that she was moving from mere misery into depression. The Livingstones heard nothing from her for months – and, in June 1853, Arthur Tidman received the second of two letters from the children's grandfather. His words are charged with anger and concern, and he leaves little doubt that Mary has deeply offended him. The rift has now become a row.

'Mrs Livingstone does not write to us, nor are we anxious that she should, neither do we wish her to know that we are enquiring about them. Yet we love the children very much – I addressed a note to you yesterday enquiring about our grandchildren, having no other way of getting any word about them as their mother was pleased to forbid all communication with us no less than three different times. We received a note from her this morning which I enclose, but owing to her remarkably strange conduct since we became acquainted with her we have resolved to have no more intercourse with her until their [sic] is evidence she is a changed person.'

Until there is evidence she is a changed person ... something in Mary had clearly changed, as this was not the conduct of the calm, capable frontier wife, 'the sturdy little black-haired woman with the bright, kind smile' who was liked and respected by all the transient guests at her Kolobeng homestead; who was admired without caveat by the man who, more than anyone other than Livingstone himself, had observed her character in the most desperate circumstances. This was not the woman who had waited with William Cotton Oswell in the Mababe Depression while her children cried for water and all their lives were placed in the custody of a team of thirsty oxen.

Neil Livingstone concludes his letter: 'We are all, however, sorry for the poor boys and if you and Mrs Livingstone can arrange matters we are quite willing to receive Robert and Thomas, put them to school and do all in our power for their spiritual and temporal welfare'. No mention of Agnes. Even in Scotland, with its progressive education system, grounded in the social-welfare programmes of the Protestant Reformation which made provision for 'a school in every parish', the education of girls was considered less important. Missionary families, however, needed women who could teach. Mary Smith of Dukinfield, Ma-Mary, was herself the beneficiary of an academic education in a religious context, and saw to it that her daughters had the same.

Where was Mary Livingstone? Lost. Emotionally if not physically. She had taken the children to Hackney, then a genteel village outside London, where she rented cheap lodgings and made contact with some Nonconformist friends of her parents. But the simple certainties of the Moffats' Christianity had been overtaken, in their long absence from the United Kingdom, by religious controversy and a new mood of scepticism. Charles Darwin had set the cat among the doctrinal pigeons; and, for all that she was new to radical ideas, it's just possible that Mary's experience of the natural world found some resonance in his theories of evolution and the origin of species.

All her life, she had absorbed the failures and successes of the bush: how the fittest impala ram acquires the largest harem of females; how the male weaver bird which fails to build a perfect nest also fails to find a mate; how the Kalahari ground squirrel, in a pretty example of adaptation, holds its tail over its head like a parasol to forage in the sun. Instinctively, if not scientifically, Darwinism may have made some sense to her, with its implications nibbling at beliefs which, for other reasons, she was finding hard to sustain.

At this stage, Mary's 'strange conduct', noted but not described by her father-in-law, could not be put down to shaky faith, and is another puzzle. Neil Livingstone wants evidence 'that she is a changed person' before he deals with her again. To a disciple of temperance, perhaps only strict sobriety can effect the kind of change he has in mind. Nobody knows when Mary started to use alcohol as a prop, but it's not improbable that her introduction to uncomfortable Scotland also introduced her to the comfort of the brandy bottle. It was considered quite acceptable for ladies to use brandy to relieve seasickness (which it doesn't) – and Mary had just arrived from a long voyage. The fraudulent remedy might still have been in her luggage, temptingly available, affecting her moods, inciting her 'strange conduct' in the teetotal household, where brandy fumes would not go unnoticed; and, once in Almada Street, she would be free to buy more, further depleting her meagre financial resources.

The evidence of just how drink-dependent Mary became doesn't exist. The only person who ever claimed to have seen her 'quite besotted' was the Reverend James Stewart, her unwise choice of shipboard companion on the way to the Zambezi. Her recurring facial paralysis, affecting her speech, may have sometimes given people the impression she was tipsy, if not drunk; and it seems she never became so dysfunctional that she couldn't look after her children. Alcohol, of course, could have exacerbated the unexplained illness – almost certainly clinical depression – which was treated free of charge by a doctor in the Westmorland town of Kendal, where she and the children were taken in by Quaker friends of her parents at the end of 1853. But, in the Victorian age which produced the slum gin shop and the temperance movement, any respectable woman who was known to drink outside normal social events would have been censured, unless she was able to disguise the prescription of brandy as 'medicinal'. Mary may simply have used brandy as routinely as many women today use wine – to relieve stress.

Around this time, she was given harrowing news of Kolobeng in a letter from Livingstone, and with some insensitivity he spared her no details. By this time, of course, Sechele and his people had withdrawn to their new capital at Dimawe, where their territorial war of attrition with the Boers came to a head in open conflict – with predictable success for the well-armed Boer commando, which took many children into captivity to use as labour and bargaining chips. There had been a breach in Sechele's relationship with Livingstone after the missionary deserted the Bakwena for the Makololo, but it was soon repaired, and he was appalled by the Dimawe disaster. He wrote to tell Mary that he had recorded the names of 124 children who were still held hostage. She would, he said, know most of them, as they had been her pupils.

The Boers had also ransacked their homestead at Kolobeng and left it a shell. Everything in it was either destroyed or stolen, including Livingstone's books and papers. 'They brought four wagons down and took away sofa, table, bed, all the crockery, your desk ... smashed the wooden chairs and took away the iron ones.' They even broke the 'good iron door' he had made for Mary's termite-mound oven.

The desk she had brought from Kuruman; the sofa which was their one extravagance; the only settled home of her married life had been violated. Its desecration meant more than merely the loss of household goods and cherished furniture. In the grounds of the homestead was the grave of her daughter, Elizabeth.

Mary's disintegration gathered momentum, her debts mounted. The beseeching letters to the LMS became more and more urgent. By February 1853, she was again soliciting an advance on her stipend. 'I trust you will not refuse as I have no one else to look to.' She was conscious she was sometimes spending unwisely, on impulse, buying things for her husband that she had no way of sending him, as if to bridge the long gaps between his letters and to bring him closer to her. This was a woman who had grown her own vegetables, made her own soap and candles, used beads and barter as currency and sewn the family's clothes from cloth ordered by her husband from Cape Town or Britain. For Mary, city shops were not so much useful novelties as bewildering booby traps, their choices difficult to negotiate. What's more, she had little idea of how much services should cost, once paying £10 to a laundress who had seized the opportunity to exploit this naïve, ill-at-ease colonial with the odd accent who had so recently arrived from the Dark Continent, where she had had Bakwena girls to slap her linen on the rocks of the Kolobeng River.

'I would beg of you to be lenient with me', she wrote pitiably to Livingstone's employers. 'I don't attempt to justify myself. I may not have been so discreet in the use of my money.' When the LMS refused to release any more funds from her allowance, she pleaded: 'Will you kindly let me have fifteen pounds of Mr Livingstone's salary. I will acquaint him of it, and make it up.'

She needed guidance, she needed succour, and here is another riddle: she did not turn for help to the obvious person. Her sister Helen had been settled in south-east England for years. When she was 18, Helen had accepted the proposal of a wealthy silk merchant whom she met during the Moffats' long visit to the United Kingdom, and was now the mistress of a large country house in Kent. She had two children of her own, and had taken into care her two youngest sisters, Bessie and Jane, who were in England to be educated. But a woman in her position would have had a generous staff of servants to help with guests and child care. Nobody knows if Mary and Helen even contacted each other. Janet Wagner Parsons says in passing that they didn't get on, but offers no fuller explanation.

After a summer of hardship in Hackney, the nomads moved again to another temporary home in Lancashire, near Ma-Mary's childhood home of Dukinfield. When she first arrived at Southampton, Mary had been met by Arthur Tidman, by all accounts a kindly man, who had helped her to deal with the utterly foreign process of rail travel; and the family had broken their journey to Glasgow at Manchester with friends of her parents. Now one of them arranged bed and board for the five strays in a village outside the city; but this more comprehensive support system did little to ease Mary's chronic shortage of funds. By November she was almost penniless, on the brink of collapse, desperate enough to send Agnes to the Braithwaites of Kendal, where soon afterwards she and the other children arrived. Miss Braithwaite sent them their rail fare.

This Quaker family opened their hearts and their home among the Lakeland hills to them and saved Mary's sanity, but not before she endured two months of unspecified illness, 'long and severe', as she told Tidman, which was treated by their doctor, who 'kindly refused any remuneration for his services'. The children were also taken in hand. Tom had a recurring bladder problem which had first presented itself on their Kalahari treks (perhaps the impure water which saved them all in the Mababe Depression was not quite as harmless as Livingstone sunnily claimed) and his health improved in the stable comfort of the Kendal house, while Agnes and Robert were enrolled in a Quaker school. Years later, Livingstone was to acknowledge that the Quakers were often successful with 'wayward boys like Robert' – perhaps a tacit admission that he himself had failed his son.

The Braithwaites remained anchors in the uncertain waters of all the Livingstone lives. In her book *Wives of Fame*, Edna Healey writes that their importance to Mary during this period 'cannot be underestimated', and explains something of why she was received with such uncritical kindness: 'Old Mrs Braithwaite was perhaps one of the few women who could really understand Mary's problems. As a young woman she too had left her children and husband to follow her "inner light" in the wilds of America, had travelled with her Quaker message hundreds of miles alone on horseback. Now, in her old age, she and her husband presided over a successful family.'

Her son Charles was a lawyer who not only helped Mary sort out her affairs but also became Livingstone's lawyer. Her daughter Anna was physically handicapped, and her gentle nature and unlimited attention were exactly what Mary and her unsettled children needed. But unaccountably, as if trapped in a cycle of packing and unpacking, starting and stopping, as if driven by the need for perpetual motion, Mary left Kendal for Epsom in the early summer of 1854. There, another friend of her parents found her rooms. She took with her Tom and Oswell, while Robert and Agnes remained behind at their Quaker school. Her life since she married Livingstone had been that of a wanderer, and increasingly a vagrant. Perhaps she simply couldn't break the habit. Perhaps she wanted the freedom to prepare for her next move.

In one of her begging letters to Tidman she had told him she was now fit for a sea voyage, and entreated him to advance her the money for a passage to the Cape, as she was sure Livingstone would be able to meet her there in August. She knew he had reached the west coast of Africa and the Portuguese port of Loanda (now the Angolan capital of Luanda) and was on his way back to Linyanti. She knew nothing of the obstacles and hardships of his journey, which included months of malarial attacks and bouts of rheumatic fever, or the heroic persistence which drove him on; and, as far as she was concerned, his 'two years' of independent travel were drawing to a close. She did not know that he had been offered a passage home from Loanda on a British warship and had refused it. He was indeed on his way to Linyanti with his team of Makololo porters, but only to continue his exploration of the Zambezi eastwards, to the Indian Ocean coast.

The long-suffering Tidman was again required to persuade the directors of the LMS to advance her the most meagre of funds, while two of her children were being supported by the Braithwaites in Kendal. Somehow, still virtually penniless, Mary endured another desolate year until she received a letter in September 1855 apologising for 'a delay I could not shorten ... I have written to you by every opportunity and am very sorry your letters have miscarried ... I cannot be long now'. Finally, news of Livingstone, his epic journey and its phenomenal revelation arrived from Quelimane, where he emerged from the interior in May 1856 – four years after he had left the Cape. He had walked across Africa. He had seen the smoke that thunders, and called it the Victoria Falls. He was coming home a great man.

Mary was waiting. She waited another six months before Livingstone arrived from Quelimane, where waiting for him was news from the LMS which incensed him. In a letter, the directors told him that they would no longer underwrite activities only 'remotely connected' with the spread of the Gospel. Although the dispatches of his observations and calculations on his journey had gone ahead to the Royal Geographic Society, he was not yet fully aware of how his triumph as a geographer would eclipse his 'failure' as a missionary. He was broodingly preoccupied with the open blight of slavery in the Portuguese territories of Angola and Mozambique, despite the best evangelical efforts of their Jesuit priests. (There was nothing sectarian in Livingstone's faith.) He had never been more convinced that the only way to defeat the slave trade, in which Portugal's colonial administrators were complicit, was by opening up opportunities for legitimate commerce. Literally. He had failed to find a viable route from the Atlantic coast to the upper Zambezi; now he was turning his attention to the Indian Ocean, into which the great river debouched.

As he sailed home he was grappling with fury and disappointment at the LMS letter and with its implications for his future and his ambitions – a state of mind which seems to have obscured any happy expectations of the forthcoming family reunion, and may have made him careless of at least one letter to his wife. When the brig *Frolic* was delayed by a storm, he informed Mary that 'patience is a great virtue', adding a detail which must have been cold comfort: the brig's captain had 'been six years away from his family, I only four and a half'.

When the ship finally docked at Dover on 9 December 1856, he was welcomed as a hero. Where was his heroine? She was waiting at Southampton, where she had expected him to disembark. The bungled arrangements for their reunion, which took place two days later in London, were symptomatic of the bungled life she had led since they last met, and symbolic of her helplessness without him.

In the last few weeks of anticipation, however, she had become inspired. Mary's handwriting is a spidery scrawl, difficult to read, perhaps reflecting her reluctance to commit her thoughts to paper. But now she had composed a poem, which has survived. It is doggerel, but it does its job. The lines overflow with love, hurt, reproach (despite a denial), pleading and prophecy. To the cynic, it might be read as emotional blackmail.

A hundred thousand welcomes, and it's time for you to come
From the far land of the foreigner, to your country and your home.
Oh, long as we were parted, ever since you went away.
I never passed an easy night, or knew an easy day.

Do you think I would reproach you with the sorrows that I bore?
Since the sorrow is all over now I have you here once more.
And there's nothing but the gladness and the love within my heart,
And hope so sweet and certain that never again we'll part.

A hundred thousand welcomes! How my heart is gushing o'er
With the love and joy and wonder just to see your face once more.
How did I live without you all those long long years of woe?
It seems as if t'would kill me to be parted from you now.

You'll never part me, darling, there's a promise in your eye;
I may tend you while I'm living, you will watch me when I die.
And if death but kindly lead me to the blessed home on high,
What hundred thousand welcomes will await you in the sky!

It was enough for the moment to restore their relationship. But nothing Mary said or wrote would ever be enough to divert her husband's attention for long, or to change his nature. Only her death did that.

Keith is refuelling and restocking the Land Rover. We have one last journey to make before we go our separate ways, Keith to drive back to Johannesburg, me to travel home from Maun on three flights. Our final expedition will take two days, and, although its first leg is not the longest of our long road trips, it is the slowest and trickiest. We will see little tar after we leave Maun and head north-east along the fringe of the Okavango Delta – the route the Livingstones and Oswell should have taken on their expedition to Sebetwane's country, and the route of their return. We will enter Chobe National Park at its Mababe Gate and drive along the Magwikwe Sand Ridge, skirting the dry, trackless, treacherous heart of the Mababe Depression until we see the Ghoha Hills and the first trees of Chobe Forest Reserve. Then, if there's plenty of daylight, we will know that we're in time to cross the Chobe River at Ngoma Bridge, where the border posts close at 6pm. And we will spend the night in Namibia.

'And if we're not in time?' I ask Keith.

'We camp. There's a public campsite at Savuti. By the time we reach it, we should know whether we're going to make the border by six. But if we do have to overnight at Savuti, it will leave us short of time for the return trip, and I know you've a flight to catch.'

Why are we going to Namibia? I've already had an argument with a local white Namibian who insists that Livingstone never set foot in his country, land of the Namib Desert and Skeleton Coast. But, if the site of Sebetwane's capital of Linyanti lay between the Chobe and Zambezi rivers, as all the history claims, then he and Oswell must have crossed the Chobe into what is now the Caprivi Strip: the long, narrow finger of Namibian territory which pokes eastward from its parent body between the borders of Angola, Botswana and Zambia. There is actually a district and village called Linyanti in the Strip – Keith has learned about it on his first Livingstone safari – but today Linyanti is also the name of a wildlife reserve on the Botswana side of the river, which to add to the confusion is a river with three different names. The south-east border of the Caprivi Strip is defined by the Kwando, the Linyanti and the Chobe – the same river at different stages as it spills through the marshes and floodplains where the Makololo lived and died.

It is this muddle of names, waters and borders, I've concluded, which has convinced my obstinate Namibian that Livingstone left not one footprint on his country. Mary Livingstone is another matter. Mary never crossed the Chobe, by all accounts. When she met Sebetwane, the chief paid her the honour of visiting her at the wagon camp on the south bank, where he then became ill before dying on the journey back to Linyanti. Such is the shifting nature of the Kwando/Linyanti/Chobe water system that, to my knowledge, nobody has identified the spot where she waited while her husband and Oswell explored the Makololo territories and reached the Zambezi. But her campsite must have been close to the stretch of Chobe waterfront near Ngoma Bridge. I need no other excuse to visit again this most beautiful of African rivers.

Linyanti is Livingstone's business, and this is not his story. But a visit to the Caprivi Strip will return me to the banks of the Zambezi, where Mary's story ended and mine began.

20

The Road to the Zambezi

'So you see the orders have come'

Her husband was home, or at least back in Britain. They had no home now, and Livingstone was no more inclined to find one. He was already planning his return to Africa, and his staging post was a rented house in Hadley Green, at that time a village north of London. Here, however, they were reunited with their scattered children and recovered a brief but rewarding period of family life; here, with an advance from the publisher John Murray, they enjoyed their first taste of prosperity, while the great, the good and the British public clamoured to honour the obscure Scot who had walked across Africa to save its soul from paganism and its people from slavery; and here, Mary entered a world more comfortable and secure but as daunting as ever. She had become the wife of a celebrity.

Within a week of Livingstone's return, while they were still in lodgings in Chelsea, he was presented with the Royal Geographic Society's Victoria Medal. It was Mary's first experience of fashionable society – and, indifferent to her wardrobe, she looked the oddity she was to remain to its arbiters of taste. She also seemed indifferent to the speeches which not only honoured her husband but finally acknowledged her contribution to his achievements. At the end of the RGS ceremony, Lord Shaftesbury turned the spotlight on her:

'That lady was born with one distinguished name, which she has changed for another. She was born a Moffat and became a Livingstone. She cheered the early part of her husband's career by her spirit, her counsel and her society. Afterwards, when she reached this country, she passed many years with her children in solitude and anxiety, suffering the greatest fears for the welfare of her husband, and yet enduring all with patience and resignation, and even joy, because she had surrendered her best feelings, and a sacrifice of her own private interests, to the advancement of civilisation and the great interests of Christianity.'

'Enduring all with patience and resignation, and even joy ...' Was it the 'even joy' which caused Mary to remain stony-faced throughout this eulogy? Much has been made of Mary's impassive appearance at the many public functions they attended – 'There were plenty of beady-eyed observers', according to Margaret Forster, 'who later scribbled their impressions – were fascinated by Mary's blank expression. She reacted to no compliment, moved not a muscle at any applause for her ... A nod was the most she ever managed, when urged to acknowledge tributes.' Forster interprets her response, or lack of it, as the submissive modesty of a wife who believed that all praise belonged to her husband. I'm less sure. Her recurring facial paralysis, little understood, may have been one reason why she 'moved not a muscle'. But a reservoir of resentment, a private contempt for the unctuous claims for her character and virtue made by people who didn't know her, who had no idea of her ordeals in either Africa or Britain – or her lack of choice in Livingstone's adventures – may have been another. Mary was not the same woman who had left Cape Town.

One breach was healed. Neil Livingstone, Mary's father-in-law, had died while his son was on his voyage home and the family visited Hamilton, where his mother and two sisters put behind them their history with Mary, and from then on did what they could to support her children. Robert, Agnes, Tom and Oswell were encouraged to get to know the father they hadn't seen for nearly five years. In the house overlooking Hadley Green (a pleasant stone building, now called Livingstone Cottage, with a plaque to salute his brief tenancy), the younger ones played round his desk while he wrote *Missionary Travels and Researches in South Africa*, producing 1,000 handwritten pages in six months. He took the children for walks in Hadley Wood, no doubt using his naturalist's eye to introduce them to the exotica of this alien bush, and with some pride paraded them before the old friends with whom they had all shared the Kalahari. William Cotton Oswell renewed his friendship with Agnes, still called Nannee, the infant tea-party hostess of Lake Ngami; and Thomas Steele met his namesake, whom his father still called Tau. (Poor Tau certainly didn't have the constitution of his Setswana nickname, the word for 'lion'; his delicate health must have competed for supremacy with Robert's mutinous behaviour during his mother's sleepless nights.)

But Livingstone was also busy. He was later to write to Robert, as he left for Africa, that while he was in England 'I was so busy I could not enjoy much the company of my children'. He was not only meeting his book deadline with the iron will he brought to every commitment, he was also dealing with the demands of fame: lectures, receptions, university ceremonies, interviews with the press, an audience with Queen Victoria – all manner of public events which caused him to complain (disingenuously, according to Tim Jeal) that 'this lionising' was not to his taste, and that he would rather be dining with friends than feasting with the Lord Mayor. 'Livingstone thoroughly enjoyed his new life,' concludes Jeal, 'and his much-vaunted claim that he disliked publicity comes strangely from a man who insisted on wearing his distinctive peaked cap wherever he went.'

Mary was often, but not always, with him. When he travelled to Dublin to lecture, he complimented himself, half-seriously, on his uxoriousness: 'I am just admiring what a good husband you have got. No sooner does he land in Ireland than he sits down & writes to his wife.' When Mary did play the consort to the national hero, she continued to ignore the expectations of his public. She refused to collude with the extravagance of mid-Victorian fashions, whether through indifference, obstinacy or irreversible blindness to style. She rejected the crinoline, preferred stout cotton to silk and – a grave social solecism – wore a straw bonnet indoors as well as out, even at evening assemblies. She seemed blessedly oblivious to the toxins swirling round the drawing rooms of London society. She received much oleaginous attention as the celebrity wife, but behind her back she was judged dull, charmless and hopelessly *démodé*. At one 'dress assembly' a commentator observed, not without sympathy, that 'Mrs L, with a straw bonnet of 1846 and attired to match, made a most singular exception to the brilliant costumes'. She was compared to a 'badly dressed housemaid', much as a celebrity WAG today might be despised for her chav's shell suit.

Livingstone was also collaborating with Sir Roderick Murchison of the RGS to secure government sponsorship for the Zambezi Expedition taking shape in his mind. He had given up hope of persuading the LMS to fund more activities which, as they put it, were only 'remotely connected' with spreading the Gospel, and he now decided to leave their service. He was seriously disaffected with its directors and had no intention of pursuing his earlier ambition to find a mission site on the Batoka plateau to secure Makololo conversion, if and when he had persuaded the tribe to move from Linyanti.

The Zambezi was surging through his tunnel vision. But the LMS were now committed to a Makololo mission, and believed that the project was and would be supported by Livingstone's experience and contacts at their capital. His earlier enthusiasm for the Makololo spurred them on and indirectly caused the greatest loss of life of any single venture in LMS history. The society even followed the example of Livingstone by authorising its two missionaries, Holloway Helmore and Roger Price, to take their wives and children with them to pestilential Linyanti, where they were under the impression that Livingstone would meet them to perform a diplomatic role if his Zambezi Expedition had got upriver to the Victoria Falls. The meeting never took place.

The awful deaths of Helmore, his wife, Mrs Price and three of the five children were a catastrophe which remains controversial to this day. Only Roger Price and two of the Helmore children survived. Against the advice of Robert Moffat, the missionary families with their Tswana followers and servants set off from Kuruman in July 1859 while Livingstone was still on the lower Zambezi, thwarted by the Kebrabasa rapids. The ill-fated party came close to including among its number Mary Livingstone.

She was back in Africa, but not on the Zambezi. She had given birth to her sixth and last child at the Moffats' homestead – the only baby her husband was not on hand to deliver. Anna Mary, named after Mrs Braithwaite of Kendal, was the child conceived shortly before the Zambezi Expedition left Britain; Mary's pregnancy was diagnosed by Dr John Kirk on the SS *Pearl* somewhere between Sierra Leone and Cape Town. 'A great trial to me', as her husband mentioned at the time, obliging him to leave Mary with her parents while he continued to the Zambezi.

The stable interlude of Hadley Green had been short-lived. It was happy enough, but it can't have been worry-free. Within a few months of her husband's return, Mary was pregnant again, but miscarried; her only miscarriage, as far as anyone knows. She was painfully aware that their family life was still held hostage by Africa. It wouldn't last. Perhaps she took some comfort from making one close friend and confidante who valued her not for her parents' sake or her husband's celebrity but for herself. Mary Fitch was the wife of a Highbury merchant who provisioned the Zambezi Expedition, and she and her family had the good sense to preserve some of the letters Mary later wrote from Scotland and Africa – letters a little wry in tone but without the humiliating content of her correspondence with the LMS.

There were clouds on her horizon, and her horizon was a far one. The funds were released, the plans were made, the date was set for the new river-borne offensive on the interior and the slave trade, and Mary would be part of it. She had to choose between husband and children. The youngest, six-year-old Oswell, would go with them. The other three were put in the care of their Scottish grandmother and aunts in Hamilton, while Livingstone appointed trustees to manage his income from *Missionary Travels* and his children's expenses. (One of them was the innovative chemist James 'Paraffin' Young, a friend from his student days in Glasgow and pioneer of the shale-oil industry in central Scotland.) Robert, now 12, was removed from his Quaker school in Kendal and enrolled in Hamilton Academy. Agnes was nearly 11, approaching puberty – a time when most daughters need their mothers with new intensity. Tom was nine and still in poor health. Mary had to choose – but, as George Seaver said of her, she had no choices, only situations. She could not be left alone again.

For the sake of his own reputation as much as his wife's emotional health, Livingstone, now well briefed on her erratic behaviour during his absent years, was determined to take her with him. But not under sufferance; he made a virtue of necessity, and turned her presence on the expedition into propaganda. On 13 February 1858, Sir Roderick Murchison, now president of the RGS, organised a grand banquet in London's Freemasons' Hall to allow the society's (all-male) membership to honour their departure. There, he announced that 'the daughter of that faithful missionary Mr Moffat' would travel with her husband and 'lend materially to the success of the expedition'.

The daughter of that faithful missionary Mr Moffat was sitting in the gallery with some female friends, 'in a stout lindsey dress and thick bonnet'. She was toasted by the Duke of Wellington – and, when one of the diners called for three cheers for Mrs Livingstone, she acknowledged the tributes with a curtsey but no emotion. When Livingstone rose to thank his hosts, all looked upwards again as he cited the assets which qualified Mary to join the expedition. 'My wife is familiar with the languages of South Africa, she is able to work, she is willing to endure and she well knows that in that country one must be able to put one's hand to everything ... glad I am that I am to be accompanied by my guardian angel.'

The mood was overwhelmingly optimistic, almost hubristic. A month later they were on their way to the Zambezi.

Another dawn departure. Maun, like the rest of Botswana, like most of Africa, is up and about. The National Parks and Wildlife Services office in Sir Seretse Khama Road opens at 7am, and Keith has taken the precaution of asking their advice on conditions in Chobe National Park and available space at its campsite, should we need to spend the night there. 'There's a lot of water on the road to the park,' they tell us, 'but you should be OK with 4WD.'

As we head north along the wooded banks of the Thamalakane, we exchange tar for gravel, and a few miles past Shorobe village we reach the Buffalo Gate – the gate in the infamous veterinary cordon fence which slices through the Delta from north to south. At Sanyoko village, a policeman pops out of his house with a warning. The road to Mababe Gate is

flooded. Things change quickly now that Delta waters are in charge, prob-
ing into every dry channel and empty ditch.

'The bridge ahead is broken, too dangerous to cross. You must go back
half a kilometre and find a track to the right. It leads to another bridge,
just a few logs, but the water is shallow there and you should get across.'

Our directions, as ever, are less than adequate to the shifting paths of
the riverine forest. When we leave the Chobe road, we soon find ourselves ensnared by sludgy tracks which defy the intelligence of satnav. The
bridge of logs, which is more a pontoon of sticks, crosses one of many
streams and takes us deeper and deeper into woodland. Keith elects to
follow the compass on his satnav – we know we must keep heading north-
north-east – and we find a promising track. But soon we come to another
Thamalakane tributary, which he decides to ford. 'But first,' he says, 'I'll
test the depth of the water. Quite a few of our self-drive Land Rovers have
been stranded when their drivers just plunged into creeks like this. Even
Land Rovers have their limits.'

There is only one way to test the depth of the water. I take the chance
to stretch my legs while Keith gets *his* legs wet, wading barefoot into the
turbid stream until it reaches his shorts. The satnav has at least told us
we're now on the eastern border of Moremi Game Reserve. Unlike South
African game reserves, its 2,000 square miles of woodland and wetland
are unfenced, and naturally the wildlife doesn't know to stay within them.
I look round, hopeful and alert, recalling the lessons of my field guiding
course in the Masai Mara: always know what's happening in the bush;
look, listen, look, sniff the air. I mentioned this once to an army officer,
and he nodded sagely: 'Situational awareness'. A rustle and flash of spotted hide make me jump. Only a bush buck.

Keith judges his snorkel exhaust pipe and 'aggressive' off-road tyres up
to the task, and we rock down one steep bank, surge through the water
and grind up the other, where I glimpse a huge boulder rolling away from
us through the trees. We have disturbed a bull elephant on his way for a
drink. So much for my situational awareness.

At last we find our way back to the Chobe road at Mababe village –
and when I see the name my pulse speeds up. We reach Mababe Gate, the
southern access to the park, before noon. 'Park' is such a civilised word;
an inadequate term for the protected wildlife redoubts of Africa, although
they do get managed. Once we pay our park fees, wave goodbye to the
lonely gatekeepers and cross the invisible border into Chobe National
Park, we are on our own in a wilderness. The track ahead offers nothing
but soft sand and stunted mopane forest for forty miles, until we reach
the public campsite at Savuti. No distance on tar roads; but this plodding

route along and beside the Magwikwe Sand Ridge, the western beach of the Mababe Depression, gets little traffic. Chobe's honeypots for wildlife and visitors are the riverfront, Savuti and the Linyanti wetlands south of the river. Much of our route will follow the margin of the Mababe Depression, which is the bed of an ancient lake where there is still no road and little water.

We set off supervised by six giraffes, an elegant sorority of mothers and daughters. I never see giraffes without thinking of Karen Blixen, who described their freakish beauty better than anyone. 'Their queer, inimitable, vegetative gracefulness,' she wrote, 'like a family of rare, long-stemmed, speckled, gigantic flowers ...' But they are the only mammals we see until we leave the park and re-enter the world of domestic livestock. This is a disappointment. Chobe's elephant population, a concentration of some 50,000 animals in the dry season, is among the highest in Africa, although we have mixed feelings about meeting any of them on the road, where we are funnelled between thick ramparts of mopane. Elephants can hold you up; it is not a good idea to try to barge through an elephant road-block, and we must reach Ngoma Bridge and border post before sunset.

Like the vegetation, the birdlife is on the homogeneous side. The trees are seemingly reserved for the exclusive use of grey hornbills. As the Land Rover trudges on through the sand there are few distractions, and I find myself thinking not of Mary Livingstone but of Isabella Price, who also crossed the Mababe Depression but died on the return journey, a victim of the rout of the Makololo Mission. Like Mary, this missionary wife was also pregnant when her ox-wagon left Kuruman, and also gave birth in the bush. Unlike Mary, she kept diaries. Although Holloway Helmore had served in Bechuanaland for twenty years, Roger and Isabella Price were new to Africa – inexperienced, ill-prepared (there was no doctor in the party) but exalted by their mission to the farthest reach of LMS ambition, until the pages of Isabella's diary become a memoir of unimaginable suffering.

On the journey to Linyanti, without the jaunty hindsight of Livingstone, she gives voice to the agonies of thirst, the ordeal of feeding spoonfuls of water to the four tormented Helmore children in temperatures of over 40 degrees. (Unaccountably, they had elected to follow the same desperate route which the Livingstones and Oswell had taken nine years earlier.) She was often ill with fever and diarrhoea, and gave birth to her first child, Eliza, two months into the trek, but she complains little about her own discomforts. When they reached the Chobe and met Makololo scouts sent to help them cross the river, her diary is almost jubilant. 'Oh! How sanguine our hopes were then! What joy filled our hearts that day when we thought that that was the beginning of a great work among those dark and benighted heathen!' At Linyanti itself, her entries become nightmarish.

They arrived in February 1860 and spent four months at the Makololo capital, where Sebetwane's son, Sekeletu, a weak and unpopular shadow of his charismatic father, had become chief. There they expected to find Livingstone, and there Sekeletu expected to welcome a Moffat. The absence of either disappointed the missionaries and confused Sekeletu, who became suspicious and unhelpful. One by one, the mission party, European and Tswana, fell ill. Within three weeks of reaching the malarial enclave between the Chobe and the Zambezi, Isabella Price is writing: 'All are now down with this nasty slow fever, with exception of Roger, myself and Konate; every one of the Helmores, poor things, so that one can not help the other ... Sekeletu has sent me a girl for a nursemaid ... and now I can devote my time to the poor invalids.' A few days later, the first Helmore child died, and the following day Isabella and her baby daughter were so ill that she could do nothing for the others.

It got worse. 'March 9th. Ah! Providence, how mysteriously art thou dealing with us! My own sweet little one has today taken her flight from us ... I seized her to my bosom and gave her a press. Then laying her on my lap found her eyes were fixed and she ceased to breathe ... Ah! I do feel lonely tonight ... When I think of her sweet little face beaming with smiles upon me, I feel it is hard to part with my precious ... my heart bleeds at the parting.' No blame is apportioned. 'My heart's desire now is that I may become more holy and devoted to the service of my Master.'

Eliza Price was six months old. By the middle of April both Helmores and two of their children were dead, and Roger and Isabella Price were so weakened they began to plan their retreat from Linyanti with the two surviving Helmore children. They had been unable to persuade the Makololo to move to a healthier site, and the Makololo, themselves steadily haemorrhaging men, women and children, broke their own rules of hospitality and honesty. Before he sanctioned their departure Sekeletu demanded oxen, wagons and most of their possessions, leaving them the bare minimum for their return to Kuruman. Isabella Price and the children had only the clothes they wore. On 26 May, before they crossed the Chobe, she wrote the last entry in her diary: 'Roger and I do not know what it is to have a day's health ... Roger is so thin and pale that he looks more like a dead man than a living one and I am so thin I have been obliged to plaster my poor bones and have lost the use of my legs.'

Five weeks into their return journey this valiant young woman died.

Her husband recorded: 'I buried her the same evening under a tree, the only tree on the whole of the immense plain of Mababe.'[1]

Mary Livingstone was at Kuruman with her son Oswell and the new baby when the Makololo missionaries first arrived from the Cape. Livingstone didn't learn of the birth of Anna Mary for another year, but it had occurred to him that Mary and the children might travel overland to meet him on the Zambezi, either with Robert Moffat and his son John, who were to travel on a separate mission to Mzilikazi and the Matabele, or with Helmore and Price. When Mary heard that they hoped to rendezvous with Livingstone at Linyanti, she seriously considered joining them. But her father thought that the timing and composition of the Makololo expedition were flawed; Anna Mary was only months old; Mary's parents were both unhappy about sending their daughter and grandchildren on another Kalahari trek; and she was missing her other children. For all the temptation of her husband's relative proximity (they were, at least, on the same continent) she decided to return to Britain.

Would Mary's presence have made much difference to the outcome of the Makololo Mission? Her experience of desert trekking, her fluent Setswana, her advice on the treatment of malaria, even her memories of the route to the Chobe River would have helped. Her status as Robert Moffat's daughter and David Livingstone's wife would almost certainly have made the Makololo more co-operative.

On the other hand, the anopheles mosquito might have killed her with the other casualties, two years earlier than it did.

'I stayed near here a few years ago', I tell Keith. 'But I flew in from a Delta camp, so I didn't use this road.' I look again at the map. 'In fact, it was about thirty miles west of here, a private camp in Linyanti Wildlife Reserve. There were no roads anywhere except the track from the airstrip and the game tracks.'

---

1 Roger Price, with the aid of his compass, found his way with the two surviving Helmore children to the Thamalakane River, where they were helped by Chief Letsholathebe. On the journey back to Kuruman, they were met by a rescue party led by Robert Moffat; and, as Price recovered his strength at the Moffats' mission, he got to know their youngest daughter, Bessie, whom he married the following year. They both spent their lives in mission work in Bechuanaland, latterly at Kuruman, where Price died in 1900.

We have reached the national park campsite at Savuti in time to take stock and use its toilets, which are sited with the showers in something that looks like a concrete bomb-proof bunker. This unlovely structure is not bomb-proof but elephant-proof. Elephants are fastidious, often choosing the clean, piped water of boreholes over muddy water holes to quench their thirst; and, until the ablutions block was built inside a circular concrete rampart, they regularly trashed the plumbing.

The landscape here is more open, with scatters of acacia woodland and low hills which are sites of San/Bushman rock art. A few fellow travellers are taking siestas at their individual campsites under camelthorn trees, and we wave to those who are still awake. They will do their game-viewing in the late afternoon at the nearby Savuti Channel, which, like the Boteti, is a river that died and came alive again. This was where I first learned a little of the mysteries of the Delta water systems, the rivers which once fed and flowed from the great Kalahari superlake, and how a place that was green and soft and plentiful could turn gaunt and harsh and brown for no apparent reason; or at least none that is clearly understood.

'I remember thinking that Savuti was scorched earth to the Delta's sweet water. We drove along the channel between the skeletons of trees. It had been dry since the early 1980s, when the water disappeared in the space of three years, but at the camp they were hopeful it was on its way back. Maybe because there had been another tiny seismic shift in the land.'

The Savuti Channel reached television as *The Stolen River* after two naturalists, Dereck and Beverly Joubert, chronicled the shrinking of its water between 1979 and 1982. They watched and filmed the impact on wildlife: 'Genets, servals, civets and honey badgers feasted on the dead fish. Hordes of fish eagles and marabou storks circled the ailing channel, defying all ornithological laws. Elephants began digging desperately for stolen water ... the species crowded in together, predators with prey, all players on a common stage ...'

The empty channel gave me one of my best leopard encounters: two cats flirting, their spots dancing before the eyes of our headlights, the male wrinkling his lip and nose to savour the pheromones which told him the female was ready to mate as they retired discreetly into the bush. Today it has water again, and drains into Savuti Marsh, at the north end of the Mababe Depression. Livingstone called the marsh a 'dismal swamp' – but dry or wet it's now valued for its wildlife. Near here Lloyd Wilmot had his anarchic camp, which paid little heed to park rules or the health and safety of its fearless owner. But we jolt onwards. Unless we are waylaid by the unexpected, we should reach the Ngoma Bridge before the border closes; but we've another seventy miles to cover, and we can't afford to be tourists. The road surface has been firmer for the last hour or so. Now, as we approach the Ghoha Hills and Chobe Forest Reserve, it turns to thick, heavy sand, slowing the Land Rover to the speed of a plough.

I've been eager to glimpse the approach of the wooded hills which the Livingstones and Oswell reached with relief, after they'd cleared the Savuti Marsh and Mababe Depression now lying behind us to the south-east. There are three of them, the worn stumps of volcanoes which were active long before the Kalahari superlake turned to desert; and they are not high, about 300 feet. To the struggling trekkers they seemed like mountains. When they came upon the first of the group, Livingstone recorded: 'This being the only hill we had seen since leaving the Bamangwato we felt inclined to take off our hats to it'.

The closest hill stands like a sentry near Ghoha Gate, and its flank is studded with baobab trees. Here we leave the park and enter the forest reserve, an enclave of community-managed livestock and hunting areas, much of it vegetated dunes. The sand does its best to hinder us, but we know we are now on the final haul to the Chobe floodplain. 'As we went north,' Livingstone continued, 'the country became very lovely; many new trees appeared; the grass was green, and often higher than the wagons; the vines festooned the trees, among which appeared the real banian [banyan] … with its drop shoots, and the wild date and Palmyra …'

Sand gives way to gravel. At the village of Kachekau we leave the forest reserve for a minor road which eventually becomes tar. I have almost forgotten what it is like to drive on a hard surface. The sun is low enough to slide its beams across the first pools of the floodplain, then the first floodwaters of the river itself. As the Chobe spills from its channel and spreads between the flat frontiers of Botswana and Namibia, expanding the border by at least a mile, it reaches our roadside verge, where naked baobabs and lean flat-topped acacias, more like sculptures than trees, stand black against the wash of luminous blue.

I feel something close to rapture: not the religious rapture of Isabella Price, for whom the river promised 'the beginning of a great work among those dark and benighted heathen', or the less exalted joy of Mary Livingstone, for whom the river delivered refreshment for herself and her children; just the mild euphoria which comes to most people in the presence of light and beauty.

Mary is in Scotland with her five children; she is often depressed, possibly drinking too much, toiling with Robert's teenage rebellions and Tom's fragile health, but showing signs of independence. She has a decent family income at last; and, although she still squanders money and keeps no accounts, she has rented a comfortable house in Glasgow, only fifteen miles from Hamilton and her in-laws. She has almost begun to make a life for herself; she draws even closer to adolescent Agnes, cherishes her new daughter and has found a tutor for Tom, who has been unhappy at school. The tutor is the Reverend James Stewart, eager to please, eager to offer support when Robert runs up debts, quarrels with his college lecturer, abandons his medical studies and disappears for a week.

Mary is distraught, but copes. She finds 'poor misguided Robert' in Hamilton and continues to cope when others think otherwise. Her public behaviour is under the scrutiny of many eyes, some friendly and concerned, some disapproving and meddling. Reports reach her husband, who is plagued by problems on the Zambezi, some of them of his own making. He has sacked his second-in-command, a naval officer called Norman Bedingfeld, and the ill-used Thomas Baines. His brother Charles, an ordained Nonconformist minister and American emigrant who has left a wife and children to join the expedition, has been a troublemaker. The rapids of Kebrabasa have proved implacable, and the little steamship *Ma-Robert* has exhausted its stamina. Livingstone sends his engineer, George Rae, to inspect her replacement, the *Pioneer*, and to supervise the building of the 'flat-pack' *Lady Nyassa*. When Rae arrives in Scotland, he meets Stewart, observes his influence on Mary, considers their relationship unseemly and insinuates as much in his letters to Livingstone. From Rae, the explorer also learns that his son Robert has developed 'vagabond ways', but does little to address the problem.

Mary's shaky new independence is, in a sense, reinforced by her crisis of faith. She has started to think for herself and to question the sacrifices she has made. What if none of it is true? What if her husband's 'great work', for which she has compromised her health, risked the lives of her children and meekly surrendered any measure of control over her own destiny, is the labour of a great lie? Science is the spirit of the age, and she numbers scientists among her close acquaintances. One of them is James Young, genius of the shale-oil industry, who is living not far away on his Polbeth estate in West Lothian. Does 'Paraffin' Young debate Darwinism with Mary? Does she put her doubts and complaints into the letters which his descendants believe were burned?

Reports of Mary's public scepticism and open criticism of missionaries and mission life certainly reach Young's old friend Livingstone, but not through any existing letters written by Mary. Some letters do survive from this period, to the Braithwaites and other friends, but they are inoffensive accounts of her movements and concerns for the children. One minor outburst of resentment did reach her mother in Kuruman – the only direct evidence that her doubts had begun to focus on her husband's neglect of her. She told Ma-Mary she did not 'think it duty' for him to leave her year after year; and it's safe to assume her mother agreed.

It is not safe to assume much else. Like everyone who has written about the last years of Mary's life (and much that went before), I am making deductions about her state of mind which can't be verified by her own testimony. It is Livingstone's letters which reveal that he knew his wife needed spiritual support, that her behaviour was often disturbing and sometimes presumed to be fired up by alcohol. It is Livingstone's letters which urge her to pray, to recover God's inspiration. He also writes to 13-year-old Agnes, warning her that he might have to send for 'Mamma'.

In London, the rumours and accounts of Mary's instability reach one of the expedition's benefactors, the philanthropist Angela Burdett-Coutts, who was kind to Mary during the months of Livingstone's 'lionising', and has the confidence of her class to remind him of responsibilities far beyond the Zambezi, the Shire River and Lake Nyasa. When he receives a reprimand from Lady Burdett-Coutts instructing him to look to his wife's welfare, he takes action. He writes to Mary telling her (not asking her) to book a passage to the Cape with George Rae, who will escort her onwards to the Zambezi with the *Lady Nyassa*.

There is an edge to the tone of the letter she writes to her friend Mary Fitch. 'I received a letter from Livingstone dated 28 March, 1861. In it he says "embrace the first opportunity to come out ..." So you see the orders have come.'

For the first time in their marriage Mary considers defying her husband. She procrastinates. She finds reason after reason to postpone her departure. Anna Mary has been ill. Anna Mary is too young, much younger than her siblings were when their mother first left them for her interrupted voyage on the expedition ship *Pearl*. Robert is too old, poised on a perilous cusp between wayward youth and wilful man. They need her. They all need her. Livingstone's ageing mother and unmarried sisters are willing to take them in, but can they supply the critical, complex emotional support which only loving parents have the understanding and commitment to provide? George Rae takes ship without her, and imports his baggage of gossip and innuendo to the Cape.

Mary's little mutiny falters. Another medical missionary is on his way to the Zambezi; and, with his encouragement, she finally books her passage.

Racked by anguish and guilt for the wretched choice she has had to make – no real choice, just another situation for this most obedient of wives – she leaves Southampton with the Reverend James Stewart on the Royal Mail ship *Celt*. It is 6 July 1861. She has just over nine months left to live.

We are in Namibia. I'm sitting in the jungly garden of a lodge beside the Zambezi, on the land which became the graveyard of the Makololo, among the floodplains and lagoons between the Chobe and the Zambezi, near their confluence in what is now the Caprivi Strip. The people who live here today, fishermen and farmers of sorghum, pumpkins and maize, move with the water levels between seasonal homes, and they are not Makololo. They belong to Zambia's Lozi tribe, and I'm looking at Zambia across the deep, wide water, a spectral river in the milky light of dawn, trailing scarves of mist.

The Makololo are long gone. They barely outlived Mary Livingstone, who lies 600 miles downriver. When Livingstone finally returned to Linyanti after the disaster of the Makololo Mission, he found that the death rate among the tribe had accelerated. His brother Charles was with him, and in 1862 Charles Livingstone wrote: 'There were not more than 50 men alive of the true Makololo; soon they will all be dead. I presume that the kingdom of Sebitoane is all in pieces now.' It took another three years before the remnants of the tribe were overwhelmed and killed by their vassals from the Barotse plains, ancestors of the Lozi who now fish and farm and service birdwatchers and anglers in tourist lodges on the upper Zambezi.

There remains a village of Linyanti, a humble, unvisited place about four miles north of the Chobe. This obscure mud-and-thatch outpost is almost certainly the site of Sebetwane's capital, although nobody can tell us for sure, either at the village itself, where we find no English-speakers, only puzzled smiles and curious stares, or in Katima Mulilo, the eastern capital of the Caprivi Strip, a confident, attractive town on the Zambezi. The Makololo have been forgotten. There has been a long and sometimes violent turnover of events in their old territory since Sebetwane welcomed Livingstone and Oswell and crossed the Chobe to honour the daughter of Moffat. They themselves were colonists, immigrants displaced from their highveld homeland on the other side of the Kalahari by the Mfecane. Their genocide was the result of an alliance of anopheles mosquitoes, Matabele raids and rebellious Lozi tribesmen, whom they had oppressed.

More colonists followed. The Caprivi Strip is a post-colonial anomaly. This long spear of Namibian land was once part of the British protectorate of Bechuanaland, but was handed over to Germany when the European powers sat down at the Berlin Conference of 1890 to reorganise their parcels of African properties. In the scramble for Africa six years earlier, Germany had annexed South West Africa and laid claim to Zanzibar, off the East African coast. The German chancellor, Count George Leo von Caprivi, was determined to negotiate access to the Zambezi in the hope, like Livingstone, of using the river as a corridor to the east-coast trade routes. In a bizarre piece of horse-trading, Britain swapped a northern slice of Bechuanaland for the island of Zanzibar in the Indian Ocean and the little archipelago of Heligoland in the North Sea.

After the First World War the Caprivi Strip was repossessed by the British and restored to Bechuanaland, but in 1929 it was again returned to South West Africa, at that time in the control of South Africa. When the colony and its African population of Khoisan and Bantu tribes became independent in 1990, its freakish appendage, like the rest of the country, became Namibia. But its troubles weren't over. The long civil war in Angola destabilised its Angolan borderlands; and, until that brutal conflict ended in 2002, it was avoided by most tourists. But the Caprivi Strip has desirable neighbours and easy access to the Okavango Delta, Chobe National Park and the Victoria Falls. It could not be ignored for long. At its eastern extremity, the 'malarial swamps' of the Makololo have been redefined as important wetlands with their own riverine wildlife reserves.

And it has a share of the Zambezi. With the Nile, the Congo and the Niger, this is the mightiest of Africa's rivers. A totemic waterway. Its name fizzes on the tongue and in the imagination. 'At the end of June, 1851,' writes Livingstone in *Missionary Travels*, 'we were rewarded by the discovery of the Zambesi, in the centre of the continent ... We saw it at the end of the dry season, and yet there was a breadth of from three hundred to six hundred yards of deep flowing water. At the period of its annual inundation it rises twenty feet in perpendicular height, and floods fifteen or twenty miles of lands adjacent to its banks.'

It is almost the end of June, and where I sit close to the river the Zambezi is restrained by its banks. Its breath is cool on my skin, its liquid syllables fill my ears, its ambiguous smell of decay and fecundity reaches my nose. I can feel its pulse and its indifferent power. It is at least 500 yards to the Zambian forest on the far side. This is the river that made the reputation of David Livingstone, then unmade it. The failure of his expedition after six dreadful years was filleted in a *Times* editorial. 'We were promised cotton, sugar and indigo ... and of course we got none. We were promised trade; and there is no trade ... We were promised converts and not one has been made. In a word, the thousands subscribed by the Universities and contributed by the Government have been productive only of the most fatal results.'

Livingstone recovered his lost reputation. His wife had only her life to lose. I've travelled overland more than 700 miles from Kolobeng, even farther from Kuruman where, nearly 150 years ago, Ma-Mary waits to hear news of her first-born child's latest adventure. But it is her son John who, in February 1862, gets a few words from his sister on the Zambezi; and they are more typical of Mary than anything she wrote while she was in Britain. 'Livingstone is very well, not much altered. The Zambesi is a fine river, rather rapid. Shall write when time allows. L's clothes want looking over and remaking. My hands are full.'

She is back in Africa, where her hands, like her heart, were never empty.

Epilogue

Too young to remember her voice. 'My name is Anna Mary, last-born of Mary my mother, deceased of the desert fever while I was but a "wee bairn" ...' Unlike their brothers, who carried the greater burden of their famous father's expectations ('the demand for strength so peculiar to the Scots', writes Parsons), the two daughters of Mary and David Livingstone more successfully survived the loss of their parents at an early age. They both married, had children and were able to create the family life they had missed. As adults, they found the stability and contentment their mother craved and their father learned, too late, that he had sacrificed. The softer, humbler, kindlier Livingstone whom Stanley met on the shores of Lake Tanganyika in 1871 had had plenty of time to reflect on his failures as a parent. He had admitted regretting 'that I did not feel it to be my duty, while spending all my energy in teaching the heathen, to devote a special portion of my time to play with my children'.

After their mother died in 1862, Agnes, Tom, Oswell and Anna Mary continued to live with their aunts and grandmother in Hamilton, while Robert set off on his own journey. It was two years before Livingstone returned from the wreck of the Zambezi Expedition; and he stayed only briefly in the house in Burnbank Road, where he found his mother failing and confused and met Anna Mary for the first time. It was not a happy household. His mother didn't know him, Robert was missing, his other sons barely recognised him, and his five-year-old daughter was a stranger. He took comfort in Agnes, whose good nature and gentle manner had endured, and who was now turning into a lovely young woman. 'I have never seen her beauty mentioned elsewhere,' writes A. Z. Fraser in *Livingstone and Newstead*, 'and yet it was an undoubted factor in her life at this time, since it interested so many strangers in her at first sight.'

Agnes stayed with her father at Newstead Abbey for seven months between September 1864 and April 1865 while Livingstone, with another commission from John Murray, worked on a sanitised account of the Zambezi Expedition. (The death of Mary is reported tersely in this book, unlike the incontinent outpouring of grief and regret in his letters and journal.) The Webb family of Newstead, whose network of friends included William Cotton Oswell, were to remain generous and warm-hearted hosts to Agnes and her siblings in the years to come, while Oswell, who called Agnes 'my adopted one', never faltered in his support. All were needed. After making arrangements for Agnes to complete her education in Paris, Livingstone left his children and Britain for the last time. With the support of Sir Roderick Murchison and the RGS, and with additional funds from 'Paraffin' Young, he returned to Africa in August 1865.

During the eight years he spent looking for the source of the Nile, his letters to his children have a tenderness absent from his earlier ones. He had plenty of time to assess his performance as a father. To William Cotton Oswell, who would soon help to carry his coffin into Westminster Abbey, he wrote: 'I hope you are playing with your children instead of being bothered by idiots'; and when Oswell read Livingstone's last journals he wrote to Agnes: 'The dear old fellow, how quiet and gentle he has become ...' As people age, they often review their past through a prism of quiet grieving for missed opportunities, irredeemable mistakes; the iron man of Africa had on his conscience not just Mary's death but also the tragedy of his son Robert.

When his mother died Robert was 16, already causing problems with his volatile temperament and rackety behaviour (not unusual in teenagers) but by no means past redemption. He cared deeply for his mother – and, after the episode of his 'disappearance', when he vanished from his medical school for a week, he was ashamed of the trouble he'd caused, and proposed he should join the navy. But the board of trustees appointed by Livingstone to supervise his children's education refused to allow him to enlist. Even then, if Robert had been given a few years of reliable family life in Glasgow, maturity might have saved him. He might well have settled down, resumed his education and become the doctor that Livingstone wanted him to be. Instead, Mary's death tipped him into a cycle of heavy drinking and dissolute ways in 'bad company'.

Livingstone, still on the Zambezi, was not indifferent to his son's well-being and future, and decided he should come to Africa, making funds available for his passage. But the boy squandered the money, his father lost patience, and it wasn't replaced. There followed a chain of events which showed Livingstone, too late, that his lost, troubled, errant son was not only trying hard to prove himself to his father but also had much of his father's steel in his character.

Robert found the fare for a steamer from one of Livingstone's friends but disembarked in Port Elizabeth destitute. In July 1863, Mary Moffat of Kuruman heard that her eldest grandson, whom she had last seen when he was six, had arrived in Natal, 'without money, almost without clothing', on his way to join Livingstone on the Zambezi. But, when he reached Durban (then called Port Natal), he got a letter from his father ordering him to come no farther north.

'I am now in great affliction about Robert', wrote Ma-Mary to a friend. 'If he had any introduction to anyone he made no use of it. Ellen [his aunt by marriage] got her brother to seek him out. He went and stopped with her until about six weeks ago when he got £1 from her to go to the Bay and get his clothes and had never since been heard of after nine days absence.'

Reluctant to be dependent on the new young widow of his Uncle Robert, the 17-year-old somehow made his way to Cape Town, where three months later his grandmother next heard news of him, 'waiting his father's pleasure'. Ma-Mary, who was still mourning the loss of two of her adult children and a baby granddaughter, wrote him a loving letter, 'full of warmth', according to Mora Dickson. 'She neither preached at him nor recriminated, neither did she show much understanding of how he might feel about his mother's death, his father's isolation and his own lonely, adolescent uncertainties. But he lay heavy on her heart. He was the oldest grandchild, the first-born of her own dearest Mary, and she felt herself to be the only mother he had.'

The letter was sent to the city's Sailors' Home, where she heard he was living. 'Tell me why you so soon got weary of the old fatherland, dear old Scotland, with which so many of us have been associated and which we are proud to acknowledge as the land of our ancestors. Tell us what is your aim now ... Dearest Robert – do write the very first post.'

He didn't. In November, she wrote to a friend at LMS headquarters in Cape Town asking for more information about 'our poor unhappy grandson', relaying a message which again urged him to get in touch. 'I am quite aware that he may be ashamed to do so ... Give our tenderest love to him as the First-born of our own dear First-born.'

But Robert had vanished. Nothing was heard of him for at least a year until Livingstone, preoccupied with the terminal stages of the Zambezi Expedition, learned that he had worked his passage to Boston, where the USA was at war with itself. There, he had been press-ganged – forcibly recruited into the Union Army to fight against the Confederate forces of the southern states. Livingstone's response to this news was frustration and anger – the emotions of a parent who could do nothing to save his child from danger. 'That bad boy', he wrote to John Kirk, 'will be made manure of for those bloody fields.'

It was another year before Livingstone returned to Britain, where, this time, there were no honours waiting, although his final act in winding up the Zambezi Expedition was remarkable. Without any real experience of seamanship, with an untrained crew, with only enough coal for five days' steaming and without the engineer George Rae, he sailed the forty-foot *Lady Nyassa* – the collapsible steamer designed for lakes and rivers – across the Indian Ocean from Zanzibar to Bombay; a distance of 2,500 miles, which he completed mainly under sail just before the monsoon gales blew in. There he sold the little vessel and embarked for London, where, in October 1864, he at last got a letter from Robert, who had stayed in touch with Agnes, his closest sibling.

If any document told Livingstone that he had underestimated his oldest son, it was this one. It shows dignity and courage, it owns up to his wasted privileges, and most of all it shows the greatest respect for his father's values. It is heartbreaking.

My dear Sir,

Hearing that you have returned to England I undertake to address a few lines to you, not with any hope that you will be interested in me but simply to explain the position …

From Port Natal I went to Cape Town where your agent Mr Rutherford advised me to find employment on board a brig that brought me to Boston, America. Here I was kidnapped and one morning, after going to bed on board ship, I found myself enlisted in the US army.

I have been in one battle and two skirmishes, and expect to be in another terrific battle before long. God in his mercy has spared me as yet. I have never hurt anyone knowingly in battle, have always fired high, and in that furious madness which accompanies a bayonet charge and which seems to possess every soldier I controlled my passion and took the man who surrendered prisoner.

The rebels are not likely to hold out much longer, as we have nearly all their railroads. My craving for travelling is not yet satisfied, though had I the chance that I threw away of being educated, I should think myself only too much blessed. I have changed my name, for I am convinced that to bear your name here would lead to further dishonour to it. I am at present in this hospital, exposure and fatigue having given me ague fever.

The letter was signed Rupert Vincent, New Hampshire Volunteers, 10th Army Corps, Virginia, but both the handwriting and Agnes confirmed the identity of its author. He had told his sister more of the conditions in his field hospital: nothing to eat but raw pork; few medicines; endemic dysentery. He blamed nobody but himself for finding himself there, refused to desert as many were doing, but hoped he might be given an honourable discharge for '£60 or so'. Livingstone turned to the American consul in London and the influential Sir Roderick Murchison, but his appeal for help came too late.

Back in action, Robert was wounded and captured at Laurel Hill, in Virginia. He died in a hospital for prisoners-of-war six weeks later, on 5 December 1864, although his death was not confirmed at the time. It was to be seven years before Livingstone learned for certain what had happened to his son; and the news was brought to him by Henry Morton Stanley on the lakeshore at Ujiji. He had mourned Robert silently, and the silence continued. Robert's name was not mentioned in the eulogies which followed Livingstone's death; his brief life was for long ignored by those who carried the torch for the Livingstone myth. The only photograph of the teenage Robert surfaced as late as 1933, and it shows a handsome, obstinate, angry face; the eyes avoid the camera's stare, the mouth is tense and resentful.

The boy who tried to write himself out of history, who changed his identity to spare his father's name 'dishonour', was buried anonymously in a mass grave – 'made manure of for those bloody fields', as his father had predicted. He was barely 19.

Loose Ends

Edinburgh, September 2011

The city is dressing down. The Castle rock and its summit esplanade are stripped of the huge, beflagged structure of seating, scaffolding and stairs which supports the massed spectators of the Military Tattoo. In the gardens of Charlotte Square, workmen collapse the marquees which host writers, broadcasters, publishers and bibliophiles at the Book Festival. Musicians, dancers, actors and an eclectic army of other performers at the Edinburgh International Arts Festival and its massive shadow, the Fringe, pack their bags with their memories and disperse around the world. No more fireworks. No more street theatre. No more buskers, queues and cavalcades. The Scottish capital's summer cabaret of high and low culture is over for another year.

As the vitality subsides, the quotidian life of the city catches its breath and reclaims its public spaces and private homes. Hospitality has been put on hold for all but Festival visitors. As my socially selective husband often opines, 'The trouble with living in Edinburgh is that everyone wants to come here in the summer'. Like many other locals, Marion and Lewis Carlin have had a houseful of family and friends during August, but as the light deepens and the air sharpens they reinstate an invitation. On a September morning, I drive through streets which seem eerily empty to the south side of the city; to a whitewashed villa in a pleasant suburb which rises towards the Pentland Hills. Here, I am welcomed with warmth, coffee and a storm of information by an expatriate Zambian: the great-great-granddaughter of Robert and Mary Moffat, and therefore, the great-great-niece of Mary Livingstone.

There are upwards of fifty direct descendants of Mary and David Livingstone living in England and Scotland, and one or two in America. But there are many more Moffats, descendants of Mary's siblings, mainly scattered throughout Britain and Africa. Marion Moffat was born in the Copper Belt of Zambia in the days when it was still the British territory of Northern Rhodesia. Her father was the grandson of Mary's youngest brother, John, who succeeded Robert Moffat at Kuruman. After graduating in 1930 with a law degree from Glasgow University, Marion's father qualified as a barrister at Grey's Inn and entered the colonial service in Northern Rhodesia. Like other Moffats, he made his mark in public life; during his work for the government in Lusaka, he set up the native courts service and spent ten years as native courts adviser.[1]

Marion has lived in the United Kingdom for over forty years, and her voice still carries a light patina of Zambian accent. She has the friendly, open, energetic manner which I've come to associate with many of the 'lost tribe' of European Africans; and, although she has the look of a happy woman, she has never stopped missing her parent continent. 'You don't want to know me in February or March. That's when I get my most acute attack of Africa blues. On the whole I've got used to the Scottish winter, but I know how Mary Livingstone must have felt about the lack of light when she first arrived.'

After school in Lusaka and Cape Town she came to Scotland, like her father, for a university education. She graduated with a BSc at St Andrews, then moved to Aberdeen to do an MSc at its school of agriculture. She saw her future back in Zambia, on the land which her family farmed – until she met a young man from Foyers, in Inverness-shire, a neighbour at her

---

1 The Native Courts Ordinance 1937 established 'native' courts which were run by and for the indigenous people of Northern Rhodesia. Their jurisdiction was both criminal and civil, but the courts were not allowed to impose the death penalty; nor were they allowed to try witchcraft cases without permission.

digs in Albyn Terrace. Lewis Carlin was serving an apprenticeship in the design office of the Aberdeen yards of Hall Russell shipbuilders. One day, he invited her to join him on an outing to the beach. 'And that was it. I've never been back for anything longer than a holiday.'

They were married in 1970, and, after homes in other shipbuilding cities ('Our daughter is a Geordie, born in Wallsend'), settled in 1984 in Edinburgh, where Lewis took a post in the offshore drilling-rig division of the shipping group Ben Line. Now retired, with IT and research skills honed while he was working at the British Ship Research Association in Wallsend, where he was trying to encourage British shipbuilding to computerise, he is Marion's chief online researcher. She has become the family historian. 'I'm trying to bring together all the elements of the Moffats' history. It's mainly for the grandchildren, and anyone else in the family who's interested, but it's not all my own work. Lots of family members and other people have been helping me.'

I've been given their contact details by their cousin, Botswana's best-known Moffat: Dr Howard Moffat, the medical man who is given a walk-on part in the Mma Ramotswe novels by his friend Alexander McCall Smith. It's my hope that Marion can satisfy my curiosity about her great-great-aunt's grave. Four years have passed since Gaia Allison, Mike Muyafula and I made our way to Chupanga and placed our blossoms on the tomb beside the Zambezi. Although I've contacted several other Moffat/Livingstone relatives and done some digging in the National Library of Scotland and at the David Livingstone Centre at Blantyre, I've yet to find the answer to three questions which intrigue me. How did the grave evolve from simple cairn and wooden cross to brick tomb, iron headstone and boundary pillars? Who were the 'Livingstones of Africa' who attached the metal plate recording their 'respect and admiration'? And what is the provenance of the fine-link yellow metal chain which Rod and Ellie Hein of the mission Afrika wa Jesu found exposed in a pillar when they were clearing undergrowth in the aftermath of the civil war?

Marion and Lewis already have an interest in the grave, but, until I arrive with my questions, they haven't made it a priority. They are familiar with the photograph taken by John Kirk after Mary was buried, when her grave was marked by a heap of stones and a wooden cross, and with a photograph taken in 1993 by a friend of a friend. Keith Shannon was working for the UK government in Mozambique and 'chanced life and limb' to visit the graveyard when Chupanga was still in the hands of Renamo rebels and the region hadn't been cleared of land mines. It is Shannon's photograph I have seen in the Livingstone museum in Blantyre, where he deposited it with an account of his visit.

Now I'm able to show my new researchers the images I took in 2007, and they set to work with enthusiasm to find out more about the grave as I finish the final chapters of this book. I've given them the e-mail address of Rod and Ellie Hein of Afrika wa Jesu, who also help, as does Keith Shannon. Within weeks, they come up with answers and possible explanations to satisfy my curiosity – and more. For this, they must take full credit.

Although Livingstone called the village where Mary died Shupanga, it was always Chupanga, or at the very least Chipanga – a name first recorded by Jesuit priests shortly before 1700, meaning fortress or place of defence. He mentions the Catholic church, later the focus of the Jesuit mission founded in 1896; and he was almost certainly aware that Shupanga House, although called a rest house, had a long history as a slave prison for captives waiting their transfer and export. It was a slave holding-pen between 1785 and 1870, according to the Heins' investigation of records – which means that it was still being used for that purpose, if only occasionally, when the Zambezi Expedition occupied it and Mary died in it.

Livingstone returned to Chupanga before he left the Zambezi, and he himself set in motion arrangements for having the improvised grave made more permanent. Marion and Lewis have traced a letter, written seven months after Mary's death, which asks his old friend 'Paraffin' Young, one of the trustees of his UK resources, to investigate materials for a new headstone – iron or granite, to withstand the climate of the lower Zambezi valley. The headstone may have been made in Britain and shipped out, perhaps not until some time later; or it may have been commissioned from the Portuguese, as the Portuguese inscription on one side repeats, with one or two small differences, the information of the English inscription. Local tradition dates it from 1890 – but, if there had been no headstone when Agnes Livingstone Bruce paid her first visit to Chupanga in 1898 (or thereabouts), she would almost certainly have taken matters in hand. She had the funds to do so, she must have known her father's wishes, and it's unthinkable that she would have neglected to secure her mother's grave and mark it with a substantial headstone.

Africa and their parents' history never became mere memories for the surviving Livingstone children. But the daughters built upon their legacy with more achievement and influence than the sons. Thomas, called Tom, nicknamed Tau for his tawny mane, grew up an amiable, even-tempered young man who followed his father's example (and wishes) and studied medicine in Glasgow. But the health so undermined by his infant years in the Kalahari remained delicate. After he qualified as a doctor, he went to work in Egypt, where he died, unmarried, when he was 29.

Oswell, whom Livingstone called Zouga, did not have a long or easy life. The boy born under a camelthorn tree beside the Boteti struggled and failed to win his father's abiding approval. When the RGS mounted a relief expedition for their vanished explorer in 1872, Oswell volunteered to join it. He was 19 and in the middle of medical studies, also commissioned by his father. When the rescue attempt was abandoned after Stanley sent word to the world that he had already found Livingstone, something of the old, censorious impatience re-entered his correspondence to his youngest son. The intense, shy, slight young man was chastised for achieving nothing which might allow him 'to hold up his head'. Oswell did marry, but like his mother was poor at managing money. He died in St Albans, in Hertfordshire, when he was 40, leaving one daughter and an indigent widow.

Anna Mary, so much younger than her brothers and sister, was left alone with her ageing aunts in Ulva Cottage with no recall of the mother who said goodbye with a gift of red shoes (she remembered the shoes), and with few memories of her father – until the day came when, as she told Hans Christian Andersen, she was 'obliged to take the sad journey to London to see what's left of him buried in Westminster Abbey'. After the funeral, she visited the Webbs of Newstead with her aunts, who are charmingly, if patronisingly, described by A. Z. Fraser: 'They were nice, sensible-looking, elderly women, looking very square and solid in their deep mourning; their dark, strong faces not unlike that of Dr Livingstone. They spoke little, and when they did so it was, unlike their brother, in broad Scotch; but they were not without a certain homely dignity of their own, amidst their unwonted surroundings. I do not think any English women in the same circumstances could have acquitted themselves so well, or shown such self-possession; for so far as I know it was the first time they had ever even crossed the Border ...'

When she was 23, the child who loved best the stories of the tin soldier and the ugly duckling married Frank Wilson of Kendal, a nephew of her mother's saviours, the Braithwaites. (Her grandson, Neil Wilson, maintained his links with Kendal and lives there today.) As Anna Mary grew up she became conscious of all that both her parents had sacrificed; and when she visited the place of her father's death at Chitambo, she 'came under the spell of camp life and *ulendo* [travel], the stillness of the trees, contrasting colours and the great vaulted sky that made a sanctuary of the woods where he died'. Before the First World War, she and her husband worked for the Church Missionary Society in Sierra Leone. Her son Hubert and grandson David both became medical missionaries in what is now Zambia. Her daughter Ruth, a nurse and midwife, also lived and worked there.

It was in the Zambian town of Livingstone, in 2005, that I met her eldest grandson, the late Dr David Wilson, when we both attended the commemorative events surrounding the 150th anniversary of his great-grandfather's arrival at the Victoria Falls. By then, he had retired to the Clydeside town of Helensburgh, and he had few memories of his grand-mother, who was often out of the country when he was a boy. She, he said, had even fewer memories of her father. Anna Mary, born at Kuruman, raised in Hamilton, was the longest-lived of the Livingstone children; and in 1929, ten years before she died, she attended the ceremonial opening of Scotland's National Memorial to David Livingstone in Blantyre.

In my conversations with Marion and Lewis, we talk most about Agnes Livingstone Bruce, Nannee, who of all the children was closest to both parents and twice visited her mother's grave at Chupanga. They suggest that, on one of her visits (the second was around 1902/3), Agnes may have been responsible for adding to Mary's tomb the plate with the inscrip-tion: 'With respect and admiration from the Livingstones of Africa'. They believe the typeset is Victorian and was stamped rather than engraved, but the plate still puzzles them. Would Agnes, would any Livingstone child, not also include a message of love? And they point out that the Portuguese version of the same message is slightly different. Translated, it can read either 'of' or 'for' the Livingstones of Africa, leaving open the possibility that the plate was later attached by the Jesuit priests who ran the mission.

The mystery of the yellow metal chain embedded in a boundary pillar remains unsolved. 'But it was common for bereaved Victorians to leave personal mementoes at the graves of their dearest relatives, and it was also common on someone's death to subdivide a long chain into sections for each child. We think the most likely explanation is that Agnes left the chain on one of her visits, possibly at the same time the headstone and pillars were added.'

Agnes had sound reasons beyond Mary's grave for visiting this region of Africa. Across the Zambezi, up the Shire Valley, in the Shire High-lands, were the vast estates of her husband, Alexander Bruce. Like her father, Bruce was an idealistic colonist who energetically pursued Living-stone's vision of Christianity, civilisation and commerce, and who had seen the British presence in Nyasaland finally expel the slave trade. But his property was destined to become the scene of the first serious upris-ing in the Nyasaland protectorate; and the Livingstone name was tainted by the events which led to its hideous outcome. One of the estates was at Magomero, site of the ill-fated Universities Mission to Central Africa, in the shadow of the monolithic mountain of Chiradzulu.

By 1915, Bruce and Agnes were both dead, the Nyasaland estates had passed to their son, also Alexander, and the Magomero property was managed by a very different breed of colonist: William Jervis Livingstone, a Livingstone cousin whom history describes as arrogant, ruthless and sometimes violent. Magomero was also the home of the man whom Malawi today honours as its first freedom fighter: the Reverend John Chilembwe, a Western-educated Baptist minister and inspired political activist. In the certain knowledge that it would fail and he would probably lose his life, he meticulously planned a rebellion against his colonial neighbour, who often withheld wages from his plantation workers and burned the rural churches and schools established by Chilembwe. The preacher ordered all white men to be killed but gave firm instructions that women and children were to be treated with respect, which they were. But William Jervis Livingstone was beheaded in front of his wife and small daughter, and his head exposed on a pole in Chilembwe's church. Its minister was shot while trying to escape to Mozambique.

Agnes's husband was also a founder of the Royal Scottish Geographical Society, which was launched in Edinburgh in 1884. Henry Morton Stanley gave the inaugural address. A. Z. Fraser says that Agnes seized on the idea, which came from John George Bartholomew of the Edinburgh map-making company. She enlisted Bruce's support on a Sunday afternoon in the fashionable seaside resort of North Berwick, on the Forth estuary. Her Paris experience and the influence of Newstead had turned Agnes into the most sophisticated of the Livingstone children; and, after her marriage, she lived in Regent Terrace, one of Edinburgh's grandest Georgian streets, where every house has an uninterrupted view to Arthur's Seat, the volcanic hill which dominates the city. Her granddaughter Diana married Ray Harryhausen, Hollywood master of special effects, the man who designed and funded the lion sculpture at the David Livingstone Centre.

As I'm about to leave Edinburgh's south side, Marion Moffat asks: 'Do you know Agnes is buried just down the road, in Morningside Cemetery?'

I'd had no idea Mary's elder daughter was so easily visited. Yet still 'poor Mary lies on Shupanga brae and beeks fornent the sun'. On the banks of the Zambezi, 6,000 miles away, her grave still waits to be fully recognised among all the Livingstone landmarks of Africa, as her memory waits to be fully honoured.

She has her champions. We are not finished with Mary Livingstone yet; nor is history.

Archive and Bibliographic Acknowledgements

Archival research is something of a mystery to me. I would like to register my sincere thanks to the archivists of the National Library of Scotland, who helped me track down copies of the few personal letters of Mary Livingstone which have survived, and to the other staff at the NLS, who are invariably obliging. Mary's correspondence with the London Missionary Society was easier to find, as it is held in a collection in the LMS archives at the School of Oriental and African Studies in London, with copies in the NLS. Thanks are also due to the archivist at the David Livingstone Centre, Blantyre, for identifying contemporary photographs and sketches from the museum archives.

I am also grateful to the publishers, authors and literary agents who hold the copyright for the following books for giving me permission to quote from them. The titles are listed in alphabetical order.

Beloved Partner, Mora Dickson (Kuruman Moffat Mission Trust, 1989).

Beyond the Shadow, Ellie Hein (Christ for Nations, Inc., 2000).

David Livingstone: The Dark Interior, Oliver Ransford (John Murray, 1978).

Good Wives? Mary, Fanny, Jennie and Me, 1845–2001, Margaret Forster (Chatto & Windus, 2001). Extracts reprinted by permission of the Random House Group Limited, and by permission of the author and the Sayle Literary Agency.

Livingstone, Tim Jeal (William Heinemann Ltd, 1973). Extracts reprinted by permission of Yale University Press (2001) and by permission of the author.

The Livingstones at Kolobeng 1847–1852, Janet Wagner Parsons (Botswana Society and Pula Press, 1997). Extracts published by permission of the author.

Livingstone's Lake, Oliver Ransford (Thomas Y. Crowell, 1967).

Wives of Fame: Jenny Marx, Mary Livingstone, Emma Darwin, Edna Healey (Sidgwick & Jackson Ltd, 1986). Extracts reprinted by permission of Peters Fraser & Dunlop (www.petersfraserdunlop.com) on behalf of the Estate of Edna Healey.

Every effort has been made to clear permissions. If there has been any error or omission, please contact the publisher, who will include a credit in subsequent editions.

Further Reading

A Cruise in the 'Gorgan', W. C. Devereux (London, 1869).

David Livingstone: Family Letters, 1841–1856, ed. I. Schapera (London: Chatto & Windus, 1959).

David Livingstone: His Life and Letters, George Seaver (London: Lutterworth Press, 1957).

David Livingstone: Mission and Empire, Andrew Ross (London: Hambledon & London, 2002).

Great Lion of Bechuanaland, Edwin W. Smith (London: London Missionary Society, 1957).

Kirk on the Zambesi, R. Coupland (Oxford: Clarendon Press, 1928).

Lives of Robert and Mary Moffat, J. S. Moffat (London: T. Fisher Unwin, 1885).

Livingstone and Newstead, A. Z. Fraser (London, John Murray, 1913).

Livingstone the Doctor, M. Gelfand (Oxford: Basil Blackwell 1957).

Livingstone's African Journal, 1853–1856, ed. I. Schapera (London: Chatto & Windus, 1963).

Livingstone's Private Journals, 1851–1856, ed. I. Schapera (London: Chatto & Windus, 1960).

Missionary Travels and Researches in South Africa, David Livingstone (London: John Murray, 1857).

Narrative of an Expedition to the Zambesi and its Tributaries, D. and C. Livingstone (London: John Murray, 1865).

Starlings Laughing, June Vendall Clark (London: Doubleday, 1990).

The Story of the Universities Mission to Central Africa, H. Rowley (London, 1866).

William Cotton Oswell, Hunter and Explorer, W. E. Oswell and Francis Galton (London: William Heinemann, 1900).

The Zambesi Doctors: David Livingstone's Letters to John Kirk, 1858–1872, ed. R. Foskett (Edinburgh: Oliver & Boyd, 1964).

The Zambesi Expedition of David Livingstone 1858–1863, ed. J. P. R. Wallis (London: Chatto & Windus, 1956).

The Zambesi Journal of James Stewart, 1862–1863, ed. J. P. R. Wallis (London: Chatto & Windus, 1952).

Index

PLEASE NOTE: David Livingstone is abbreviated as DL and Mary Livingstone as ML in the subheadings.